Nathan Lynch is a writer and international speaker who has spent two decades investigating the hidden world of dark money that fuels organised crime, corruption and violent extremism around the globe. His work peels back the layers of complex financial crime schemes. He is certified by the US Department of Justice's elite CCIPS Cybercrime Laboratory and is a program expert with the Financial Services Volunteer Corps, which provides support to developing countries to help them combat the scourges of money laundering and other serious financial crimes.

Nathan has trained police, government officials and bankers across Asia and the Middle East on the techniques the world's criminals use to conceal and clean their dirty money.

THE
LUCKY
LAUNDRY

NATHAN LYNCH

HarperCollins*Publishers*

HarperCollins*Publishers*
Australia • Brazil • Canada • France • Germany • Holland • India
Italy • Japan • Mexico • New Zealand • Poland • Spain • Sweden
Switzerland • United Kingdom • United States of America

First published in Australia in 2022
by HarperCollins*Publishers* Australia Pty Limited
Level 13, 201 Elizabeth Street, Sydney NSW 2000
ABN 36 009 913 517
harpercollins.com.au

A catalogue record for this book is available from the National Library of Australia

ISBN 978 1 4607 5991 2 (paperback)
ISBN 978 1 4607 1337 2 (ebook)
ISBN 978 1 4607 4399 7 (audiobook)

Cover design by Darren Holt, HarperCollins Design Studio
Cover images by shutterstock.com
Author photograph by Matt Hind (London)
Typeset in Minion Pro by HarperCollins Design Studio
Printed and bound in Australia by McPherson's Printing Group

To my dearest Taz, for your relentless love and support.
For our little treasures, Zara and Jordan:
One day we will pass you the flame of Aussie democracy.
Treasure it, marvel at it, nurture it.
For it is the greatest of human inventions.

*

In memory of Joy Geary.

Contents

Backpacks, Banking and Blood

No one truly knows whether Pete Hoang, a professional money launderer, had enough time for his life to flash before his eyes. If he did, one thing's for sure: it would've been a wild, stop-motion replay of 38 crazy years. Gambling, girls, rented sports cars, luxury apartments, business-class travel, champagne, danger. And cash. Lots of grubby, powder-coated cash.

But the last thing the orphan-made-good saw on this earth wasn't the inside of a penthouse suite, the face of a beautiful woman or the interior of a luxury vehicle. It was a barrel of cold steel, staring him down at close range.

For a man who flitted between complimentary suites at the best casinos across the Asia-Pacific, his final resting place was ignoble: a pool of blood, a footpath, outside an apartment block in a quiet street in Croydon Park, Sydney.

Seconds before those five slugs of lead ripped his face open and tore through his slender body, Pete saw a man race from the apartment block. He'd been very careful – paranoid, even – in the past few weeks. Friends were worried about him. At dinner two nights earlier, he seemed distracted. The exuberant, effervescent kid who extracted himself from Vietnam at the age of 20 was not himself.

Pete had reason to be worried. He was facing federal money-laundering charges in a Victorian court. Worse still, he'd lost a bag holding $1.5 million. Seized. Taken by the Australian Federal Police (AFP) at Crown Casino in Melbourne, his favourite haunt. His luck had finally run out. Pete was in deep debt and even deeper trouble. He had no one to turn to for help. The only family he'd known during his life in Australia were now hunting him.

In the last 48 hours of his life, Pete was preoccupied by pings on his Phantom Secure BlackBerry phone, the encrypted device that an international organised-crime syndicate had once gifted him.

In that slow-motion millisecond, standing on a gum-pocked footpath in Dunmore Street at 1 am on a Sunday morning, he knew he'd been set up.

And then, a flash …

*

Sydney Airport, 1997

The Australian immigration official smiles — properly smiles — and looks at Tan Minh Nguyen-Tran with a relaxed, welcoming face. Tan is super nervous, but taken aback. Immi guys aren't meant to do that!

As far back as Tan can remember, people have been ruthless. Dog eat dog. Tan was raised an orphan in a small farming community in Da Nang, Vietnam. He battled his way out and made it overland to Indonesia, where he scored a new identity and a passport. In all those life-and-death adventures, across the porous borders of South-East Asia, the 20-year-old orphan has never seen a friendly person from the government. Unless they are chasing graft.

Around him, families bustle through turnstiles with piles of suitcases, laughing and joking with airport staff. Aussie accents twang across the airport PA. There is a buzz in the air.

'Hi, and welcome to Australia,' the official says. 'Can I have your passport please?'

Tan slides the magic green book across the counter, calmly, just as he mentally rehearsed during the flight. He won't need his prodigious memory for this task.

'What's your full name, please?'

'Petrus Keyn Peten.'

'Date of birth?'

'December 7, 1975.'

'Nationality?'

'Indonesian.'

The man inspects the document. Thump, thump, flip. It's stamped. 'Enjoy your stay.'

The parentless kid from central Vietnam walks through the gates and into Australia, his new life in front of him. A different sort of sunshine fills the arrivals hall, amplified in its intensity through giant panes of glass. The mercurial kid from Da Nang is reborn: an Indonesian student in Sydney!

The giant airport clock above the baggage claim area ticks methodically as he watches his bags meander along the carousel. *Come on.*

Little Tan from Vietnam doesn't know it yet, but in the Lucky Country, time is going to prove more elusive than money. The second half of his life has just begun.

*

When Petrus Keyn Peten arrived in Sydney on a false student passport in 1997, he knew exactly what to do. The people who'd sold it to him had told him the drill. Within a few short months he had applied for refugee status, under the name Minh Tan Nguyen.

The rootless young man began to find his feet in Sydney, a big foreign city. It was a place where anyone could make it – with the right connections, a good work ethic and a little bit of street smarts. Minh had plenty of the latter two, and he knew where to find the first. He flitted between apartments, a job here and a hustle there; changed his name three more times; and within four years he could call himself a citizen. Pete Tan Hoang: Aussie.

Fourteen action-packed years later, the adventure was over.

An hour after midnight on Sunday morning, 7 September 2014, a pub-goer walked past a slight Asian bloke curled up on the footpath. When he reached the Croydon Park Hotel, he told the doorman there was a customer passed out drunk in the gutter on Dunmore Street. They might want to check on him. A few minutes later, the security staff from the hotel found Pete's body, cold and without a pulse, with five bullet holes in his head, neck and left arm.

Ambulance staff raced out but could only pronounce him dead. It wasn't a difficult diagnosis. Pete's face was so disfigured that the Department of Forensic Medicine, in nearby Glebe, would eventually have to identify him by his fingerprints.

He was carrying the buzzer for a rented Nissan GTX sports car. The Phantom Secure phone that Pete had used to arrange the midnight meeting was still charged and locked in his pocket. When police eventually cracked it open, they found it empty. All the data, including Pete's messages with his killer, had been remotely wiped.

*

The police ordered an inquest into the killing. This was not surprising, considering Pete was facing federal money laundering charges and had extensive links to organised crime, and there was no sign of a killer. The verdict was handed down by New South Wales coroner Les Mabbutt in July 2018.

Mabbutt, a handsome 57-year-old former cop, was still haunted by his early days in the police force, when he'd made 'death knocks' to distraught families. He did a law degree by night to get away from it all. And now here he was, handing down a verdict of 'Homicide by unknown person or persons' for the life of Pete Tan Hoang.

In this case, there was no distraught family, no crying wife, no shattered kids. No one turned up to mourn the loss of the orphan boy from Da Nang. All Les could do was refer the case to the Unsolved Homicide Squad, where it still sits unsolved today.

In reality, the only family Pete knew had been the ones who pulled the trigger. He had become just another statistic in the world of organised crime. A dispensable bagman whose life was extinguished to ensure he wouldn't rat on those at the tip of the dirty money pyramid. The last time Pete's killer was spotted, he was jumping into the passenger seat of a waiting hatchback, which sped off into the inky blackness of Sydney at night.

Pete had lucked out in the great game of life. And like a roulette wheel, the game would now roll on without him.

Welcome to the Lucky Laundry

The Lucky Country. The envy of the world. A nation of open plains, open smiles, open arms and open borders. Pure air, pristine beaches and even relatively clean politicians. A place where the world's hopeless and oppressed can come to make a fresh start. A land of democracy, good governance, bountiful resources and plentiful opportunity. A nation where hard work and a spirit of enterprise will guarantee a roof over your head, a backyard if you want it, top-tier health care and a solid education for your children.

'What is this mythical paradise?' you might ask. It's Australia, once upon a time. This was the land Down Under in 1964. A post-war wonderland under the predictable but steady leadership of Prime Minister Robert Menzies. It was also the nation characterised in Donald Horne's epoch-defining book, *The Lucky Country*.

Of course, the 'lucky country' moniker was at best a backhanded compliment. It stuck because it was true. Those who bothered to dive into the tome soon understood that, for Horne, Australia was a victim of its own good fortune. This was a place where the hard graft of innovation played second fiddle to surfing one's way through wave after wave of dumb luck. If necessity was the mother of invention, it seemed the Aussies of the 1960s didn't really need for much.

According to Horne, Australia was 'a lucky country run mainly by second rate people who share its luck. It lives on other people's ideas, and, although its ordinary people are adaptable, most of its leaders (in all fields) so lack curiosity about the events that surround them that they are often taken by surprise.'

Ouch. Well, if the Akubra fits …

*

Fast-forward half a century from Horne's day and modern Australia is a very different place. Many of those open plains, once viewed from the cockpit of a Boeing 707 Flying Kangaroo, have been paved with tiles or covered in Colorbond roofs. There are greenfield developments in a patchwork grid as far as the eye can see. Open smiles have been replaced by the emotionless protection of medical masks. Open arms have been supplanted with social distancing and big-city scepticism. And our open borders have been replaced with bumper stickers on souped-up utes saying 'Fuck off, we're full!' In Canberra, Arthur Calwell's invention of the three-word immigration slogan – 'Populate or perish,' he cried in the late 1940s – has evolved into an equally concise modern battle cry: 'Stop the boats!'

The dream of the quarter-acre block, of the double-brick cottage with a lawn for the kids and a Hills Hoist, is now so alien as to be a parody. The ideal of a home in which to raise a family has been overtaken by mortgages delivered by an army of 'brokers' from the deregulated, globalised banking sector. Australia's average household debt, measured against gross domestic product (GDP), has reached an historic 123 per cent. A nice, neat number, but Australian households have been lured into one of the greatest debt traps the world has ever seen. Most of this borrowing has not funded enterprise. It's been borrowed to buy homes at prices that spiral ever-upwards. Modern Australians borrow from the rest of the world to buy each other's homes, abetted by a banking sector that clips the ticket on every dollar borrowed when they rack up the interest bill each month.

It's an illusion of national wealth: credit masquerading as productive endeavour. Families that are petrified of missing out have locked themselves into 30 years of dual-income wage servitude. Their mortgage contract has obliged them to sign up to a new social contract, one that requires them to outsource the raising of their children to government-subsidised daycare centres so they can maintain two high-paying, full-time jobs in the city. In return, young families in Sydney or Melbourne may be able to scrape together a deposit for an apartment in a decent area, close to their work. This national property addiction is pro-cyclical and self-reinforcing, driving the market ever upwards.

Australian households are now the second-most indebted on earth, after those in Switzerland. We've quite literally gone property mad.

*

Aussies have been very good to the national housing market, investing more than $9 trillion of their wealth into residential real estate. The housing market, in turn, has been very good to Aussies. In the 50 years since Donald Horne was surveying the social landscape, housing prices have multiplied more than 85 times. In 1970, the median house price in Sydney was $18,700. Half a century later it's $1.6 million. Even during the Global Financial Crisis of the late 2000s, Australia defied the world's troubles. Anyone lucky enough to invest in bricks and mortar (the family home, plus one for the retirement fund) has enjoyed preposterous returns over the past five decades.

For those with a 'foot on the ladder', the family home has become many things in addition to a place to live and raise a family. Property is the great Australian path to prosperity. It's an asset class, a form of security, an ATM redraw facility, and something to show off at barbecues. It's the pride and joy of every Australian – and with so much wealth tied up in bricks and mortar, housing policy can also swing elections. Governments are loath to touch the engine of the Australian economy, regardless of how unstable or inequitable it is making our broader society. The hopeful opposition leader Bill Shorten learned this lesson the hard way in 2019.

These days, Australia is the land of the lucky – provided you're not unlucky enough to be chasing your first home.

Despite those difficulties, every weekend, young Australian families bid at property auctions against anonymous bidders and buyers' advocates. These families bid valiantly with a combination of their hard-earned savings, government grants, the proceeds of judicious investments, and sometimes even gifts and inheritances from parents. The vast majority of this money is leveraged up by the world's most profitable banks through the wonder of credit – a promise to repay, secured against a mortgage and a lifetime of future earnings. Aussie families use this credit to buy into their simple dream: home ownership, financial security and self-determination.

But there's another side to the housing boom. Look past the picket fences and you'll often see a different type of resident, a more shadowy purchaser. These owners are often listed on property titles as companies, which are in turn the trustees of offshore vehicles in secrecy jurisdictions like Samoa or the Cook Islands. These trusts may even have 'flee or flight' clauses, which mean they immolate and disappear the moment a tax authority, a jilted spouse or a criminal investigator asks any questions. To a financial crime investigator, these complex financial structures are mere ghosts.

Who are these new neighbours who have popped up all over Australia, as they have in Canada and London, with the metaphorical lights off and blinds drawn? And what of those anonymous buyers? Who are the people hiding behind dark sunglasses, and behind even more opaque foreign trusts, standing discreetly at the back of property auctions? Who do those professional buyers' agents in property deals truly represent?

In many cases, no one in Australia knows. Because no one is really required to know. Everyone in the transaction chain (except the bankers) is allowed to turn a blind eye. They can park their suspicion behind a thick wall of customer privacy, professional discretion and self-interest. This is one reason why Australia is so attractive to investors who seek secrecy, discretion and security. It's also a primary reason that we have become one of the world's most attractive destinations for money launderers. Forgiving laws, gaping loopholes, earnest advisers and a squeaky-clean international reputation have made Australia a place of choice for illicit funds. Despite a federal crackdown on the foreign ownership of established houses, there are still many ways for crooks to score a piece of the action. Foreign criminals and government kleptocrats can go to town on new builds. They can jump into commercial property, farmland, dairies. In one case, the AFP seized a 3000-acre property near Tasmania's stunning Musselroe Bay that was linked to a $23 million investment fraud in China.

With the right advice, buyers can easily conceal their ownership. Real estate agents will happily turn a blind eye to a foreign 'cash purchaser' who is ready to sign a contract; those unconditional cash deals mean the agent's commission goes straight in the bank. Ka-ching. In some cases, agents have even provided fraudulent bank letters to assist a foreign buyer to move their funds through a local proxy buyer. With so much money at stake, and so few checks, there are many ways to skin this criminal cat.

Australia has become so accommodating to kleptocrats, in fact, that countless local families have been forced into the rental market to make room for them. Who are they renting from? Even that's unclear in some cases – such as the student accommodation building named Dudley International House in Caulfield East in Victoria, which was used to launder $4.75 million in kickbacks to Malaysian officials. Or the Sydney apartment blocks, Tasmanian dairy farms and a Hilton Hotel whose foreign owners only came to light when they were exposed in the Pandora Papers leaks in October 2021.

If Donald Horne were alive today, he might say the modern Australian 'lacks curiosity' about the source of this flood of unexplained wealth. He might say Australians are 'implausibly in denial' about the influx of foreign money, which is so critical to powering the country's post-banking-deregulation economic miracle. He might suggest the professional facilitators are also blind to the good fortune that allows undisclosed buyers to make cash offers on multi-million-dollar waterfront palaces, after a weekend's gambling at one of Australia's equally accommodating casino complexes. When good fortune shines in the land of the lucky, it's deemed rude to ask too many probing questions.

In our comparable regional neighbours – Singapore, Indonesia, Malaysia, New Zealand, Hong Kong – questions must be asked of any prospective wealthy property purchasers. Not here Down Under. Unfortunately, this means that many trusting modern Australians – in a world that has grown deeply suspicious of cash offers on real estate – are too often 'taken by surprise'.

*

It's abundantly clear that not all of the money that props up the world's most buoyant property market is the savings of hardworking Aussies. A significant slice of that $9 trillion is the proceeds of criminal wealth.

This is money tainted by the stench of foreign corruption, tax evasion, drug deals, environmental crimes and human trafficking. This crooked loot has been transformed, like tungsten into gold, by the alchemy of the modern world's dark-money laundromat. It's been washed and tumbled across borders, pressed through secrecy jurisdictions, preened by an army of willing professional advisers, and then put proudly on display like a plastic-clad business suit hanging in a dry-cleaner's window.

The sheer gravity of the world's 'black economy', worth around US$2 trillion each year, ensures an incessant flow of illicit money. It's like the dirty, muddy river water that one sees surging downstream after a rainforest has been clear-felled; the money gets progressively cleaner as it is filtered through the world's major financial ecosystems, passing along tributaries, drawn by ocean currents, until it reaches our shores. By the time this criminal liquidity feeds into the Australian housing market, it's as clear as tap water. Who really knows what the true source was of that cash gushing into Australian housing sales? Was it from an underground aquifer or was it the outflow from a dirty criminal deal?

Australians have always believed in character and integrity. In honesty. A fair go. It's one of the reasons Aussies are so well liked around the world. But our generally trusting nature has also made Australians vulnerable to attack. It has made us a prime target for the international criminal underworld. Australia's high levels of public trust, and the facade of our 'clean' economy, makes it an ideal place to park the proceeds of human trafficking, illicit drug production or bribery.

Every now and then, however, this facade crumbles spectacularly. On 3 August 2017, the country awoke to news that the nation's proudest financial institution, the Commonwealth Bank, had become a wash-house for international crime syndicates. The system was so efficient that the criminals didn't even need to speak to a teller. Technology handled the cash deposits for them. Drug syndicates, Middle Eastern terrorists and other major crime groups had managed to move billions of dollars – to this day, no one knows the exact amount – through the same bank that was giving primary-school kids their first Dollarmite account.

Australians were shocked. Police surveillance footage showed money mules sitting on milk crates on the footpath outside a suburban Commonwealth Bank branch, stuffing the ATM with bricks of green and gold banknotes from a dishevelled backpack.

A year later the rot spread to Westpac. The nation's oldest and second-most profitable bank was caught moving funds for the country's worst sex offenders, facilitating unspeakable crimes against children in the Philippines. On top of that, Westpac had also been running a cross-border financial sluice gate that allowed multinational clients to book Australian revenue in low-tax countries such as Singapore. The money slipped through the fingers of the Australian Taxation Office (ATO) and landed in the hands of more forgiving offshore tax collectors. Who knows what happened to it then? It certainly didn't pay for Australian roads, schools and hospitals, as it should have. Billions were lost to Australian taxpayers, humble wage earners who would have to make up the shortfall through their own taxes. As with the Commonwealth Bank, Westpac's poor compliance controls and bad bookkeeping meant the ATO would never be able to shine a light on this corporate tax evasion. The bank records had never existed to begin with.

After that, the dominoes started to fall quickly. First it was Crown Casino in Melbourne and Perth, then The Star in Sydney – the country's two largest casino groups. All were embroiled in scandals involving junket operators, criminal money, proceeds of corruption, bikie gangs and Asian triads. Australians were less surprised to see grainy footage of 'high rollers' at Crown Casino unbundling millions of dollars, in neatly bound bricks, from another Aussie icon: the supermarket cooler bag. One prolific gambler moved $100 million in a single week through the pokies at The Star.

Even the country's sporting clubs were implicated in systemic money laundering, after authorities discovered that criminals were washing vast sums of money through the nation's beloved pokies. Management had looked away, feigning ignorance, as tax evasion and criminal cash kept the nation's community sporting clubs afloat. At least the listed casino chains weren't having all the fun.

In this instance, however, Donald Horne was wrong. Australia's 25 million honest citizens weren't just surprised, they were shocked and appalled. They weren't complacent – they were bloody furious. How could a country that detested political corruption become the 'safety deposit box' for corrupt politicians from across Asia, the Pacific Islands, Africa and Europe? How could Asian triads and Mexican drug cartels swap synthetic drugs – near-worthless chemicals – for some of the country's finest freehold real estate? Australia was losing its precious farms and waterfront development sites to criminal gangs, in return for fleeting chemical highs.

How could one of the world's richest countries, a bastion of financial integrity, find itself in a position where its politicians would lie to the world for 15 years about impending law reform that would close these loopholes? Was all this pretence intended to uphold the system that had turned Australian housing into one of the world's criminal Ponzi schemes, or did some of Australia's leaders so lack curiosity about the events that surrounded them that they were unaware of the risks of the global criminal economy? More to the point: how could Australians be certain they weren't paying more for their family homes because they were going head-to-head at auction with a drug dealer or a foreign kleptocrat? Could Aussies still believe in the fairness that had been the foundation of the nation's social contract for more than 200 years?

The truth is, they couldn't.

And they still can't to this day. Since 2006, those 'Tranche 2' federal money-laundering law reforms have been handballed from one incoming prime minister to the next. The Ponzi scheme that is Australian property has outlasted six of them.

At best, Australia's leaders 'so lack curiosity' about the events that surround them that they're unaware of the risks of the global criminal economy. At worst, Australia's leaders have a horse in the race and are knowingly complicit in this global scam. There's no doubt that the nag called 'Self Interest' is running its little heart out.

Welcome to the deep, dark world of the modern criminal economy. Turn the page, if you dare, and join me on a journey to the heart of the international black money hydra that has wrapped its serpentine limbs around the Lucky Laundry.

ONE

Into the Dragon's Den

Bill Majcher is familiar with the buzz of walking into the dragon's den. Truth is, he's drawn to it. The thrill, the intellectual battle, the chase, the catch. And, hopefully, the prize at the end.

Bill has been out of the undercover intelligence game for two decades – or so I'm told. But he still has nerves of steel. Peeling back the layers on a delicate financial crime enterprise, going covert, gathering evidence, reverse-engineering the structures that are used to conceal some of the world's biggest financially motivated crimes, playing a character in a celluloid thriller – it's what he still lives for.

'When I discovered the undercover world, I was like a duck to water. I had a knack for it, you might say,' Bill says with a grin.

Bill still carries a lean figure that belies his 35-plus years on this intriguing, addictive beat. He's always impeccably groomed, with sharp blue eyes that hint at his Polish heritage. Bill is an old friend from the anti-money-laundering world, which is one of the world's most tight-knit professional communities. Every time I'm passing through Hong Kong we'll grab lunch, a beer, maybe even a night out if he's banked away some credits with his family. Tonight, Bill has invited me for a beer or three at a grimy, noisy, buzzing bar in Hong Kong's Wan Chai area. It's a triad-owned establishment, naturally. As well as selling beautifully crisp beer, this bar's helping to manage some of its owners' 'cash problems'. Cash-intensive, over-the-counter businesses are very useful for diluting the revenue from other, less salubrious enterprises.

*

Vancouver, Canada, 1990

'What the hell am I doing here?' Bill wonders. Sitting in a filthy toilet with his dirty shirt sleeve rolled up, a rubber band wrapped tightly around his left bicep and a syringe filled with 50cc of No. 4 China White heroin, in his right hand.

Bill looks down at his left arm. He can see the bright purplish track marks that suggest he has a strong affection for heroin.

Just a few short years ago, Bill was finishing university and working as a Canadian Eurobond trader in the City of London. He was a hotshot. A young bond trader with the world ahead of him. Yet here he is now, shooting up heroin in the skid row of Vancouver surrounded by some of life's greatest losers.

Right now, Bill has an urgent decision to make. Is he going to shoot up first or let his new companion, Joe, take the hit? Joe is anxiously crowding him out in the bathroom, eyes shining with addiction as he anticipates the warm pulse.

Joe's recently been released from prison for armed robbery. He's anxious to reintegrate into his old network. But he's even more anxious to take his share of the heroin Bill has just purchased from some of Joe's friends. Eight nasty people, big, with acres of tattoo, leather and muscle between them. People who are waiting right outside the bathroom.

Some of these friends are already hostile towards Bill. Perhaps suspicious of this new guy on the dope scene. From his training, though, Bill is aware that whatever happens in the next few minutes in that dirty stall will have an impact on his physical wellbeing. It's China White, or fight and flight.

In that moment, Bill hears the words of one of his management professors: 'You've now entered the due diligence phase of the deal.'

No matter how well you've been trained, the initial course for undercover agents — or UCs, as they're known — can't prepare you for everything. And here in this dirty, graffiti-lined toilet cubicle with a freshly released drug addict, Bill needs to act on instinct.

Joe's one job — one simple job — was to check Bill out, make sure he's not from 'the filth'. Joe is there to watch Bill shoot up. Undercover cops might do lines of coke, they might sleep with escorts supplied by a cartel, they might do weed, but very few would shoot up high-grade street junk.

Yet intelligence operatives can read a mark quickly. They're adept at playing their targets. They have a forensic ability to identify and exploit vulnerabilities, weaknesses, minute moments of opportunity. Bill sees his opportunity in Joe's hungry eyes; he's visually salivating over that bag of China White. The gang might have given him a task but Joe, first and foremost, is a hopeless junkie.

Bill moves the syringe to his arm, toys with it. 'Foreplay,' he says and laughs.

Joe is itching for it.

'Here, pal,' he says. 'You take the first hit. I can wait. Looks like you need it more than me.'

Bill hands over the rig and Joe can't resist. He opens his forearm, a junkie's act of lonely seduction, taps a vein, slides in the dart and draws back. A crimson hurricane swirls inside the plunger. The tail of the dragon. As the needle slides down, Joe is transported. He's riding it away, barely clinging on to the life he no longer wants. He's warm. Safe. He's home.

Bill takes the needle, which has about 30cc of heroin left in it. He plays the role, preparing the next hit expertly. This much he was taught during his UC training a few months earlier. As Joe goes on the nod, Bill turns and quickly wraps the needle tip into some toilet paper. The idea of getting nicked with that dirty barb petrifies him more than the beating he's just escaped from Joe's buddies outside.

Bill turns around, exhales, and kicks open the door. He's passed his first test as an undercover agent. The rush is undeniable. Incomparable. He's scored the information he came here for, and the evidence is in the bag. In that moment he's hooked. It's an addiction that will define the course of his life.

Welcome to the game, William Majcher.

*

Bill's first and foremost a family man now, though that wasn't always the case. Guys with careers like Bill's tend not to have families, or to start them late. Their work is always tinged with danger. Covert operatives effectively sit outside the law. They live in a grey zone of rubbery rules. They have to juggle multiple narratives in their head. They may have to go to extreme measures to win their target's trust. They do things that aren't conducive to a white-picket-fence life.

Operatives like Bill also spend many of their waking hours with a death sentence hanging over their heads. If they get exposed while engaging with a drug cartel, there's an automatic $100,000 bounty shining like a sharpened guillotine above their necks.

So why do UCs like Bill take these risks? If they turn to the 'dark side' they can earn millions working for a cartel, just like Pete Hoang had done in Sydney. Their 'tradecraft' in the art of money laundering is forever in demand in the underworld.

The truth is they love the thrill. But more importantly, they have a belief. People like Bill want to uphold a system of rules and consequences that make our world work. They view the risks they take as the price we must pay for a civil society.

*

When we meet in Wan Chai, I'm hunting some information on the tentacles of the Aussie laundromat. I want to find out how billions of dollars from Asia's criminals, every year, are sluicing their way into the Aussie economy. Ever reliable, Bill has some wild tales to share. This time though, I'm even more blown away than usual, as he tells me about some of the work he's been doing on behalf of a company linked to the Chinese Ministry of Public Security. The MPS! It sounds incredible. He tells me he's now a 'gun for hire' on the hunt for some of China's missing billions.

After he left the Royal Canadian Mounted Police in 2007, Majcher needed a change of scene. He was approached to come to Hong Kong and roll out a global network for a merchant bank. A few moves later and Bill decided to open his own business specialising in asset recovery and financial investigations.

Hong Kong was very good to Bill. '*Xìngyùn dì dìfāng*,' as the Chinese might say: a lucky place. But he had always had his eyes on the biggest prize in the business. The whale among whales for asset recovery agents: the MPS.

After years of relationship-building, he was approached by a senior adviser to the leadership of the MPS-linked State Administration for Foreign Exchange (SAFE) in China. They were very concerned about 'capital leakage'. China is one of a few formerly 'hard line' communist countries that heavily restricts money from leaving its territory. It's a way to ensure that a lack of confidence in the economy can never snowball into a total economic collapse – the downfall of many a quasi-dictatorship. SAFE wanted to determine how so much money was moving in and out of China without its knowledge.

'It's not all about the outflow,' Bill explains. 'China's government is also very concerned about illegal capital inflows. They understand that billions of dollars flow outside of the country, outside of the purview of the government, as the by-product of corruption and criminality. That money comes back into China without them seeing it and fuels further corruption and criminality. It's a two-way street.'

But it gets better. The scent of this dirty money, he tells me, has led him straight to some of the whitest beaches on the planet: Queensland, Australia.

TWO

A Shady World of Greys

Bill Majcher landed in Brisbane in late 2018, looking like a typical Canadian expat on vacation. In reality, he was in town on behalf of SAFE: hunting whales. He walked the streets of the Gold Coast taking photos, checking the sights. Occasionally, he would wander into a real estate office and enquire about properties. He had a list of addresses he wanted to check out. Foreigners were barred from buying established Australian houses, but no one in the real estate game seemed reluctant to help out a prospective buyer. As far as the agents were concerned, the Aussie foreign ownership laws were the buyer's problem to navigate.

What the agents could never have guessed was that Bill was actually chasing the proceeds of multi-billion-dollar corruption scandals and investment frauds on the Chinese mainland. If he could find assets and 'repatriate' them he would get to keep a slice. Everyone was a winner. Except the kleptocrats of course.

*

As Bill explained this to me in that noisy Wan Chai bar, his eyes darted over my shoulder to a table next to us, where two people were speaking quietly in Mandarin. They seemed to be doing more listening than talking. He dropped his voice to a whisper so that he's almost drowned out by the sonic boom of the bar's PA system. Old habits die hard.

'The majority of flight capital out of China goes to English-based countries: the United States, Canada, Australia, New Zealand and the United Kingdom,' Bill says. 'They go there because English is the international language. Many of the children of the Chinese billionaires or millionaires are going to English-based universities. They've set up or established a presence in these English law countries.'

In addition to these myriad lifestyle benefits, he tells me there is one crucial dealmaker for setting up in a country like Australia. The Anglophone countries – all of which have legal systems built upon the English common law tradition – have an essential quality that the Chinese kleptocrats are seeking: respect for property, and strict limits on extradition.

'They understand that English law has a fundamental basis that makes extradition difficult. To extradite even the most heinous criminal in the world from a country such as Canada takes 10 or 12 years. So that creates a lot of opportunity for an economic criminal at least, to try to extend that deferral and build the financial base for the family outside of China,' Bill explained.

Was this part of the reason why Australia had become one of the Asia-Pacific region's most attractive and welcoming laundromats?

The Chinese government seemed to think so. Its novel solution was to use bounty hunters like Bill to track down these billions in stolen assets. Australian authorities had cracked down immediately, treating some of these as cases of foreign interference. Did the government view bounty hunters like Bill Majcher, acting on behalf of a public-private partnership in Beijing, any differently?

*

Before arriving in Australia, Bill notified the AFP that he'd been presented with a civil recovery mandate from the Chinese government. The MPS, he explained to the Feds, was growing tired with the formal channels. Their relationship with the Australian police was solid but the process was too slow.

Bill told the AFP that the money he was charged with recovering had been stolen – either through corruption or massive Ponzi schemes, where as many as 100,000 Chinese citizens had been defrauded in a single hit. The AFP advised him that they were swamped with criminal files concerning China, and if the civil process could be used to lessen the burden, they would be supportive.

The notion that a Chinese-funded bounty hunter was roaming Australian streets might have shocked many Queenslanders, had they known about it. What should have shocked them even more, however, was just how easily Chinese criminals, public servants and politicians could snap up Aussie property. How could Australians be sure that the person bidding against them at a Saturday auction wasn't a buyer's agent for a Chinese kleptocrat? Or a triad? The truth was, they couldn't.

For more than a decade the Australian government had been sitting on legislation to prevent this from happening. The laws were to be known as 'Tranche 2' of the *Anti-Money Laundering and Counter-Terrorism Financing Act 2006* (known in shorthand as the AML/CTF Act). In 2006, Prime Minister John Howard had made a commitment to the international community to pass laws that would prevent lawyers, accountants and real estate agents from turning a blind eye to dodgy deals. The policy had bipartisan support from Labor – tri-partisan, if you included the Greens – and was believed to be a fait accompli.

But in Canberra, a lot can go awry in the corridors of power. Since the first tranche of the laws was passed, there had been years of earnest talk. Cans were judiciously kicked into election 'caretaker periods'. The policy promise turned out to be even more elusive than a carbon tax. By 2018 it had outlived six Australian leaders: Howard, Kevin Rudd, Julia Gillard, Rudd (the sequel), Tony Abbott and Malcolm Turnbull. This was a genuine example of bipartisan cooperation in pursuit of political incompetence.

Peter Whish-Wilson, the former investment banker and surfing Greens senator from Tasmania, was horrified. He described this debacle as a 'timeline of inaction' that embarrassed Australia on the global stage. During an impassioned speech to parliament in 2019, made to a near-empty chamber, Senator Whish-Wilson said lobbying from 'vested interests' had once again betrayed Australians who wanted to be able to own a home in their own country.

'The reason we haven't cracked down on the dark heart of money laundering in this country … is because vested interests have lobbied so hard to stop this from happening,' he railed.

In 2017, Transparency International (TI) had identified Australia, Canada, the United Kingdom and the United States as the top four locations for laundering money through real estate. TI singled out Australia as the worst, however, as it had failed to address all 10 major legal loopholes that facilitate the laundering of criminal funds. According to Whish-Wilson, there was 'plenty of evidence to suggest that a large part of the recent spike in Chinese investment in Australian real estate and in many other parts of the world is money laundering'.

How could this be possible in an English common law country that markets itself to the world as having a clean economy with low levels of political corruption?

*

Despite Australia seeing something akin to Mr Sheen when it looks in the mirror, there are many in the international community who view things differently. A team from the Paris-based Financial Action Task Force (FATF) had visited Australia in 2014 to prepare a major report on the country's effectiveness in the fight against financial crime. The FATF is housed within the influential Organisation for Economic Cooperation and Development (OECD) and is funded indirectly by its members, including Australia. The global body was tasked with setting standards, identifying vulnerabilities in the financial system and measuring the effectiveness of each member state's controls. The report, released a year later, was a mixed bag. To Canberra's horror, the FATF made it clear that Australia was 'an attractive destination for foreign proceeds of crime, particularly corruption-related proceeds flowing into real estate'.

AUSTRAC, the report acknowledged, was one of the most effective and innovative financial intelligence units (FIUs) in the world. It did an excellent job of policing money laundering through the sectors it could oversee: banks, financial services, casinos and bullion dealers. AUSTRAC was portrayed as a little-known national treasure, hunting down society's worst criminals through financial intelligence and quietly supporting an array of state and federal agencies with their investigations.

Yet the federal government was forcing this 300-strong agency to fight the Goliath of global organised crime with one arm tied behind its back. AUSTRAC had only half the powers it needed. It was overseeing 14,000 businesses when it should have been overseeing 100,000 more, spread across the 'gatekeeper professions' and high-value goods dealers, such as jewellers and car yards. This is where the dirty lucre was likely to be flowing.

It was a brutal assessment. Yet after this international bollocking, only platitudes and commitments – not laws – flowed from Canberra.

In the face of this apathy, the blows to Australia's international reputation kept coming. In December 2017, the OECD issued its Phase 4 Report on Australia's implementation of the Anti-Bribery Convention. This report recommended that Australia should 'address the risk that the real estate sector could be used to launder the proceeds of foreign bribery'.

Another major multilateral body, the International Monetary Fund (IMF), released a Financial Stability Action Plan, which stressed the need to regulate the gatekeeper professions. These Designated Non-Financial Businesses and Professions (DNFBPs) could drive a range of economic, social and political risks in Australia by fuelling the black economy.

The IMF said Australia should urgently 'expand the AML/CTF regime to cover all DNFBPs starting with trust and company service providers, lawyers and real estate professionals as they have been assessed as presenting higher money laundering and terrorism financing risk.'

*

As Bill walked around the Gold Coast with his list of properties owned by foreign kleptocrats, his eyes were also blown wide open. He knew his home country of Canada was a target for Chinese criminals, but here in Australia it was next-level. There was simply no oversight. Everyone in the real estate transaction chain could feign ignorance when a wealthy buyer from China appeared, willing to pay cash for a premium residential or commercial property.

Behind the scenes, the AFP's Criminal Assets Confiscation Taskforce (CACT) was doing what it could, but this was slow, cumbersome work. The agency had recently seized $15 million in real estate, jewellery, wine and assets that were acquired with the proceeds of crimes perpetrated in China, including investment frauds. While it was a big number, the officers involved knew they'd only made a small dent.

Over the next two years, the team would seize almost $450 million in criminal assets. Once again, this wealth would be tied up in art, luxury vehicles, jewellery, designer clothing, handbags, premium wine and electronics. But there was one asset class that stood out above all the others combined: real estate. For every million dollars the CACT seized, $575,000 was held in commercial or residential real estate. Australian property was, by far, the criminal's asset class of choice. Money launderers had perfected the art of infiltrating Australia's economy, via gatekeeper professions, to acquire the country's finest high-value goods and property.

Criminals and their advisers were also developing new tricks to circumvent the AFP's asset forfeiture teams. They would go to extreme lengths to conceal the true ownership of these properties. They would hide assets behind offshore shell companies with straw directors, or pay someone innocuous in Australia an annual fee to pose as the purchaser of land. If anyone at the AFP or the Foreign Investment Review Board (FIRB) looked into these deals (which statistically was unlikely), they would see that an Australian citizen was the legal title holder. Tick.

Money-laundering experts, meanwhile, said it was no surprise that the assets in the AFP's seizures all sat outside the reach of the Australian financial intelligence world. AUSTRAC didn't have oversight of these sectors, such as property, art, jewellery and cars. Nor did AUSTRAC have oversight of the lawyers, accountants and estate agents who helped to structure these complex deals. And when it came to concealing ownership behind a thick corporate veil, international criminals could afford the best of advice.

*

On the sunny shores of Queensland, Majcher was horrified to find Australia had fallen behind the rest of the region – indeed the world – when it came to bringing gatekeepers within the net. He said the 'Tranche 2' law reforms would be crucial for Australia to have any hope of turning back the tide of criminal money that was surging down from the Middle Kingdom, the Middle East and other high-risk regions.

'Lawyers, realtors, and immigration agents are, in my view, the most engaged parties facilitating these dirty money channels,' he said. 'So why on Earth is nothing being done?'

With the benefit of his close ties to the Chinese police, Majcher had gained a unique insight into how these scams worked. In many cases, crime gangs were taking advantage of the voracious appetite in China to get money out of the country, in breach of capital controls. This worked nicely alongside the voracious appetite in Australia for illicit drugs. It was a perfectly symbiotic relationship between vendor and customer. A professional launderer simply had to act as the intermediary to bring these two groups together, like a financial dating agency, so they could swap their funds.

Triads in China knew there were many people who wanted to get their money out of the country. These people would happily hand over their precious yuan in China, in return for the ownership of houses in Australia. These houses might have been purchased with the cash generated from drug sales in Australia by Chinese-linked drug dealers. Typically an offshore corporate entity would own the real estate assets, so the shares in the corporation might change hands but – on the property title at least – the corporate owner would remain the same.

Once again, the veil of corporate secrecy, aided and abetted by gatekeepers, was proving to be the criminal's dearest friend.

Beijing, meanwhile, was growing increasingly annoyed. The MPS took the view that Australia was deliberately offering a safe haven for kleptocrats and other financial criminals, including those who had absconded from China with the proceeds of investment frauds. Interest in commercial recovery services (or bounty hunters) had reportedly grown under operations Sky

Net and Fox Hunt, which sought to strike fear into the hearts of corrupt officials. China wanted these criminals back to face the firing squad – but if it couldn't get the offenders, it at least wanted their assets.

Some of these bounty hunters acting for China had been caught operating in a very murky area. Their tactics had been likened to intimidation or standover work, rather than 'asset recovery'. Some were using heavy handed approaches to intimidate Chinese nationals or dual citizens living in Australia. People had received 'knocks on the door' from bounty hunters claiming to be acting on behalf of the Chinese MPS. There were allegations that Chinese spies had also been harassing former officials and their families to the point where they packed up and returned in fear. There was strong evidence that China had been leaning on extended family members back home to persuade kleptocrats to return.

Some of the people China was pursuing in Australia, Majcher knew, were employees of state-owned enterprises with annual incomes of around $30,000, who had *somehow* amassed fortunes worth up to $500 million. 'From my perspective, the legal system in the West is rooted in the principle that an accused is innocent until proven broke,' Majcher quipped. 'I have shared that viewpoint with some individuals in the MPS and received no disagreement.'

*

Of course, there is another major player in the world of money laundering: the banks. Banks are the main conduits for international financial flows. They can play a critical role in either facilitating financial crime or hardening the system against attack. They have unique power in the 'public-private partnership' that is financial intelligence. They also have huge legal obligations to detect and report any suspicious activity – such as foreign kleptocrats on meagre public-sector salaries buying luxury Australian homes without a mortgage.

The partnership between law enforcement, the financial intelligence agencies and the banks relies heavily on trust. The banks can only see a small slice of the picture – their own customer base – while the authorities can see a bigger picture but often lack that granular detail. In the cut and thrust of business, however, sometimes the importance of that trust can be forgotten.

THREE

The Glitch in the Machines

Two years before Bill set foot on Aussie soil, with his list of names, a covert operative from the other side of the law was working the beaches 900 kilometres further south.

It was January 2016. A balmy summer's day in Sydney. Holidaymakers were massing on Bondi Beach in rows of tanned skin and lycra to soak up some rays. The aquamarine Sydney Harbour was awash with full-sailed white yachts. But Van Kien Do wasn't feeling festive. He was hard at work, trying to launch his new business. Worse still, the technology was failing him – and his boss, Thi Lan Phuong Pham, was highly unsympathetic.

Pham was barking orders into a burner phone to Do, on the other side of Sydney. Mr Do was acting as what the policing world would call a 'smurf', named after the miniaturised comic book characters. Just like their blue-skinned counterparts, smurfs act as individuals doing small tasks to stay unnoticed while they collectively accomplish a much greater goal. Tasks like buying pseudoephedrine for use in producing meth or, like Do, depositing bundles of cash into ATMs – bundles too small to set off any alarm bells. This is the stock-in-trade of the humble smurfs, the ultimate proletarians of the criminal underworld.

Suddenly, Pham let out a cackle of laughter. The Vietnamese hotelier was safely at arm's length on the other side of Sydney. From her vantage point, on the other end of a Viber call, it all seemed rather comical. It was her accomplice Do who was getting himself on CCTV footage, handling the dirty cash, mixing with bikies and gun runners, and apparently taking all the risks. Unbeknown to the embattled Do, his boss was also creaming 80 per cent of the profits from their criminal scheme.

What Pham didn't know, at that point, was that she wasn't nearly as safe as she thought. Pham and Do had already come to the attention of Strike Force Bugam, a partnership between the New South Wales Police and the Australian Criminal Intelligence Commission (ACIC). The joint-agency task force was targeting organised crime and money laundering and Pham's operation was sitting squarely in their gunsights. Every word she said in Australia, every text message she typed, was being recorded and monitored.

Pham would eventually fly home to her young son in Vietnam, where she would manage that side of the operation: bringing in new customers and arranging cash drops for criminal syndicates. But even there, the Australian authorities would be watching and waiting.

*

For decades, Australian police had known that money was the vascular system of the criminal body. Each year, the cops were getting new laws and new tools to help them track, trace and target the proceeds of serious and organised crime. But they also had a problem: as their detection tools became more sophisticated, the criminals were always becoming smarter. It was a cat and rat game – and all too often the rats were winning. The sheer volume of work meant the police could only pursue a handful of their major targets.

'We only catch the dumb ones, or the unlucky,' was an all-too-common refrain I'd heard from law-enforcement officers.

In this instance, however, the cops had an edge on the crooks. Detective Sergeant Warren Lysaght, of the NSW Police, had become obsessed with the intellectual battle of money laundering. Lysaght was a burly cop with square shoulders and a tightly cropped beard. He loved rugby, a laugh with his mates, a beer and his family (not necessarily in that order). On his phone, his profile picture was the monochrome outline of a skull. This was not some 'who dares wins' bravado, but the X-ray of his own fractured cranium after a tough day on the rugby field.

Detective Sergeant Lysaght was engrossed in this job, tracking major criminal groups and thinking multiple moves ahead. It was a game of underworld chess. He was working day and night with a tight group of colleagues on the Pham case, which was in turn blowing open a new understanding of criminal tradecraft. The ACIC and the AFP had taken a sudden interest in the case when weapons started moving around the country. The Feds wanted to take it over. But fortunately for Warren and his team, the NSW Police were firmly backing Bugam. They would see this case through to the end.

Strike force operations have impressive names, but the reality is often quite different. The sensitive nature of this criminal intelligence work means that it needs to stay tight. Often a strike force will involve a close team of colleagues – mates who trust each other like spouses, and can work together almost as closely. Within the cone of silence of Strike Force Bugam, it wasn't uncommon for secure messages to fly around at 1 am about a surveillance job the next day. Wives and kids often had to accept that the job took precedence over family activities.

The vehicles they were tracking, filled with drugs, weapons and cash, moved unexpectedly, which meant everyone remained on high alert. This camaraderie of strike force work and the thrill of the hunt were what had drawn Lysaght to the job, and he was still there two decades later.

Detective Senior Constable Ray Malkoun was one of the tightknit Bugam team members. He was also one of Lysaght's best mates and the father of a young family. Malkoun had contracted cancer during the operation and was recuperating at home following some invasive surgery and aggressive chemotherapy. Despite his colleagues' demands, they couldn't keep him off the case. The other team members told him to rest and promised they'd close the job without him, so he could recover, but he wouldn't hear of that. Malkoun was still working on it from home, despite his doctors' orders. The case had come to represent something much bigger than dismantling a single syndicate. They were breaking new ground, discovering new criminal typologies that would lead to the discovery of other criminal networks. They were part of the continual fight to keep an international criminal scourge out of Australia.

Each of the Bugam cops would have stepped in front of a bullet to save a colleague. They were dedicated and intelligent professionals, and they were unified by the fact that their targets were the most ruthless of organised criminals.

*

Strike Force Bugam was part of a new wave of investigations that used financial intelligence to trace and disrupt criminal syndicates. In the traditional model, coppers would solve a crime and seize the money. They would then build a profile of the criminal network through the indelible trail of money movements. The Bugam boys turned this model on its head. By starting with the laundering syndicate and following the money backwards, they were finding new criminal offences that would previously have gone undetected. The sophisticated financial intelligence they used, known as 'graph analytics', helped them build a picture of these interlinked criminal networks. They had a saying: dirty cash always leaves behind a smell.

Using intelligence from AUSTRAC, and the ACIC, the police were able to find deep connections among these illicit money flows. They then used this to crack other crimes, with the money trail leading to gun runners, hitmen, crooked cops and more members of underground syndicates.

The commander of Strike Force Bugam, Detective Superintendent Scott Cook of the NSW Police, said in November 2017 that the approach also had another objective: upending the risk-reward equation for serious criminals by seizing their easily earned assets. 'By focusing on the cash or other proceeds of crime,' he said, 'we're hitting them where it hurts most: profit.'

*

Back in November 2015, the Strike Force Bugam investigators began looking into links between money-laundering syndicates and what's known as 'cuckoo smurfing'. This is when a syndicate, or a money transfer agent, acts as an intermediary for a person who wishes to purchase Australian property with foreign currency. The buyer is not aware that, when they hand over their foreign currency, they will receive criminally tainted Australian dollars in return. The criminals behind these schemes may offer exceptionally good exchange rates as they're seeking to wash their ill-gotten cash through a legitimate transaction.

The Bugam investigation would lead them directly to the trail of Thi Lan Phuong Pham. What they found was disturbing. Money remitters in Vietnam were acting as fronts for a major global laundering operation. They would offer to move legitimate funds to Australia for their customers, but instead would dump criminal funds into their Australian accounts. Often the money would arrive in dribs and drabs as mules worked their way down a train line of ATMs across North Sydney. When it all eventually arrived, customers were usually relieved they had not been defrauded. Like China, Vietnam has foreign exchange controls, which prevent citizens from sending large amounts of money abroad. This drives people into the arms of these *hawala* networks and underground remitters.

Hawala, or *hundi*, as it is also known, is the world's cheapest and oldest way of moving money across borders. It's an informal and untraceable network of money changers who are spread like an invisible mesh around the globe. These systems have served mankind for more than a millennium, having emerged in the Middle East and the Indian subcontinent as far back as the 8th century. Their history has outlasted empires, with multi-generational alliances allowing transfers to take place instantly, and with no digital trail.

It's a business that relies on trust. The *hawaladars* – who often operate out of legitimate businesses such as grocery stores, newsagents and delis – simply keep a written ledger and settle their transactions periodically. Settling ledgers could involve a friend travelling with gold disguised as jewellery, diamonds inside toothpaste tubes, a single large bank transfer disguised as a trade invoice, or these days – proving the adaptability of this hidden global network – a cryptocurrency transaction.

In Australia, *hawala* and *hundi* have been largely replaced by the formal financial system, as all cross-border transactions must be regulated and reported to AUSTRAC. Remitters must register with the financial intelligence agency and have a compliance program. That sort of rigour is not conducive to the informal nature of the ancient *hawala* system.

Yet despite the penalties and risk of jail for *hawaladars* in Australia, still the networks persist. In some ethnic communities, the appeal is the speed and the low cost. In some instances, the appeal is primarily cultural – that's particularly so among foreign workers. In other cases, users are actively seeking anonymity for their outbound transactions, ranging from simple tax evasion on Australian cash earnings to the financing of terrorist groups like ISIS.

In Pham's case, the customers had no idea their clean funds in Vietnam were being substituted with criminal loot in Australia. Some would discover this the hard way when the AFP froze their accounts as the proceeds of crime, well after a criminal gang in Vietnam had disappeared with the legitimate funds.

In the case of Mrs Pham, police discovered the hotelier had been acting as the coordinator of a major offshore syndicate. The 42-year-old single mother travelled to Australia in January 2016 on a one-year visa. During that time, she attempted to set up a network of smurfs, who would launder her clients' money under instructions from abroad.

*

Van Kien Do became Pham's first Australian accomplice. He was introduced to a shadowy figure known as 'The Accountant', who would provide him with the details of cash pickups. After collecting the money, Do would deposit the funds into bank accounts through ATMs, branch tellers and direct bulk cash drops. It was a slick operation.

One of the goals of this criminal 'specialisation' was to separate the money from the crime. Ever since the days of Al Capone, organised-crime groups had known it was dangerous to handle their own dirty linen. More recently, proceeds of crime confiscation laws had made it crucial for gangsters to avoid the 'vertical integration' of their criminal supply chains. 'Separate the money from the crime', had become an underworld mantra.

Unfortunately for Pham, by the time she arrived in Australia the authorities were already on her case. The Vietnamese national bought a mobile phone and a SIM card, which police immediately secured a warrant to bug. During stakeouts and phone surveillance, the police monitored Pham's every move as she taught Do the delicate craft of cuckoo smurfing (a reference to the cuckoo bird, which deceives other birds into raising its young).

Pham took Do to a number of banks and showed him how to place cash into ATMs, intelligent deposit machines (IDMs) and through branch tellers without arousing suspicion. She taught him to break the money into amounts under the $10,000 currency reporting threshold, to move between branches, and to ensure he regularly bought new SIM cards and burner phones. They communicated using Viber in the belief it would protect them from police surveillance.

The deal was that Do could keep one per cent of the proceeds, in cash, for himself. For the boy from Vietnam, who was struggling to make ends meet in Sydney, it seemed too good to be true.

'Should I transfer the whole amount or can I retain my commission percentage?' he once asked Pham. He was due to receive a bag containing $200,000.

'Yes, of course. If you receive two, you'll have to forward only one ninety-eight,' his handler replied.

'Okay, so I can keep two?'

'That two is yours. Leave it aside,' Pham said.

Sadly for Do, this lucre would not come without a price.

*

When it came to putting money through the spin cycle, Do was not a natural-born criminal. During one of his first cash placements, on 17 January 2016, he was stuck at a Commonwealth Bank smart ATM, unable to deposit the funds. He tapped at the LCD screen but nothing happened. Do called his boss, perplexed and nervous.

'Press the button on the bottom left!' Pham instructed her hapless accomplice.

He tried again. 'But no message appeared,' he assured his boss.

'Then the machine is broken,' she said, before breaking into a hysterical laugh. 'Cut and run!'

It was an ignoble start to Do's lucrative new career, but the embattled money mule was not ready to give up. He was aware this was a sure path to either prison or riches, and he was willing to keep rolling the dice.

Later that month, Do was told that a 'Caucasian man' would turn up at his house to deliver $200,000 in cash. For Do, who knew the individual was linked to organised crime, this was a frightening proposition. Do was given a Vietnamese 500-dong note to use as a 'token'. He was told that the bagman would have a copy of the note's serial number, and this would validate his identity.

These 500-dong notes proved to be a common – and very effective – form of ID among the laundering syndicates and their criminal clients. These people didn't know each other, and it was likely they would never meet again. Swapping serial numbers on banknotes was the perfect way for the gangsters to make sure they were handing their bags of money to the right bagman.

Still, Do was nervous that these characters would learn where he lived. 'Hey, tell me,' he asked Pham, 'if someone comes to deliver things, should I let them in?'

'Yeah, you should,' Pham replied, from her location well away from the physical cash drop. 'These people are okay. Let them come inside, the house is better.'

She explained how the transaction would work. 'They'll give you a bag, just like a bag of gifts … We'll only check [the amount] after they've gone. If something is short, tell me so that I can let their bosses know. So far, we've been doing right all the time. If we do something wrong, nobody would want to see us again.'

'It's okay. I understand that,' Do replied. 'We need to maintain good credibility.'

'That's right. Our company has very good credibility,' Pham assured her loyal smurf.

Do had good reason to be cautious. Getting caught by the authorities was the least of his worries. The organised-crime group he and Pham were working with was a serious operation. It would go on to launder $42 million between March and August 2016, in proceeds from illicit drug and firearm sales. Members of the syndicate included bikies and an ex-copper.

*

In mid-February, Pham returned to Vietnam, satisfied that Do had the Australian work under control. 'The Accountant', who went by the name Hoa, would give Do instructions, with account numbers, BSBs or physical locations for cash drops. Do, ever the entrepreneur, began to build his own network of smurfs to work under him.

Over a six-month period, Do collected and laundered $2.75 million from criminal groups. In doing so, he netted $27,500 in cash commissions. Not yet a fortune, but it was easy money for someone trying to survive in Sydney. And their operation was growing.

Pham's deal was even better. She was raking in four times that amount, and doing so from the safety of Vietnam.

FOUR

Banged Up, Abroad

By the end of their first year in the money-laundering game, Pham and Do's hustle was booming. After a patchy start, they were pretty confident they had this game wired. It was money for jam.

They had worked out that the Commonwealth Bank's smart ATMs – Intelligent Deposit Machines (IDMs) – were the best. As long as the machines weren't full, they accepted the most notes. If a machine had just been emptied, you could wash up to $600,000 in a single sitting, at any hour of the day or night. Dirty money would disappear into a hole in the wall and, in real time, corresponding numbers would appear in an Australian bank account. Pham could even watch the money appear in her own accounts, from Vietnam.

Those criminal funds might end up being used to buy a house or invest in a local business. In some cases, the dirty dosh was used to buy government bonds as part of the Special Investor Visa (SIV) program. This was the ultimate irony; in effect, the government was helping to launder the proceeds of the illicit drug and firearms trade, and handing out five-year visas while they were at it.

If it wasn't for the constant police surveillance, Do would have been riding high. As fortune would have it, the syndicate had an even greater stroke of luck that worked in its favour: the Commonwealth Bank was suffering from systemic failures to detect financial crimes. Deposits through the bank's IDMs – those not-so-smart ATMs – were not being recorded on the bank's central transaction monitoring platform. This meant that billions of dollars worth of transactions were taking place in the dark.

Two of the most crucial financial intelligence reports are 'threshold transaction reports' (TTRs) and 'suspicious matter reports' (SMRs). TTRs need to be submitted for any transaction of $10,000 or more. SMRs are filed whenever a bank comes across something the layman might call 'suss'. In Pham and Do's case, hundreds of these reports should have been filed with AUSTRAC, which could then examine the transactions with an eye for illegal activity. But for cash deposited via the bank's IDMs, none of these critical reports were being filed.

If it weren't for Strike Force Bugam and some diligent financial intelligence work, Pham and Do's syndicate might have flown completely under the radar.

*

By the end of 2016, Pham was extremely happy with how her Aussie business was running. She was trousering four per cent of everything that moved through her clients' accounts. In Vietnam, this represented a huge sum of money. For the

Bugam team, however, the pressure was mounting. They were under intense duress to wrap up what had been an in-depth and expensive operation – but they were waiting for Pham to return to Sydney.

There was a growing belief within the police chain of command that Bugam should swoop on Do. Detective Sergeant Lysaght knew this would tip off Pham, though, which would ensure she never returned to Australia. There was also pressure to hand the case over to the AFP, which had greater resources for long-term organised-crime jobs that crossed state and international borders. The team kept monitoring the chatter on the intercepts, hoping for a break.

In January 2017, their moment arrived. Pham said she wanted to return to Sydney to oversee her operations and catch up with her loyal accomplice. The pair had a plan to expand the business and needed to speak in person. And what could be better than a work trip to beautiful Sydney at the height of summer? Strike Force Bugam had been patient; now Pham was swimming into their net.

When Pham arrived in the country, it was their time to strike – with force. On Wednesday, 18 January, the police swooped on Do, taking him into custody. They kept Pham under surveillance, predicting she would panic and try to flee Australia. Sure enough, a day later, they tailed her to the airport.

Pham stood in line, calmly preparing to fly away. The Vietnamese money launderer knew she was taking a big risk flying out that day. But what choice did she have? It seemed the game was over.

In the queue behind her stood a burly man. Detective Sergeant Lysaght wanted one last coup: access to Pham's phone.

His plan was to wait until she used a PIN code to unlock her device, then he would pounce, ensuring he had access to the treasure trove of evidence. To his amazement, though, she didn't reach for her phone.

Before Pham reached the front of the queue, she felt a tap on the shoulder. She was under arrest.

When Lysaght seized her phone, to his surprise he found it was unlocked after all. Ha! It was the perfect end to a triumphant day.

The first thing Lysaght did after the arrest was report back to his colleague, Detective Senior Constable Ray Malkoun, who was still on leave, fighting to stall the relentless march of terminal cancer. The men were jubilant. It had been an incredible, roller-coaster operation. They had broken new ground in the understanding of criminal laundering syndicates, and they had caught the 'controller'.

Tragically, Malkoun's health was not looking great. Deep down, Lysaght knew he would soon be at his dear friend's graveside, promising through tears to be there in person – for both of them – when Pham was sentenced in court.

*

The members of Strike Force Bugam were celebrated within their closed-door world. Both the NSW Police and the ACIC had executed a difficult job, from start to finish.

Detective Inspector Stuart Sweeney, from the NSW Organised Crime Squad's Money Laundering Unit, said the investigation highlighted the need for good intelligence – and strong inter-agency cooperation. 'While borders can present some investigative challenges, the ever-increasing collaboration of law enforcement across the globe is showing that being outside the jurisdiction will not save you,' he said.

Pham certainly believed she had distanced herself sufficiently from the scene of the crime. In a police interview she was brazen, denying all knowledge of the scheme. She claimed to not even know Van Kien Do. When the police handed her a surveillance photo of her and Do together at an event, she continued in her denial. 'He looks like a singer from the USA!' she told the investigators.

The ruse didn't last long. The evidence collected from mobile phones, security camera footage and stakeouts was undeniable. This was a sophisticated money-laundering operation and Pham was going to do a long stretch in Australia at Her Majesty's pleasure (and taxpayers' expense).

*

The lessons from Bugam shone a light on a very inconvenient truth about the ever-evolving criminal landscape. Since the introduction of the anti-money-laundering regime and the 'proceeds of crime' seizure laws, criminals were loath to hold cash. Their goal was to move their loot as quickly as possible to a dedicated laundering syndicate, such as Pham's. This had given rise to an entirely new industry: the professional money launderer. It was part of the burgeoning 'crime as a service' underworld economy, powered by darknet marketplaces and encrypted chat services. These bag-handlers, money movers and underworld accountants could market themselves internationally and charge somewhere between 5 and 10 per cent for their services. Committing a predicate crime, like running drugs or a robbery, was increasingly a mug's game. The real action was in moving the vast proceeds of crime, for a small slice of the profits.

Money-laundering services like Pham's had become essential to the US$2-trillion-a-year crime industry. This wave of 'money seeking anonymity' had distorted entire economies, fed corruption and forced legitimate businesses to the wall while their criminal competitors thrived. Many cash businesses had sprouted purely as a front for placing the proceeds of crime, discreetly, into the banking system. For other cash businesses, such as coffee shops and bars, money laundering was a side hustle to pay the bills and keep the lights on in what was a tough business climate.

But, as Pham discovered to her cost, you couldn't get away with this game forever. In court in Sydney, 6800 kilometres away from her young son and family, the tough Vietnamese businesswoman broke. After resisting for months, she eventually pleaded guilty to one count of 'directing the activities of a criminal group'. The offence, under section 390.6(2) of the *Criminal Code Act*, carried a maximum penalty of 15 years in prison. She was given a sentence of six years' jail.

Her loyal but unfortunate accomplice Do, meanwhile, was sentenced to three years in jail, with an 18-month non-parole period. Members of the organised-crime group that handled the drugs and guns were also arrested and sentenced with the help of this financial intelligence.

For Pham, the daughter of a wealthy Vietnamese family, it was a tragic fall. She sobbed repeatedly during her court appearances. She didn't need to do this work. Reality had bitten hard.

For her bank of choice, the situation wasn't much better. Pham's case would eventually be buried inside a 691-page

Revised Statement of Claim in the landmark *AUSTRAC v Commonwealth Bank* money-laundering case. Pham had taken advantage of the fact that the bank had turned a blind eye to dirty money. It didn't conduct due diligence on the members of the cuckoo smurfing syndicate. It had failed to file hundreds of financial intelligence reports. And it kept criminal accounts like Pham's open for business, even after people within the bank's financial crime team had flagged them as highly suspicious.

To AUSTRAC's legal team, Pham was known simply as 'Person 81'. And soon Australians would discover that her journey – from running a hotel chain in Vietnam to running a transnational money-laundering syndicate in Sydney – was nothing extraordinary. There would be many, many more stories like hers. She was but one in a lengthy gallery of rogues.

FIVE

King Cash and the Plastic Fantastics

The sad cases of Thi Lan Phuong Pham and Van Kien Do, like that of the murdered Pete Tan Hoang, show the strange lure that colourful strips of polymer hold for humans. Like bower birds drawn to something shiny, people are susceptible to the hypnotic allure of banknotes. Their beauty – beyond the intricate artwork and microscopic lettering – is in the promises they hold: luxury, freedom, power, love, adventure, retirement or just a slightly easier life.

A stroll through the Reserve Bank of Australia's museum, in Martin Place, Sydney, offers a glimpse into the intertwined relationship between a civilisation and its currency. The lesson from history is clear. Any society that loses control of its currency is destined for collapse.

Those who work in financial intelligence, on the side of the cops, are continually amazed by the things people will do to amass money. They will take incredible risks. They will take lives. They will risk their freedom – even their own lives – for the opportunity to clip the ticket in the global marketplace of dark money.

Illegal money printing is the bane of central banks and governments the world over. Even the US 'superdollar', which is printed on a cotton-linen substrate with red and blue security fibres, has been hit by sophisticated counterfeiting attacks. This threat doesn't come only from criminal syndicates, but also from 'state-based actors'. North Korea is believed to have run a sophisticated US dollar counterfeiting program for decades, and to have used this illicit 'currency' to buy materials for its weapons program.

In Australia, however, the polymer banknote has been largely resistant to counterfeiting. But this durability has created other problems – unanticipated problems – for the police and financial intelligence community.

*

Australia's world-class scientific agency, the CSIRO, has had some big wins over the years. Without the CSIRO we might not have the essential creature comforts of wifi, extended-life contact lenses, Aerogard or Softly washing detergent for extracting stubborn grime from those sensitive Aussie Merino garments. One of the CSIRO's greatest innovations, however, is stashed in bank vaults, safes, wallets and mattresses the world over: the polymer banknote.

Back in 1966, Australia had a big problem. Counterfeiting. The country had just switched over from pounds to decimal currency – the dollars we all covet and spend our lives chasing furiously today. The first Australian dollars used cutting-edge technology: they were printed on high-quality paper with metal thread, watermarks and embossed 'intaglio' printing. But to the horror of the RBA's chairman, Dr H.C. 'Nugget' Coombs, it took the crooks just a few months to achieve a high-grade forgery. Within a year, forged Aussie dollars were accumulating in tills and bank vaults all over the country.

Being an innovative bloke, Nugget called the boffins at the Commonwealth science lab. He figured there must be a better way. And so, on April Fool's Day in 1968, a group of scientists, academics and central bankers met in the New South Wales town of Thredbo, by the ski slopes, for a top-secret meeting. Given that the meeting took place on April Fool's Day, it should be no surprise that there was no snow. But this was no junket: the RBA had brought them together for a confidential discussion about 'some aspects of banknote printing'.

Within the confines of the gathering, the RBA officials revealed the nature of their problem. Paper money was too easy to replicate. And if the problem continued, and especially if word of this got out, it could undermine confidence in the Australian economy. A scientist from Kodak summarised the problem bluntly: it didn't matter how good the fancy paper and ink was; if something could be photographed, then it could also be copied and printed.

The solution the group reached was to develop some sort of 'optically variable device' (OVD). This would be something that couldn't be photographed in its entirety because it changed with an external stimulus, such as heat or light. There was only one problem: no such technology existed. Dave Solomon, a CSIRO scientist, later recalled the project as an exciting challenge for some of Australia's top scientists. Why use paper, they figured, when they had access to new and mysterious polymer plastics? The boffins' radical ideas soon started flowing. 'We produced these OVDs in large quantities to demonstrate the practical nature of the concept,' Solomon said. 'We built a production plant in secret and printed a design provided by the RBA – "birds in flight" – using our plastic film.

'However, the number of ideas was beginning to confuse the Reserve Bank and a freeze was put on further designs. So we focused on diffraction gratings (holograms), moiré interference patterns, photochromic compounds and a label. The latter was detectable by a machine.'

The CSIRO team pumped out 50 million banknotes and 1.25 million OVDs, to demonstrate to the RBA that they could deliver at scale and on budget. To ensure they weren't inadvertently engaging in counterfeiting themselves, they printed $3 and $7 test notes. The end result, 10 years later, was a robust banknote technology that would eventually be patented and exported to the world.

As with most technological revolutions, the science outpaced the rate at which human institutions could change their thinking and behaviour. Only in 1988, after another 11 years of widespread counterfeiting, was the first modern banknote released.

What the scientists never could have conceived, however, was that by the turn of the century, money laundering would have grown to become a bigger criminal industry than counterfeiting. They had created a banknote that could, quite literally, survive going through a rinse cycle. Central bankers are kindly people, and did not anticipate how nefariously some others might behave. Criminals, on the other hand, quickly realised that these near-indestructible and almost-irreplicable wedges of cash offered them a new opportunity for profit.

Counterfeiting was now officially a mug's game. But the durable nature of this plastic dosh – which quickly became known affectionately as lobsters ($20), pineapples ($50) and Melbas ($100) – would have an unexpected impact on the Australian economy.

*

In 1988, Australia was kicking off the greatest party on Earth to celebrate the bicentenary of its settlement by the British. Led by its beloved larrikin Prime Minister Bob Hawke, the Silver Bodgie, the country was punching above its weight on the world stage. On 26 January, as streamers flew and yachts sailed around the country's turquoise waterways, Sydney Harbour was alive like never before. A palpable optimism hung in the air with the smoke that still lingered well after the colour and fury of the fireworks had subsided.

Just up the road from Circular Quay, at 65 Martin Place, there was excitement within the RBA too. The central bankers were celebrating the release of their new $10 polymer banknote: it was a way of telling the world that, at 200 years young, Australia could be a tech and financial services innovator. In this bold new era, Aussie innovators were proving Donald Horne's 'lucky country' slur wrong.

While the nation's eyes were focused on celebration, turning 200 wasn't the only big change for Australia that year. It was purely coincidental that, down in Canberra, Australia's anti-money-laundering regime was being birthed in a rare moment of bipartisan politics. The parliament introduced a new law to fight serious crime (primarily tax evasion and drug trafficking) by collecting 'intel' on cash transactions of $10,000 or more.

Back then, ten grand was a big chunk of change. Six months' pay for the average Aussie. Over time, of course, Canberra insiders knew that the magic of inflation would conspire with them to create a massive trove of financial intelligence. And it would be stored safely within flashy new IBM mainframe computers, which could crunch numbers better than a roomful of mathematical savants.

The *Financial Transaction Reports Act 1988* took effect a year later, requiring banks, casinos, car yards and solicitors to report basic intelligence to the Australian Transaction Reports and Analysis Centre, the newest kid on the block in Canberra.

Fast-forward 30 years to 2019, and $10,000 was no longer such a vast sum. The average Aussie might now blow that on a fortnight in Bali. The country had become inconceivably wealthy over the preceding three decades. But as the nation's wealth ballooned, so too did its underground economy.

Conservative estimates suggested that the nation's shadow economy had swelled to be worth some $32 billion each year. The true figure was up to three times that number, according to estimates from the United Nations Office on Drugs and Crime (UNODC). In response, the parliament proposed banning cash transactions above $10,000.

Measuring the scale of the cash economy is, of course, a guessing game. What you can audit is the amount of cash *in* the economy. The government had passed laws to treat money laundering as a problem for the commercial banks. But what about the RBA, which actually issued the currency? As you might have guessed, Canberra itself was excluded from the anti-money-laundering laws.

In truth, the RBA was happy to see the country's cash balance grow. It was the fuel of economic growth and the ballast of the banking system. The lifeblood of the economy. And because it held this view, the RBA had done precious little deep thinking to explain the scale of Australia's love affair with cold, hard, cash.

As a result of the banknote's durability, it could remain out of circulation almost indefinitely. It didn't rot. It could literally be washed. The AFP teams would sometimes find it concealed, in rolls, inside PVC pipes embedded in the walls of houses. They would discover it buried in backyards, or packed under false floors in sheds and houses. Sometimes judicious bank tellers noted in reports to AUSTRAC that the cash they handled smelled of mothballs, which criminals would discover to their detriment in court. Even so, cash was the perfect vehicle for tax evasion, drug deals, bribes and money laundering.

By 2019, Australians were hoarding a gargantuan $76 billion of the stuff. It was the 'float' of the criminal economy. It was the currency of addiction. It was the bricks of cash tied with lacky bands that funded Australia's outlaw motorcycle gangs. And it had infiltrated broader Australian society. Many a pensioner would buy a coffee with their own mothballed banknotes, while also clearing a healthy pension cheque from Centrelink.

As a direct result of its innovation, the RBA had inadvertently created the banknote of choice for money launderers, tax evaders, cash couriers, mules and cuckoo smurfs the world over.

SIX

The Missing Melbas

The plastic banknote is a boon for those wanting to store, move or hide illicit assets outside the banking system. In Australia, the note of choice for hoarding and bulk cash smuggling is the $100 note, known affectionately as 'the Melba' (the note features the face of the legendary opera singer Dame Nellie Melba).

In November 2021, the Aussie cash supply surged above the $100 billion threshold, up 20 per cent during the pandemic. The RBA estimated that between half and three-quarters was being 'hoarded'. The notes favoured by launderers – $50s and $100s – represented 94 per cent of the cash in circulation. In effect, there was somewhere between $2000 and $3000 being hoarded 'under the mattress' for every man, woman and child in the country. This raised the question: where were Australia's missing Melbas?

Steve Worthington, Professor of Finance at Swinburne University Business School, said most Australians rarely come across the highest-denomination banknotes. 'When was the last time you had a $100 note in your pocket? When was the last time you withdrew one from an ATM?' he wrote in an article in

2016, raising serious questions about the use of these banknotes in the black economy. 'From an Australian perspective, we might argue those who benefit most from $100 banknotes are either tax evaders or engaged in criminal activities or both.'

It seemed that no one at the RBA, or anywhere in government, really knew how much of this $100 billion cash mountain was being used to sluice the illicit economy.

*

In response to a request from Canberra, Australia's central bank issued a research paper that attempted to solve the mystery of the missing Melbas. The paper investigated the scale of banknote hoarding and attempted to quantify the associated illicit activity.

The RBA said in its paper that between 15 and 35 per cent of the banknotes circulating in Australia were being used to facilitate legitimate transactions. Around half to three-quarters of outstanding banknotes, they said, were simply being 'hoarded'. The RBA's optimistic assessment was that only '4 to 8 per cent of outstanding banknotes are used in the shadow economy'.

These estimates were highly questionable, however, in view of other domestic and international research. The 'big four' accounting firm KPMG studied the Aussie shadow economy in 2018 and estimated it was worth $32 billion each year. The Australian Bureau of Statistics (ABS) had already judged that the underground cash economy (that is, tax evasion) amounted to around $25 billion per year; when drug trafficking was added in, KPMG concluded, this figure rose to $32 billion annually.

Yet these sanguine Australian numbers, which suggested the shadow economy sat at a modest 1.5 per cent of GDP, were still vastly lower than independent international estimates. Research from the Institute for Applied Economic Research at the University of Tübingen in Germany, for instance, found that Australia's shadow economy (primarily tax evasion) accounted for a whopping 9.4 per cent of GDP, or more than $150 billion.

When illegal production and organised crime was added in, the number rose ever higher. The Australian National Audit Office (ANAO), in a 2002 report on the cash economy, said the cash economy 'may range from 3.5 to 13.4 per cent' of GDP. A 2017 International Monetary Fund (IMF) working paper, authored by Leandro Medina and Friedrich Schneider, said Australia's shadow economy was likely to be between 12 and 13 per cent of GDP. Even the government's own Black Economy Taskforce estimated in 2019 that the shadow economy was larger than the RBA's modest figures suggested: around 3 per cent of GDP, or $50 billion.

The RBA's estimate that 92 to 96 per cent of Australian cash was being used for lawful purposes was looking statistically untenable – even laughable.

This raised several deeper questions. Why would the RBA, as the issuer of the nation's banknotes, want to downplay their use in the illicit economy? And why, especially given the central bank had itself been implicated in foreign bribery in 2018, was it declining to include an internationally accepted range of offences (including bribery) in its definition of financial crime?

*

When the RBA's researchers asked Aussies why they hoarded cash, people came up with a range of justifications. Not surprisingly, these explanations rarely involved confessions of tax evasion, cocaine purchases, welfare fraud, money laundering or other criminal activity. Instead, the justifications included: emergency transactions; faster withdrawal times and lower fees; cash gifts; savings for large purchases; privacy and anonymity; preparing for payment system outages; and 'mistrust of banks'.

Well, at least the last of those justifications was not a fib.

'Those with large physical cash holdings may be less likely to participate in a survey,' the RBA said, dancing around the elephant in the room, 'and, even if they do, might be hesitant to respond with the true extent of their holdings.' The RBA's paper also noted: 'The existence of asset means-testing for various social benefits in Australia, and more generally the desire to hide assets from tax authorities, also provides an incentive for Australians to hold assets in a form that is hard to trace.'

Of course, any estimate of the size of the Australian shadow economy involves a degree of speculation, given the criminal world's inherent opaqueness. The central bank and other researchers cannot know for sure where illicit cash is flowing, as the criminal's fundamental aim is to avoid detection. Despite these challenges, the RBA accepted that consumers were hoarding thousands of dollars at home – as much as $15,000 for a three-child family – for emergency transactions, birthday pressies or ATM outages. This was an extraordinary conclusion for such important research into the dark economy.

*

The truth is, criminal innovation always moves much faster than the RBA. Criminal markets in Australia have evolved significantly over the past decade. Drug dealers aren't just using cash. The insidious criminal economy has spread even further to encompass payments in cryptocurrency and with contactless terminals, passing the money off as 'business income'. They are skipping the cash 'placement' stage and going directly to the layering and integration of dirty money. Many crimes are being executed online. In 2020, as the COVID-19 pandemic locked people in their homes, fraud and digital scams skyrocketed. Aussies lost an estimated $851 million to scams, a record annual amount, according to the Australian Competition and Consumer Commission (ACCC). This evolution had changed the volume and nature of 'dirty money' and the law enforcement community would need to adapt with it. Throughout 2020, the world of crime was mutating faster than the coronavirus itself, and governments were struggling to keep up.

The ACIC, meanwhile, was one agency that wouldn't be left behind. It pointed to a number of disturbing categories of criminal activity that were being excluded from official statistics: identity theft, cybercrime, investment and financial market fraud, card fraud, illicit tobacco and firearms offences, intellectual property theft, human trafficking and slavery, and child sexual exploitation. These were crimes that were corroding, and in some cases decimating, Australian society.

And the laundering of those criminal proceeds had become a lucrative industry in its own right, hoovering up between 5 and 10 per cent of the gross profits. All in all, this was a massive hidden industry.

But the RBA, the issuer of the country's $100-billion cash mountain, had failed to appreciate this evolution. Downplaying the criminal abuse of the nation's physical currency had also allowed the RBA to argue that the burden of fighting financial crime rested with commercial banks and other business sectors, not with the central bank itself. This abdication of responsibility would have huge flow-on effects for the nation, as it was self-evident that tackling the scourge of financial crime required a coordinated, whole-of-society approach.

The RBA's paper had promised to answer a question in its title: 'Where's the Money?' In truth, the report might just as well have been titled 'Nothing to See Here, Folks ... Please Move Along'.

Australia's banks and casinos, and the financial intelligence community, however, had no option to live in this comfortable complacency. They were seeing a very different scenario play out in the real economy. Its consequences would ultimately prove catastrophic – for victims of financial crime, for the banks and business community, for law enforcement, and indeed for the entire Australian community.

SEVEN

Down the Hallways
of History

Back in November 2011, Ian Narev's posterior hadn't yet had time to mould a comfortable dent in the chief executive's leather chair at Commonwealth Bank's headquarters in Sydney. Ralph Norris, his predecessor, mentor and fellow Kiwi, had groomed him for this role for years. As of two weeks earlier, the chair, and the multi-million-dollar salary that came with it, was his.

Narev might have felt like he needed to pinch himself. The son of penniless European immigrants who'd escaped the Holocaust and went on to build a life in New Zealand, was now sitting atop Australia's largest bank. The former child actor and brilliant law student had grown up alright. He was helming the country's most iconic and systemically important financial institution. In his 40s. It was an incredible ascendancy, by any measure. Over the next six years, shareholders would agree to pay Narev $43,887,682 for his stewardship of the vast banking enterprise that had worked its tentacles into every aspect of Australian life.

The Commonwealth Bank is a pillar of Australia's economic strength and prosperity. It's a symbol of the country's growth over the preceding 100 years from backwater primary producer to a member of the G20 and the economic envy of the world. It had achieved all of this with a population no larger than that of Delhi or Shanghai. If airdropped into Tokyo, Australia's citizenry would rattle around with a couple of million spare apartments; crash pads, perhaps, in case they missed the last *shinkansen* home after a night out on the Kirins.

Narev had always been bright and ambitious, and fascinated by philosophy and ethics. He felt a responsibility to make an impact with his life. When he listened to his parents' harrowing stories of the Holocaust and life in wartime Europe, he had felt a special urgency. Every fibre inside him wanted to make them proud, to justify the sacrifice they had endured to give their children a better life.

As a kid, Narev had enjoyed a stint as an actor in the New Zealand TV series *Children of Fire Mountain*. Later in life, he would draw on these early experiences to galvanise himself for a big presentation. His colleagues all agreed he was a great communicator, able to memorise entire results presentations, right down to the decimal places. His performances in front of rooms full of analysts were legendary. But Narev always felt the weight of CBA shareholders' expectations – and, to a lesser extent, Australia's entire economy – bearing down upon his slight shoulders.

*

In November 2011, Narev's name had been engraved on the chief executive's plaque for only a fortnight. Yet he would speak as the face and voice of the institution as it celebrated its 100th birthday in Sydney. This was a 'landmark event', as the corporate comms team described it.

The words 'trust' and 'culture' were hallmarks of any Commonwealth Bank presentation. As the new chief, Ian Narev – open, friendly, approachable – was now the principal advocate of that promise. The board had chosen him as the bank's public face of trust, which has always been the fundamental currency of banking.

For this milestone celebration, the country's most profitable bank had hired an avant-garde experiential communications agency, Imagination Australia, to create a walk-through experience. The open-ended brief was to 'create an exhibition and event that would commemorate CBA's history and place in Australian culture'.

The exhibition was placed in the middle, with the event space fanning out around it like a nautilus. More than 200 storylines were presented, using old film footage, written memoirs, photography and installations. Photos hung from a Hills Hoist; a Victa mower sat on a pedestal. The underlying message in the event was clear: the Commonwealth Bank was claiming its rightful legacy as a proud Aussie icon.

As Narev walked down a bright hallway at Sydney's Hordern Pavilion, on his way to open the centenary celebration, the weight of expectation hit him like a tonne of tungsten-filled gold bars. The excitement he'd felt at winning a career-defining role evaporated. He was now the new custodian of the iconic 'pillar' bank, with a nation's expectations riding on his performance.

*

Four years later, while CBA was surfing atop a groundswell of record bonuses and shareholder dividends, Narev still recalled that evening with fondness. 'I remember there was a wonderful celebration at the Hordern Pavilion. It was started with a kind of walk through the years of the Commonwealth Bank's history,' Narev said.

In a portent of fate, as he walked down that hallway in 2011, he had a strange out-of-body experience. He could physically hear the voices of history echoing in his head. 'The way I describe it is that I was walking through with my wife, Frances, going to the dinner, and all I could hear was these voices saying: "Do not stuff up this institution."'

It was a profound moment for the new chief – perhaps even the banker's equivalent of a spiritual experience.

'You get this fabulous appreciation for the history of the institution, and the fact that it was the Reserve Bank and it was government-owned. That does create different franchise benefits and a higher degree of scrutiny on certain things – and we embrace both of them,' Narev told a function at UNSW.

The deep baritone of Australian history had sent out a message. A warning for the vessel's young, bright, ambitious captain: *Do not stuff up this institution.* It was a call that had echoed through the Great Depression, the Second World War, from the farms to the beaches and the shining glass spires of Sydney. It bounced off the steel beams of the Harbour Bridge and the tiled sails of the Opera House. It reverberated with the sound of a baby's rattle; kids dropping their first coins into the metal CBA piggy bank that a nice lady in a black-and-yellow uniform gave them at school. It was the cheerful voice that responded without question or hesitation when people walked into a branch to withdraw their retirement savings.

'Do not stuff up this institution!'

*

When Narev shared this personal experience in 2015, he felt safe to do so, vindicated by four years of bumper returns. Australia's favourite bank was blowing away its competitors. In the process, it was also blowing away analyst and shareholder expectations. On a return-on-equity (RoE) basis, the Aussie battler was one of the world's most profitable banks – a beneficiary of the credit-fuelled economic expansion that was Australia's 21st-century economic miracle. Australia would go on to post three decades of uninterrupted growth, the longest run any country in history had enjoyed without a recession. The country was riding high on the rise of China to economic superpower status, and the CBA was helping turn that good fortune into a domestic debt binge.

Prior to the introduction of responsible lending laws, this was an aspirational wealth-creation model that the CBA advertised on television as 'Equity mate!' The general gist was this: load up on debt to buy property; watch the value of your asset soar as everyone else chased the same dream; then leverage those paper profits by taking on more debt to buy the other things you want. If anyone had doubted it before, they wouldn't now. This was indeed the Lucky Country, reinvented for a new century of consumption-fuelled economic growth.

In one memorable ad, a cautious homeowner with an embittered wife was counselled by his more profligate neighbour, who had drawn down on the equity in his home to buy a boat and a holiday house. The grinning neighbour had borrowed his way to both a happy wife and a happy life.

The ad was good enough to make 'Equity mate!' part of the Aussie vernacular. But it didn't look so good a few years later, when the Northern Hemisphere banks collapsed into a housing-fuelled sinkhole of debt and government bailouts. With the arrival of the Global Financial Crisis in 2008, and the resulting crackdown on profligate lending, the 'Equity mate!' ad was quietly retired and replaced with the more service-focused 'Can' campaign.

*

After the crash of 2008, there was an immediate shift in culture. Return *of* your money, rather than the return *on* your money, was all the rage again. In public, the banks were more sober, and they were also constrained by responsible lending laws that passed in 2009, which required lenders to establish that any new credit was 'not unsuitable' for the borrower. Behind the scenes, however, the money spigot stayed open. Despite the reforms, credit somehow ballooned to the point where Australian households were soon carrying the highest debt-to-GDP ratio outside Switzerland. Under a barrage of questions in the Senate in May 2017, even the chairman of the Australian Prudential Regulation Authority (APRA), Wayne Byres, admitted that alarm bells were 'going off softly' at the institution he headed.

But the Lucky Country's dream of 'Equity mate!' – free wealth obtained through the monetary magic pudding of the bricks-and-mortar ATM – was made of sterner stuff than in the

Northern Hemisphere. The housing boom continued to roll on Down Under. Paper fortunes piled up, leaving Aussie property owners and their bankers sitting atop unthinkable riches. It was the best of times – provided you owned a home and an investment property or two.

In this heady climate, it was difficult for a senior Aussie banker not to make a fortune. But even among their peers, Narev and his team at CommBank were considered banking masterminds. They were feeding Australia's addiction to foreign-sourced credit with an efficiency that would make even the British East India Company blush. Nothing could stop Australia's consumption boom; certainly not something as trifling as the collapse of manufacturing, world-beating household debt and a deteriorating national balance sheet.

The RBA's punchbowl was still out, an army of heavily incentivised mortgage brokers were spiking it from their hipflasks, and the party was roaring like the 1920s.

Narev was even being feted as a genius by the chairman of a slightly less profitable competitor. David Gonski, chairman of ANZ, quipped at a public forum that Narev's one character flaw was that he 'worked for the wrong bank'.

*

One of the big lessons Narev had learned from his mentor, Ralph Norris, was that technology sat at the heart of banking. Norris had the vision to invest in a comprehensive technology overhaul, while other banks simply milked their IBM mainframes for the last drops of profit. Under Norris's stewardship, CBA was the first bank to move to a real-time core banking system. It was a massive multi-year project, and somewhat risky, given the complexity of the business. But this punt gave CommBank the ability to move faster and more profitably, winning business from its less nimble peers, Westpac, ANZ and NAB. It had better data at its fingertips and could do things like processing loan requests more quickly than the other three 'pillars' of Aussie banking, or executing instant payments.

At the heart of this investment lay a broader push for automation. CBA was replacing humans with technology in many innovative areas, meaning it could win business without increasing its headcount. One stellar example was its investment in hundreds of Intelligent Deposit Machines (IDMs) across Australia in 2012. These allowed customers to dump their cash into the bank at all hours – after their nightclub or kebab shop closed, for instance. Unlike a 'night drop', this money would be counted, forgeries excluded and funds cleared instantly thanks to CommBank's real-time banking platform. The only thing these incredible machines seemed to lack was a cocaine residue sensor.

The owner of a Kings Cross nightclub could bank his cash takings at 2 am, and then move the money to Hong Kong before daybreak. All for $22 plus forex.

The response to this new technology was seismic. When the IDMs were first introduced in 2012, customers dropped $89.1 million of cash into them over a six-month period. Two and a half years later, the machines would rake in, count and clear $3.36 billion during an equivalent six-month window.

Narev and his team saw this as evidence that their bet on automation had been a winner. Customers liked non-face-to-face banking and were voting with their ATM cards. Over three years, an astounding $8.9 billion moved through CommBank's magic

IDMs. They promised speed and convenience, among an array of other consumer benefits.

As some less reputable customers had discovered, however, IDMs also offered another valuable benefit. They provided a lack of teller scrutiny and, therefore, the likelihood of the bank 'forming a suspicion' about money laundering or terrorism financing was greatly reduced. The IDMs didn't have brains and they didn't have the all-important 'sixth sense' of human intuition. For all their potential, the IDMs wouldn't be ringing the anti-money-laundering unit to report that a customer had just dumped a backpack on the counter full of banknotes that reeked of mothballs.

It was a launderer's paradise.

*

The Diebold Nixdorf IDM technology that enabled this instantaneous crediting of cash deposits into any CBA account was impressive. The name was not the only thing that was 'intelligent' about this investment.

The bank's spreadsheets showed it was able to create huge cost savings by pushing cash transactions out of the branches and onto the streets. The all-important institutional investors, who drove the bank's share price and bonuses, were enamoured with this efficiency strategy. IDMs were transforming CBA's customer experience: the bank was leading the charge to 24/7 banking through whatever channel the customer preferred.

'It's a consistent strategy ... invest in people, invest in technology,' Narev said during a shareholder presentation in February 2015. Those nit-picking business journos couldn't argue with the numbers. During the previous six months, productivity improvements had delivered $140 million in savings to CBA's shareholders.

The success of IDMs reflected why Team CBA were lauded, even by competitors, as the smartest guys in the room in Australian banking. Narev and other executives could point to evidence of this in the price-to-earnings premium that his bank's shares attracted, relative to the other three big banks. CBA's tech investment was so far ahead of its peers that they had no hope of catching up any time soon.

By 2015 the mass migration to mobile payments was underway and the IDM technology was starting to look old-school. Even so, the bank was still attracting huge volumes of deposits. CBA continued to trumpet its market-leading moves into a 'digital banking ecosystem', one that promised to deliver real-time banking at an 'ultra-low cost' to consumers.

Behind the successful customer-facing banking revolution, however, there were some issues with the tech. And if the business managers had bothered to ask the financial crime compliance team, they would have learned that these were some very big issues indeed.

*

The deployment of IDMs and other technology was being rushed inside the bank to meet an ambitious timetable. CommBank wanted to make the most of the march it had stolen on its competitors by harnessing the power of further investment in technology. It was seeking to expand its IDM network from 150 to 380 machines across Australia.

According to senior people in the risk team at the time, morale was sapped. Efficiency was being chased at the expense of compliance controls. Everywhere there was a cost centre, analysts within the bank looked at ways to streamline things. It was an approach to management and corporate efficiency that Narev had honed during his decade as a star performer at consultancy McKinsey.

'If you had a project and you wanted to get approval for it you had to present a business case. Things were funded on a project basis. So if you wanted the project to go ahead you had to be able to demonstrate the business benefits – and they needed to be several multiples of the money spent,' a bank insider told me, on condition of anonymity.

This approach to cost control was an organisational mantra. Regulatory risk was regarded, internally, as something to which you paid lip service to keep the regulators happy. When the risk teams left, you just went back to the real business of banking: making money.

And perhaps they had a point. Few outside the highest echelons of financial power in Australia knew the extent to which the Commonwealth Bank had captured the government and its regulatory arms. There had always been a revolving door of jobs, between poachers and gamekeepers, that kept government officials obediently subservient to their targets. This was a given. There was also the well-known lobbying power of groups such as the Australian Bankers' Association, which had poached Anna Bligh, a former Labor premier of Queensland, to lead its push into Canberra. These weaknesses in the system were well understood and could – theoretically, at least – be mitigated.

What wasn't known, however, was that in 2009 a crack team at the Commonwealth Bank had quietly salvaged the reputation of Australia's prudential regulator, APRA. At the height of the financial crisis, the Commonwealth Bank, with its healthy balance sheet, had pulled the entire economy back from the brink. And as history would prove, APRA was very, very grateful.

EIGHT

The Bankwest Affair

By 2015, the Commonwealth Bank was untouchable – and not just by its competitors. Management had engineered a climate where the regulators were too supine, too awestruck, and too timid to challenge the Goliath of Australian financial services. APRA and ASIC, each with hundreds of millions of dollars in their annual operating budgets, including special litigation funds, had become the archetypal 'captive regulators'.

In the United Kingdom, this phenomenon was known as 'tea and bickies regulation'. In the old days, when gentlemen ran the banks and their friends ran the regulators, things were sorted out face to face over a boardroom table. When they had been particularly naughty, bankers would tell colleagues they had visited the Bank of England and it was a 'no bickies' meeting. If the English central bank served your team tea only, you knew there were things you needed to fix. Urgently. And fix them you did.

Banking was a conservative man's game and public trust, as they say, was the foundation of the profession. It was well established over the British central bank's 320-year history that if trust went out the door, bank deposits soon followed.

In Australia, seven years after the financial crisis, there was no such gentleman's agreement. The banking and finance industry was an economic powerhouse that accounted for 450,000 Australian jobs. Financial services, insurance and superannuation had devoured a large chunk of the economy. The big four banks were also the nation's biggest taxpayers, and among the most prolific of political donors. The banks had more lobbyists floating around the shadowy corridors of Canberra than any other sector, including resources.

Ian Narev was driving towards his fourth straight year of bumper profits. He was commandeering one of the most profitable banks in the world.

What few people outside the powerful Council of Financial Regulators knew was that Narev and his team had once saved the Australian economy from Armageddon. In swooping to Bankwest's rescue, CommBank had also saved the regulators who were tasked with overseeing the economy. It had been an existential drama for the Australian economy – one the managers at the nation's financial regulators still remembered acutely, and one the management at the Commonwealth Bank, led by Narev and David Cohen, would never let them forget.

The regulators were cowed. AUSTRAC was an unknown quantity. Aside from a civil proceeding in early stages against the gaming giant Tabcorp for money-laundering breaches, AUSTRAC had never had cause to use its civil litigation powers.

That was all about to change.

*

In October 2008, at the height of the Global Financial Crisis, Bankwest was in a catastrophic position. The bank was an icon in Western Australia, having started out as the Rural & Industrial Bank (R&I) with a mandate to power the state's economic growth.

Back in 1895, Western Australia's political leaders believed that the gravity of the financial sector was pulling inexorably towards Sydney and Melbourne. They could not rely on east-coast bankers to power their state's hunger for capital, which they desperately needed to develop WA's incredible human and environmental bounty. Perth is, after all, 3291 kilometres (as the kookaburra flies) from Sydney. It is more distant from the east coast of Australia than Dublin is from Moscow. The R&I Bank soon evolved from a government-backed lender for farmers into a full-service deposit-taking bank. At the height of the Second World War, R&I Bank was so systemically important to the state's economy that its existence was protected by an Act of parliament.

Fast-forward to the banking boom of the 21st century, the mid-Noughties, and the UK powerhouse HBOS was on a global growth spree. It had snapped up a bunch of prized assets around the world, including Bankwest, as the rebranded and privatised R&I was now known. HBOS had a strategy. Using its massive global balance sheet, it believed it could build Bankwest to the point where it was able to have a tilt at the weakest of the Aussie 'Big Four'.

Melbourne's NAB was in Edinburgh's gunsights like a hunter tracking wounded prey. If things went to plan, HBOS could, by stealth and cunning, become the fourth protected 'pillar' of the Australian banking system. It would be a commercial masterstroke, with HBOS taking control of one limb of the financial system and giving the UK financial sector substantial influence over the Australian economy.

As they say in Scotland, *Whit's fur ye'll no go past ye!*

*

Between 2005 and 2007, Bankwest's new owners embarked on a radical east-coast expansion plan. It was opening branches that looked more like airline loyalty lounges, complete with baristas and couches, and hoovering up clients in the commercial property sector. The objective was simply to grow market share; profitability was an afterthought at best.

The bank was growing like a teenager with a pituitary disorder, while its IT backbone creaked and ached under the strain of such rapid national expansion. Managers in the bank couldn't even tell how much lending they had in particular sectors. APRA's requirement was that property lending should not account for more than 55 per cent of the bank's total book. Bankwest and the regulator didn't know it yet, but through a combination of greed, recklessness and carelessness, that figure had already swollen to around 65 per cent.

To make matters worse, APRA had an agreement with Bankwest based on what's called 'home state and host state' regulation. In effect, because Bankwest had access to its parent company's massive balance sheet, APRA gave it light-touch oversight and relied on the steady hand of the UK's Financial Services Agency (FSA).

It was a sound and sensible regulatory theory. But like many financial theories, it didn't weather the cataclysmic events of 2008 terribly well. The investor Warren Buffett once famously said, 'It's only when the tide goes out that you discover who's been swimming naked.' As anyone who has bathed in a Scottish loch knows, the Highland water can be particularly unflattering; so too with a banking balance sheet that's exposed in all its unclothed glory.

In October 2008, as the financial crisis struck the United Kingdom, the world discovered that HBOS was indeed swimming naked. The bank slipped rapidly into a murky insolvency. It was bailed out with £17 billion from taxpayers, and took the mighty FSA down with it. The UK regulator's failures left it hopelessly exposed. If HBOS was swimming naked, then the FSA was certainly wearing nothing 'neath its kilt.

As an emergency measure, Bankwest was cut loose, left to stand or fall on its wafer-thin capital reserves amid a bloodbath in asset prices. UK taxpayers weren't willing to pay for the poor judgement calls that HBOS had made a hemisphere away. The financer of the food bowl of the WA economy was now a basket case.

*

It's a beautiful, crisp day in Perth as I arrive for coffee in the ritzy Subiaco Quarter. Struggling to find a carpark, I contemplate an attractive-looking loading bay. People have told me that in Perth if you're driving a four-wheel drive and have a ladder on the roof, you can park in the best bays up and down St George's Terrace, unmolested by the city's notoriously efficient grey ghosts. Alas, at this moment I don't have a ladder handy, and a parking inspector is prowling the carpark holding what looks like a 1980s car phone.

After finding a park, I race into the cafe, flustered and sweaty in the dry late-summer heat. My host, Jeff, a former senior Bankwest insider, stands to greet me with a booming big-country-town welcome. He pumps my arm, in a grip pulsing with megawatts of West Oz bonhomie.

This is a capital city of just under two million people, who have one of the highest per-capita standards of living in the world. Did I mention it's also bloody sunny? Everyone here has a reason to smile. Who knows whether it's the resources wealth, the freedom, the fresh air or just an abundance of vitamin D? Even the young cafe staff are smiling, with their world-class uni degrees being part-funded by cappuccinos and a generous welfare system.

'So, you want to hear the inside story on what really happened at Bankwest? It's a cracker of a yarn,' Jeff assures me.

A waitress arrives and places two strong cappuccinos in front of us. Milky froth teeters on the edge of my mug like foam clinging to the edge of a Rottnest Island salt lake during an arvo sou'wester. I take a sip and marvel that, years after the boom ended, the city's finest establishments can still charge $4.50 for a crema-free cup full of tepid brown liquid. Welcome to WA, where the living is great. Provided you can accept a little hint of Dutch Disease — and the odd airport-quality coffee for airport-quality prices.

Oh, and the other thing about the people of Perth? They're fiercely patriotic, and they *really* love to talk.

*

When HBOS collapsed, there were hasty discussions behind the scenes in Australia. The Council of Financial Regulators met for crisis talks, bringing together the force of the Treasury, the RBA, APRA and ASIC. A messy collapse at Bankwest, the country's fifth-largest lender, could be the domino that triggered an Australian financial crisis. Together they agreed on a decisive course of action.

Only the Commonwealth Bank had the balance sheet to digest such a massive basket-case of banking bungles. The Aussie financial powerhouse had been salivating over Bankwest for some time, and had recently valued it at $4.2 billion.

Behind closed doors, a deal was done. Ian Narev, the bank's whip-smart young head of strategy, and general counsel David Cohen pulled together the acquisition of a lifetime. They would swing to the Australian government's aid, saving APRA (and potentially the entire financial system) in the process. Their resolute response meant that Australia would avoid the fate of other nations, such as the United States, the United Kingdom and Ireland, whose financial sectors were devastated.

Although the Council of Financial Regulators is a coming-together of equals, rulebooks are quickly shredded during a crisis. In a tightly closed room, the Treasury and the RBA took charge. The ACCC and ASIC were instructed to wave the deal through. Competition concerns were irrelevant. As were the consumer protection niceties outlined in the *Corporations Act 2001*.

CBA would need to cauterise the ailing bank's dead limbs before the entire body became gangrenous. But it could not be made responsible for HBOS's excesses and APRA's oversights. Greg Medcraft, the chair of ASIC, and Graeme Samuel, the chair of the ACCC, left the meeting with no doubt as to their instructions. This was a 'war room' meeting, and extraordinary times called for extraordinary responses.

*

Due diligence on the transaction was impossible, in view of Bankwest's woeful back-office technology and the speed of the deal. Instead, the parties agreed to establish a system of clawbacks for bad loans and unforeseen losses. Bankwest would give up its banking licence (requiring a repeal of Western Australia's *Bankwest Act 1995*) and become a sub-brand of CBA. But first CBA would need to repair the loan book. CommBank was assessing its own capital under the 'advanced approaches' for big banks in the global Basel II capital accord. This was essentially a rule that allowed banks to tell regulators – within reason – how much capital they would need to hold in reserve for a crisis. Everyone at the table, as they dissected the carcass of Western Australia's oldest bank, agreed that this toxic mess could not be allowed to contaminate its predator.

As Jeff explained to me, APRA and CBA had no hope of knowing what had gone on. This was because even the bankers themselves had no idea about the composition of their loan books. They would spend months, working after hours and unpaid, categorising their loans correctly so that APRA could understand Bankwest's exposure to high-risk sectors, such as commercial property and tourism. These assets, in particular, had been smashed by the financial crisis.

APRA maintained a brave face, characterising the CBA coup as a 'takeover'. Unfortunately, four years after the collapse of HBOS, the UK Parliamentary Commission on Banking Standards blew APRA's cover story to pieces. The UK inquiry conducted a sweeping review of the group's international activities. It found that HBOS's impaired loans in Australia had reached a staggering 28 per cent of the total loan book value. This was higher than the HBOS default rates in the United Kingdom and among the highest rates for the group internationally. In effect, one in every four loans they had issued would go into default.

The Bankwest-impaired loan rates were appalling even by the standards of Ireland, which had suffered deeply during the Global Financial Crisis. When compared with Ireland's banks, Bankwest's default rates were exceeded only by Anglo Irish Bank and HBOS itself. The inquiry heard evidence that, in Australia, HBOS sought to double its national market share. It wanted to become a new rival to the four 'pillar' banks that dominated the market. In the aftermath, the Australian impairments totalled a bewildering £3.6 billion.

'This loss is all the more striking in view of the comparative resilience of the Australian economy in the global downturn. In this period, the Australian banking sector remained profitable and no entities received any public capital support during the crisis,' the UK report said. James Crosby, then head of HBOS, said the losses in Australia were indicative of an 'appalling lending record'.

The UK report also found that HBOS Australia took the 'relatively quick and easy path to expansion without acknowledging the risks inherent in that strategy'. With Bankwest's expansion plan, it concentrated on sectors such as pubs, clubs, hotels and property development in regional areas, which worsened its default rates.

During the $2.1 billion Bankwest takeover by CommBank, APRA ensured that these facts never came to light. But inevitably someone would have to foot the bill for Australia's biggest prudential regulatory failure since 2001. Not surprisingly, Australia's financial regulators didn't disclose publicly who would be forced to pay that price. In fact, the victims only emerged – obliquely and by accident – during Justice Kenneth Hayne's Royal Commission into Misconduct in the Banking, Superannuation and Financial Services Industry, almost a decade later.

NINE

A Tale They Won't Believe

Brendan Stanford is a tough guy. A classic former law-enforcement character. He's sociable, friendly, funny, but with the kind of underlying tenacity that's forged in the furnace of the Australian Federal Police. Brendan's what you'd call a salt-of-the-earth bloke. He's a former pub owner, a father, husband and a leukaemia survivor.

Brendan has seen a lot during his working life. But the toughest thing he's ever had to endure was watching the decline of his brother, Michael, his business partner, following the Commonwealth Bank's takeover of Bankwest in 2008.

The Stanford brothers had gone into business together with the aim of buying and resurrecting country pubs. They believed that historic pubs were the lifeblood, the town square, the social heart of rural communities. Without good pubs, country towns could be lonely places.

The brothers' first foray had been a success. Brendan bought the pub in Cessnock, New South Wales, and Michael worked there. They ran it for five years and sold at a profit. Soon after, Brendan and his brother saw an opportunity to buy the Coronation Hotel in Portland, north-west of Sydney. Fatefully, they decided to finance their purchase through Bankwest. Having recently been taken over by HBOS, the Perth-based bank was beginning its march across the east coast. It was hankering for their business.

The bank offered very attractive terms to win the Stanfords' over. They signed up for a $1.2 million commercial loan, and bought the hotel for $1.6 million, with a 20-year term and a loan-to-valuation ratio (LVR) of 80 per cent.

The day they signed with Bankwest was one of celebration. The brothers had no idea they'd just lit a fuse that would lead to their financial and emotional destruction.

*

In May 2018, as Brendan bravely recounted his story before the Australian financial services royal commission, the pain of recollection was written across his face. Despite the difficult memories, he stayed composed. Stayed strong.

He told of how his brother had handled the negotiations with Bankwest over the loan in 2009, while Brendan was undergoing treatment for leukaemia. He told of how his sister-in-law offered to provide Bankwest's new owner with $400,000 to 'de-risk' the loan, to prevent a fire sale of their underlying asset. He told of how they'd argued there was no market for pubs like his in 2009, despite an extensive marketing campaign, as savvy buyers were holding out for the next distressed asset sale from a former Bankwest customer. Yet, despite this, CommBank moved in and sold the pub, along with its pokie licences, for just $525,000.

After costs, it was a pittance more than the Stanfords had offered to tip in to keep the loan facility open.

But do you know what was the hardest part to accept? They'd never missed a repayment! They knew they could have worked through the Global Financial Crisis. Things would improve; they always did. All they'd asked was for Bankwest's new owners to honour the original loan term and let them keep working. To not drive them into a constructive default, based on a ridiculous property valuation that the bank had arranged (at the owners' expense) that valued their business at a mere $250,000.

It wasn't until the counsel assisting the Hayne Royal Commission asked about the impact on his brother, however, that Brendan choked up. Commissioner Hayne then requested a break. When they returned ten minutes later, he was asked the question again.

'From the time this was instigated, I saw him struggle,' Brendan replied. 'Even after it all happened, I saw him depressed for a few years. That's why I'm here today because … he couldn't come in.'

As the drama and schadenfreude continued inside the Commonwealth Law Courts building in Melbourne, Brendan left the Hayne inquiry quietly.

It was an overcast day outside. He had previously spent many hours in courts during his time as a cop, providing evidence for the prosecution. He pulled down his dark sunglasses, composed himself, took a few deep breaths of the crisp Melbourne air and walked past the cameras. He was ready to go back to his day job.

After Bankwest, as CBA's bankers trousered ever-larger bonuses, things hadn't gone so well for Brendan. He'd found a job as a hospitality contractor and was keeping his family afloat by working in someone else's business.

He didn't want this limelight. He didn't want to appear before a royal commission. He certainly didn't want to have his story plastered all over the news. But he had to do it.

It was all for his brother, Michael.

*

The Royal Commission's hearings into the treatment of Bankwest customers had been particularly emotional. The bankruptcies, the suicides, the family breakups and the impact on children were all reminders that banking collapses do not just rip apart balance sheets. They rip apart people's lives.

Dr Andy Schmulow, a regulatory specialist, academic and consultant, believes the Royal Commission offers an unprecedented insight into the dangers of light-touch prudential regulation. But, perhaps worse, it also provides a glimpse into the level of regulatory capture at Australia's proud financial regulators.

'It's unacceptable that APRA allowed Bankwest to get to the point it was at prior to the CBA takeover,' Schmulow tells me over coffee at a sandstone university in Perth. 'My sense is that they covered themselves by offering Bankwest to CBA on preferential terms so there wouldn't be an Australian bank default at the height of the financial crisis.'

Schmulow, who wrote his PhD on prudential regulation, has also worked inside APRA. His hackles rise when he recalls the cosy and myopic internal culture at one of Australia's most important government agencies. As the GFC taught

Australians, due to the highly leveraged nature of banking, when prudential regulators fail, entire economies tend to fail with them.

'This refutes the whole narrative that Australia did incredibly well during the 2008 financial crisis because our banking system was so well regulated. Bankwest, and its aftermath, proves it wasn't,' Schmulow says, looking out wistfully over a family of Western Australia's iconic black swans on the grassy Matilda Bay riverbank.

How had it taken so long to get to the truth?

Shortly after its acquisition of Bankwest, CommBank launched an internal review to determine Bankwest's level of impaired and 'troublesome' loans. The review, dubbed Project Magellan, was set up to give CBA a clearer idea of the quality of the loan book it had taken on, as it had assumed liability for these loans when it acquired the bank.

APRA had set a number of conditions on the acquisition, such as that CommBank must surrender Bankwest's banking licence as soon as possible. As with Westpac's emergency 'takeover' of St George in December 2008, the deal was structured to conceal any concerns over the institution's solvency. It was also structured to provide the maximum reputational protection for APRA itself.

Around the same time, in London, the parent bank HBOS was being folded into Lloyds Bank. This was part of a £17 billion bailout that left the UK government holding a 43.4 per cent stake in the new entity. The deal-making with CBA was, by comparison, an act of genius.

The rescue of Bankwest was executed exceptionally well. The deal was done swiftly, discreetly and without resorting to a taxpayer-funded bailout. The transaction was approved by the federal treasurer, Wayne Swan, on the Thursday before Christmas in 2008.

'I have taken this decision after a comprehensive assessment of its impact on the national interest, with conditions that support a strong and competitive Australian banking system,' Swan said at the time. 'These conditions will also ensure the best possible outcomes for both customers and employees of CBA and Bankwest.'

That same week, as pre-Chrissy beers flowed in the Coronation Hotel in 2008, the Stanford brothers had no idea their experience would become emblematic of the hollowness of the government's assurances.

*

CommBank named its new captain at Bankwest a week before Christmas 2008. The acquirer had appointed Jon Sutton, the former head of agribusiness lending at CBA, as Bankwest's national managing director. Sutton understood regional customers deeply and was given the public mandate of 'enhancing and developing the Bankwest brand'. It all sounded very promising for the once-proud West Australian bank and its customers. But it soon became apparent that the 'acquisition' would not go as smoothly as the media releases suggested.

Soon after joining Bankwest, Sutton sent an internal memo lamenting the quality of its business lending book. It was 'poorer than original expectations and we are … actively de-risking the exposure,' he wrote in a memo to the CBA board's risk committee.

Under 'Project Magellan', CommBank raked over the Bankwest portfolio. It was looking for loans that were not yet in arrears, but likely to run into trouble. David Cohen, who went on to become the chief risk officer at CommBank, told the Hayne Royal Commission that Project Magellan set out to review at least 60 per cent of Bankwest's business customers. 'It was a combination of internal people and external people seconded in to assist,' he said. 'Broadly speaking, each of the reviews uncovered some concerns around the level of provisioning.'

In an unusual move, the project team also included receivers, members of the profession that stood to win lucrative work if people defaulted on their loans.

In response to Project Magellan's findings, CBA's executive risk committee decided to reduce its commercial property exposure by $1.8 billion. This was largely achieved by 'de-risking' the Bankwest commercial property book, which had represented more than half of its lending activity under HBOS. The Stanfords and many others were swept up in this billion-dollar purge.

*

In August 2012, Cohen had appeared as the face of CBA at the Senate's Inquiry into the Post-GFC Banking Sector. At the time, he was confident that there was no misconduct on CBA's part. In December 2015, he appeared before the Parliamentary Joint Committee and again asserted that Bankwest and its new owner had acted fairly. With the benefit of more time, however, his views would change.

Cohen told the Hayne Royal Commission in 2018 that he recently discovered the bank lacked the skills at the time to make proper risk assessments in relation to 'troublesome' loans. This had only become apparent during his preparation for his appearance at the royal commission, the CBA senior manager said.

Cohen said, with hindsight, that the credit processes Bankwest had used were 'not as diligent' as those that the Commonwealth Bank applied on its own loan applications. It also discovered that the continuing management of business banking customers throughout the life of their loans was out of kilter with CommBank's day-to-day management of business relationships.

In cases like the Stanfords, he said, CommBank now recognised that the customers had been mistreated. 'In this case, the lack of discussion with the borrower, the lack of explanation about why a sale was the only option, I think that was not reasonable.'

For Brendan Stanford, this belated apology came with a generous side serve of cold comfort.

In the wake of the financial crisis, it must be remembered, Australia's banking system was standing on the precipice of a historic collapse. The country was one single bank run from catastrophe. Financial services icon Macquarie Group had come so close to the brink that ASIC made a knee-jerk decision one weekend to ban short-selling. Major banks around the world had collapsed under the weight of their own high-risk lending. All Australians had a stake in the outcome of the Bankwest takeover, whether they knew it or not. And for the Lucky Country, the government believed that the continuation of the property merry-go-round, with ever-escalating house prices, would be the road to economic recovery.

With this political decision, the Australian public – whether they knew it or not – had entered into a Faustian pact. Housing and finance were now the engine room of the domestic economy. Rather than use the GFC as an opportunity to de-leverage, in an orderly manner, property-mad Australians doubled down. The national property market barely took a breather. The entire nation found itself gambling, once again, on the maintenance of the historic multi-decade housing boom.

Keeping the house prices elevated was now the principal job of Canberra's politicians and their economic masters, regardless of their political bent. Policies that risked pricking the bubble were cast aside or kicked down the road. After 2008, fixing negative gearing was political suicide. Avoiding a housing correction was now a matter of national interest, and it would be pursued even if it meant exposing Australia to the darkest heart of the international economy.

Australia had become the Lucky Laundry.

TEN

The Smart Laundromat

Around mid-2015, the staff of the Commonwealth Bank's Leichhardt branch, in Sydney's inner west, were at their wits' end. Those stupid 'smart' ATM machines were driving them bonkers. The team had been continually reporting suspicious behaviour, with shady-looking customers causing havoc out the front of the branch. Someone would turn up with a backpack and a milk crate, set up shop on the street and hammer away at the wretched IDMs like they were pokie machines. They were shovelling bricks of cash – bundles of $50s and $100s – into the hole in wall, sometimes until the machines jammed. This was *not* normal customer behaviour.

The bank had installed secret alarms linked to the IDMs, which would buzz inside the office if a customer spent too long shovelling money into the throat of those hungry beasts. The problem was that these alarms were going off continually, as an army of characters emptied their backpacks on Marion Street. Bank staff joked that it was ironic the branch sat opposite a dry-cleaning business.

On 30 June, the branch manager snapped. He'd been well trained in how to spot money laundering. His staff all took it seriously. They were doing their best to identify and report suspicious customers to the financial crime team. It seemed utterly absurd that out the front, in plain sight, mules for money-laundering syndicates were washing hundreds of thousands of dollars with impunity.

The branch manager sent an email to the Group Security team with a one-word subject header: 'Urgent!!!'. He blasted it out in a hurry, not bothering to clean up his typos:

> We have had people coming in and depositing about 5 times into account with $50 notes. this is just short of $10,000.00 Then that night there is a transfer sent to china for just short of $50K. The person who is making the deposit would clearly know the process as sometimes they deposit into all different accounts until the ATM is full then leave. I believe that there should be other security measures in place as this is crazy. if you review these people's accounts they have sent millions and millions overseas!!

The attentive bank staff had not only done their job, they had blown the whistle on financial crime. They could have no idea, at that point, that what they'd spotted was the tip of a multi-billion-dollar criminal washhouse.

*

Criminal syndicates are always on the lookout for new vulnerabilities in the financial system. The AML/CTF regime means that money laundering has become riskier, and more difficult, but it's also more lucrative. If you can find a cunning loophole, you can monetise the thing until it snaps shut. In the worst-case scenario, you might lose a smurf or a bag of cash to the cops. In this line of business, for your 5 or 6 per cent cut, those are the taxes you occasionally have to pay.

And so it was with the smart laundromat affair. Crooks had pretty quickly worked out that the Commonwealth Bank's IDMs were the go-to place to wash dirty sheets of polymer. Insiders knew that the machines contained two cash cannisters, both of which could accept 3000 notes. This meant a smurf could deposit up to $600,000 into a single machine before having to move down the road to the next one. No other bank was that generous to criminals.

The AFP would run surveillance and watch young people on tourist visas run the gauntlet along a line of IDMs through Sydney. Some would have a driver. Others would just work their way along the North Sydney train line, like ants on a scent. It was a similar thrill to Aussie backpackers doing their rite of passage in Pamplona for the Running of the Bulls. After their bag was empty, they would throw it in the nearest bin and knock off for the day, returning home with a pocketful of deposit receipts. For many a person from South-East Asia, $300 a day and a holiday in Australia is like winning the lottery.

And so the money continued to flow down the networks of 'smart laundromats' dotted across Australian capital cities. In August 2015, a customer fed so many $50 notes into the Leichhardt branch's IDMs that the internal alarm sounded three times in a row. A banker went outside to investigate and saw a person whom he described as a 'male who was tall with black hair of Asian background.' When the account was investigated, the branch staff found that it belonged to someone with an 'Anglo name and NSW driver's licence as ID'. As soon as the money was deposited, someone had logged in via internet banking and zipped the funds off to an account in Hong Kong. The Group Security team investigated this one and decided that the account activity was linked to a Malaysian money-laundering syndicate.

An extensive branch network, 24-hour real-time banking, smart ATMs and cheap transfers overseas had made CBA the bank of choice for launderers. One of the other benefits was that CBA accounts seemed to stay open longer than other banks. Syndicates had pretty quickly established that a CommBank online account was easy to set up with stolen ID and very rarely got shut down, despite the most egregious cash transfers.

It was this can-do attitude that made CBA very popular with South-East Asian tourists carrying milk crates and backpacks. It was an attitude that curried very little favour, however, with a small army of people within the Australian law-enforcement community. These were people who put their lives on the line, day in and day out, in the fight against serious and organised crime.

*

Over at the AUSTRAC headquarters in Chatswood, on Sydney's north shore, heads were also being scratched. The team worked closely with the AFP and knew about these vulnerabilities. What they didn't know yet was the extent of the problems. As luck would have it, they uncovered what appeared to be a small glitch with CBA's transaction reporting system. Routine data analysis in AUSTRAC's financial intelligence unit revealed that two threshold transaction reports – the compulsory reports for every deposit above $10,000 – had not been filed. This was strange, as these basic reports were bread-and-butter stuff for a major bank's financial crime team.

Those two transactions related to a cross-border transfer from a CBA account to HSBC, which itself was in money-laundering purgatory in the United States. The Hong Kong bank gave AUSTRAC the reports detailing two $20,000 transactions that should have been reported by both banks. When AUSTRAC attempted to pair the transactions with CBA's reports, there was no matching record. As it turned out, this would be the spark that set off a brushfire that grew into an inferno at Australia's most profitable bank.

Peter Clark, a senior official at AUSTRAC, ensured that the regulator followed these anomalies up with CBA.

'We made enquiries to the bank and as a result of that we became aware of other issues,' Clark said with his characteristic public-service understatement, before a Senate Estimates hearing.

At this stage, in 2015, Commonwealth Bank executives had no idea they had wandered into Australia's largest-ever money-laundering scandal. At the time AUSTRAC had never really used its civil litigation powers. A few weeks earlier it had launched civil proceedings against the gaming giant Tabcorp for money-laundering breaches, but this was in its early stages.

Anyone at CBA doing a risk assessment on the likelihood of getting fined by AUSTRAC would have deemed the agency to be a non-existent threat.

ELEVEN

The Commonwealth Strikes Back

In July 2015, following the detection of those two missing threshold transaction reports (TTRs), AUSTRAC ordered the Commonwealth Bank to conduct a money-laundering risk assessment on its Intelligent Deposit Machine channel. The review found that IDMs posed a high money-laundering risk. Inexplicably, when it applied a final rating, CBA gave its smart ATMs a 'low residual risk'. The internal review did not spell out exactly how this risk management alchemy was achieved.

The bank knew full well there were serious issues. Two months later, in September 2015, the bank's compliance team prepared a briefing paper on the reporting problems for the chief executive, Ian Narev. 'An investigation has determined that the two cash transactions were made through IDMs,' it said. 'It was discovered that the deposits were not reported because of a system coding error dating back to November 2012.'

That same month, retail banking head Matt Comyn emailed Narev to drop a bombshell. He attached an internal report that showed professional money-laundering syndicates were exploiting the IDMs. Narev responded calmly, professionally: 'It goes without saying that we need to take this extremely seriously … Whilst this is as a result of unintentional coding-related errors, the circumstances warrant very senior oversight.'

At the same time, no one inside the bank was willing to argue that these criminal syndicates weren't good for the bank's IDM-use stats. Despite a beslubbering $5.1 billion moving through the IDMs in the most recent 12-month period, Alden Toevs, CBA's chief risk officer, was also nonplussed. He sent a letter to AUSTRAC in October 2015 to reassure the agency that there had been no changes in its IDM risk profile. There was no cause for concern, and nothing that warranted an internal review.

Even when these transactions were linked to the financing of terrorism in Syria, the bank remained largely unconcerned. In one case, the accounts for a suspected terrorist with links to ISIS remained open for 18 months. This was despite warnings from police that the individual may have been involved in cuckoo smurfing to facilitate the conflict in Damascus.

The suspected terrorist, who was on an AFP watchlist, moved at least $8.1 million through the bank.

Many months later, as the bank continued its internal investigation, the true scope of the failures started to become apparent. Even so, CBA still believed it could resolve the matter with an enforceable undertaking from the regulator – essentially a commitment to do better – without any admission of liability. With APRA and ASIC wrapped thoroughly around its finger, the bank had no reason to think otherwise.

But AUSTRAC was no typical financial regulator. As part of the law-enforcement and criminal intelligence community, it was a different creature. AUSTRAC spent months investigating and attempting to resolve the problems collaboratively with CBA. The two missing transaction reports ultimately led to the discovery of another 53,504 reports that hadn't been filed. CBA took the view that the missing TTRs, which ran over three years, were the result of a single technical breach and should be treated as a minor IT issue.

AUSTRAC differed. The more the regulator looked into CBA's compliance controls, the more problems it found. Alarmed, the regulator quickly organised a targeted onsite review at the other major banks. Sources at another 'big four' institution said they had been preparing for a visit based on correspondent banking in October 2015. Without explanation, at the last minute, AUSTRAC changed the subject of the review to 'smart ATMs'. The financial crime teams were left scratching their heads as to why AUSTRAC was suddenly more interested in basic ATM controls than in the more complex issue of 'corrie banking'. They decided the regulator was just trying to keep them on their toes.

The onsite reviews did not uncover any systemic issues across the banking sector, according to Peter Clark, of AUSTRAC. 'We undertook an examination of the other major banks in terms of their IDMs,' he said. 'We were satisfied that they had thresholds that were less than the reporting threshold for their transactions and they had in place mechanisms to monitor and report.'

Some of the banks had exceptionally good controls in place to manage the risks associated with such a high-risk channel. Everyone knew that non-face-to-face cash placement would be exploited by criminals. In response, they set their 'transaction-monitoring' software and other detection tools to pick up and report anything suspicious. The most basic technology could ensure that criminals were never at an ATM long enough to need to bring their own milkcrate work stool.

In addition to its other failures, Commonwealth Bank had the highest single deposit limit at $20,000, and customers could just run one transaction after another until the machine seized. The other banks had set cash-deposit limits for their machines of $4000 to $5000. At ANZ, for example, there was a 50-note maximum. Any more than that and the customer would be forced to enter the branch.

At CommBank, however, forcing customers with large cash deposits back inside branches was not a welcome idea. That would have undermined the business case behind the push towards automated banking. There was a fundamental tension at play between the risk and commercial teams. And risk was losing, by a wide margin.

By the time AUSTRAC detected 174 allegedly late or missing suspicious matter reports at CBA, as well as missing reports relating to five terrorism financiers, the most serious type of reporting failures, the matter was escalated internally. AUSTRAC's chief executive, Paul Jevtovic, and his team were tracking the matter closely.

*

From a young age, Paul Jevtovic had a strong sense of justice. He hated it when things went the wrong way. Even as a young football fanatic, if a ref called it wrong in his own team's favour, he would own up. His father, Branko, had hammered home the need to compete with honour.

Paul was a firstborn son and descended from a culture where that carried strong responsibilities. As a boy of just 16, his father, Branko, had fled Yugoslavia as a wave of communism swept across Eastern Europe. Branko had walked to Austria and stood in an emigration line, alone, as new nationalities were handed out like raffle tickets. Branko soon discovered he had stood in the queue to Australia, the Lucky Country. Like his father, Paul would accept his duty and destiny at a young age. His love of team sport, his sense of responsibility and his desire to lead left him with an easy choice. For as long as he could remember, Paul had watched football coaches deliver inspirational speeches in the face of impossible odds. He'd watched teams rally under those words, lifting themselves from despair and kicking defeat mercilessly into the back of the other team's net.

If he couldn't be a professional footballer, in Australia in the late 1970s, for Paul there was only one other option. He wanted to join the Australian Federal Police.

At 18, he got the call. He had been accepted as an AFP cadet. The look of pride on his father's face when he graduated left him with no doubt. He'd made the right decision. Paul promised himself that he'd do his father proud. He would bring together his loves and dreams, his family's gratitude, and fight every day to protect the good life they had built here in Australia.

As time went on, Paul would see the peaks and troughs of life – and death – in the AFP. He'd see the worst and the greatest of deeds that humans were capable of inflicting upon each other. Sometimes he would treat his job as though it were something even more important than life or death. He would treat it as sport.

'You start to realise that you can inspire people,' Paul told me in 2021, from his apartment in Hong Kong. Another epic adventure had led him to the Asian financial powerhouse four years earlier, only for him to be caught in the maelstrom of a 21st-century pandemic. 'I wasn't the best football player in the world. I don't think I was even the best player in any of the teams I played in. But I realised there's something else you can bring to a team. You don't always have to be the best or the smartest. But your behaviour and example can influence and get the best out of others.'

This was a wisdom that could only come from experience. It ultimately saw Jevtovic appointed in 2014 as chief executive of AUSTRAC with an explicit government mandate to 'transform' the agency.

As one of Paul's senior colleagues said, 'He didn't have an MBA. And yet he was the most incredible leader. You would go to war for him. You'd risk your life.'

Paul's character gave his staff the confidence to stand firm in the face of some of the country's most formidable opponents.

*

CBA, like Tabcorp before it, believed it had the AUSTRAC relationship under control. In one internal email in mid-2016, David Craig, the bank's chief financial officer, told Narev that he 'had no reason to be concerned about this at this stage'. The bank's board had just met with Jevtovic, who had apparently expressed 'no concerns about CBA's intention to be fully compliant with AML legislation'.

In January 2017, Jevtovic met with Catherine Livingstone, the bank's chairperson. David Cohen, by then the bank's chief risk officer, warned her that the IDM issue 'would be raised in the meeting, which of course it was'. Narev offered to meet with Livingstone the next day to get the chair's 'instincts on how, if at all, you believe we can engage with them in advance of the final determination to influence it'.

In March, AUSTRAC again met with the bank. By that time CBA had continually missed targets and failed on its promises to clean up its act. Back at AUSTRAC, Jevtovic's mood had shifted.

A CBA staff member wrote back to Narev: 'They also said our failure to immediately and proactively tell them about these and other problems (here they were talking about the control weaknesses over multiple years, etc) is a show of bad faith that leads them to wonder what else is broken across CBA's financial crime landscape.'

*

Things were spiralling out of control. But for Australia's largest and most influential bank, AUSTRAC was an unknown quantity. It had never revealed the iron fist of powers concealed within its velvet glove of 'public-private partnerships'. In the United States, falling foul of financial crime or economic sanctions regulators could be fatal for a bank that was dependent upon access to US-dollar clearing. In Australia, the financial intelligence agency's enforcement arm was still very much in its infancy.

Commonwealth Bank was still naively confident – bordering on arrogant – about the federal agency's powers and level of determination. How could an agency with just 300 staff and a measly $70 million annual budget pose a threat to a bank with an armada of the country's finest silks and a $10 billion-per-year profit engine to draw upon? As one of the country's biggest listed companies, the Commonwealth Bank spent more than AUSTRAC's entire budget on its in-house catering each year.

At CBA's May 2017 board meeting, however, something changed. The mood had darkened. Discussion focused on whether anyone within the bank was facing personal liability. Concerns around shareholders' potential exposure would come later. The consensus was that the board members were all okay.

By July 2017, the bank's chairman and chief executive realised they were testing AUSTRAC's patience. Behind the scenes, the AFP was telling AUSTRAC about its own continual frustrations with the flagrant money laundering and terrorism financing facilitated by CBA's smart ATMs.

Perhaps the bank's most senior people hadn't realised that Paul Jevtovic, the head of this little agency, had spent 35 years at the coalface with the AFP? Every minute of his working life, he'd battled the very people who were washing their dirty millions through CBA.

The bankers desperately tried to get another face-to-face meeting with the agency's chief to smooth things over. This was how it generally worked with larger financial regulators like APRA and ASIC. After all, the senior management and boards at the country's major banks had perfected the art of regulatory capture. What they needed now was a 'no-bickies' visit to Chatswood.

To their surprise, the offer was rebuffed.

Narev was rattled. Had he miscalculated? Like that day at Hordern Pavilion, he had a premonition. This time it was a feeling that bad things were afoot. He emailed Livingstone late one evening to share his feelings of unease. Would AUSTRAC seek to make an example of them?

'This could be AUSTRAC's moment in the sun,' he wrote prophetically.

TWELVE

Shaking the Hand of Fate

Who can truly fathom the strange machinations of history, how key events take shape the way they do? So often the major twists in a nation's great story come back to the simple luck of 'the right person at the right time'. It might be a humble servant of the people who has unknowingly dropped upon the fulcrum of fate at the very moment when an act of principle and self-sacrifice is needed.

Australia has been lucky, very lucky, to have had many such people pop up in moments of significance, as if emerging from the country's red, beating heart. The miners in Ballarat in 1854. Jandamarra in the great battles for Indigenous freedom in the Kimberleys in the latter part of the 19th century. Edith Cowan boldly standing for parliament in 1921. The reformed alcoholic John Curtin rising to lead Australia during the Second World War. The Franklin River protesters in Tasmania in the 1980s. These were ordinary people who stood up, in the face of impossible odds, and did something extraordinary for the people they loved – the family, community and landscape that had given them everything that mattered.

Great countries are built upon the actions of humble, principled people who believe in the intangible values of fairness, egalitarianism, hard work, trust and integrity. These are not unique to Australia. They are human qualities.

And so it was that in 2017, in Sydney, two simple men found themselves face to face, as the leaders of their respective armies. A Commonwealth agency versus Commonwealth the bank. As fate would have it, both these men were the children of proud, brave, hardworking first-generation migrants. Both felt an enormous debt of gratitude to the parents and grandparents who had suffered and taken risks to win them freedom, opportunity and a place in the Antipodes to call home. Both men had been shaped by forebears and mentors of great character.

On one side of the table was Ian Narev, the leader of Australia's largest bank, the perfect symbol of the opportunity that exists in the Lucky Country; to come from nothing, to land in New Zealand, to move to Australia and rise to the highest spires of business and commerce, based purely on talent and merit.

On the other side was Paul Jevtovic, another boy formed from within the furnace of adversity, his character forged like steel among the raucous hammering of his father's panel-beating job in North Melbourne.

Who can truly understand the desperation and hope of brave migrants, who are willing to cross oceans to escape war, oppression, tyranny – all to provide their children with the simple treasures of peace and opportunity in a democratic country? The nugget of this experience lies in the heart of so many people who have built a home and a life in Australia.

And so it was, when Narev and Jevtovic had first greeted each other across a table in a Sydney boardroom. They had no idea of these intertwined back stories. They certainly had no idea they would one day make decisions that helped to change the character of Australia. But they had begun a connection that would send ripples through the fabric of Australian history.

*

In his last months at AUSTRAC, as Jevtovic faced the reality of the complete breakdown in public trust at Australia's largest financial institution, he knew he had a decision to make. The bank had lied repeatedly about its commitment to do better. It had prioritised multi-billion-dollar dividends over supporting the police and the government agencies in their fight against serious and organised crime. It had allowed meth syndicates to spread their poison and flee with their profits. To Jevtovic, this was simply intolerable.

The AUSTRAC chief knew that if he initiated the litigation he was contemplating, there would be consequences for himself personally, for the financial sector more broadly and for Australia as a whole. But he also knew that he needed to act. To buckle at this moment would unravel all the values and principles he had worked to uphold. Besides, he knew as a child what it felt like to be poor. He'd come from a family so humble that his parents couldn't afford to buy him school shoes. He knew it felt fine.

At that critical moment, the words of Lieutenant General David Morrison, former chief of the Australian Army, resonated in his mind: 'The standard you walk past is the standard you accept.'

In his office in Chatswood, he lifted his pen and signed a piece of paper, approving AUSTRAC's litigation against CommBank.

It was a pen full of the fire of courage and principle, that would ignite a fuse, that would soon set the entire Australian financial sector alight. With a splash of ink the litigation had begun, and another unstoppable force in Australian history had been unleashed.

*

In July 2017, no one outside the very tight legal team at AUSTRAC and the Australian Government Solicitor (AGS) knew that litigation against CBA was afoot. For months they toiled away in secret. The AFP and other agencies provided support to help AUSTRAC's tiny team build its case. Coming from law-enforcement backgrounds, they knew the importance of keeping these operations very close. This was not a 'tea and bickies' exercise.

Then without warning, on 3 August, AUSTRAC dropped its bombshell in the Federal Court. It would be a David and Goliath encounter: a 300-strong agency with a minuscule legal team taking on the country's largest company. This was an enforcement challenge that had eluded ASIC, APRA and the ACCC for decades.

Fortuitously, AUSTRAC's case was being led by Sonja Marsic, a lifelong warrior for the anti-money-laundering regime. Marsic was a softly spoken woman with long, dark hair and a disarmingly gentle demeanour. Like Jevtovic, her family shared Serbian roots.

Marsic was deeply humble despite having kicked massive career goals. Before joining the AGS, she had helped to draft the original AML/CTF Act for the Attorney-General's Department in the lead-up to its passage through Parliament in 2006. At the time, Marsic was about to go on maternity leave, and worried that she might miss the drafting of Tranche 2 of the legislation, which was to cover the gatekeeper professions, high-value goods dealers and real estate. As it turned out, she needn't have been concerned. Her daughter would graduate from high school before those laws escaped Canberra's equivalent of purgatory.

Fast-forward to 2017, however, and Marsic was leading the valiant legal team at the AGS, which was to represent AUSTRAC in this landmark civil litigation. For Marsic, the case was about much more than banking and technical matters of law. It was about forcing banks to become genuine partners in the relentless battle against the worst crimes imaginable. This was about tearing away the profit motive from drug trafficking, corruption, child abuse, wildlife smuggling and environmental crimes. She knew all too well how precious Australia's democracy was, and why it needed to be defended every day from these criminal scourges.

In another fortuitous turn of events, Australian history had shone upon its daughter, Sonja Marsic. The country was calling on her to make a decision of courage. Marsic had run the first AML/CTF test case, against Tabcorp, which ended when the betting company settled and agreed to pay a $45 million penalty. Now she was taking on the biggest target in the country. This would be the legal fight of her career. But if anyone knew the ins and outs of the anti-money-laundering laws, it was the woman who had helped to draft them. Working with the enforcement team at AUSTRAC, this was now her main event.

THIRTEEN

Spreading like Wildfire

In August 2017, the ink from Jevtovic's pen was well and truly dry on the CommBank litigation. He had left the agency; indeed, he had left the entire country. If anyone wanted a fall guy for this decision, he was up in Hong Kong. The timing was accidental but executed to perfection.

The legal team had sculpted the case over a period of months. No one would admit it publicly but the truth was, in the lead-up to filing that statement of claim against CBA, they were all nervous. They were anxious about the repercussions, and they were nervous about being shut down through subtle political interference. In the murky hallways of Canberra, these things had been known to happen. Everyone knew this case would have implications for superannuation funds, investors and the international reputation of the entire Australian banking system. At the same time, what option did they have? Allowing even one Aussie bank to wash billions of dollars for meth cartels and terrorists, while management turned a blind eye and trousered bonuses, was untenable.

There was also the risk that they might lose. This was the reality of all litigation. Marsic and AUSTRAC knew, when coming up against the most deep-pocketed of defendants, that even an apparent slam dunk could go awry. Nothing in litigation is certain.

'There's many a slip 'twixt the cup and the lip,' as the old saying goes.

Having said that, the allegations in Marsic's legal filings were brutally comprehensive. They were crafted, as though by a surgeon's scalpel, to ensure the bank had no room to hide and no desire to run the case to trial. As with Tabcorp, a settlement, a genuinely punitive fine and a commitment to overhaul the business's risk culture would be the best outcome for everyone.

And so, on a Thursday morning that August, one of the greatest battles in Australian legal history had begun. News of the litigation spread like wildfire through the Commonwealth Bank's Darling Harbour headquarters. The bank filed an urgent announcement with the ASX; shares duly plummeted. Staff read the court filings and were shocked. They were trying to work out why the bank would gamble its reputation on such a risky line of business. They were questioning why the IDM revenue was worth the potential damage, be it political, reputational or financial.

The bank had spent significant money rolling out physical alarms on the IDMs, and on transaction monitoring software in its central IT system. The operations team was set up to report TTRs and SMRs to AUSTRAC. For the country's brightest financial sparks, the numbers simply didn't add up.

To financial crime teams, there was another baffling aspect of the case. When banks allow themselves to be used in the placement stage of the money-laundering cycle, the deposits are notoriously 'unsticky'. Criminals want to move those funds on as quickly as possible. They want to move the loot from the scene of the crime, to zip across borders and muddy the trail.

This was why the IDMs had proven so attractive to launderers. Provided there were smurfs willing to feed cash into ATMs, 200 notes at a time, the kingpins behind the laundering syndicates did not even need to set foot in Australia. They could stay in Malaysia, Vietnam, Hong Kong – anywhere with an internet connection, in fact – and watch the funds landing into their fake accounts in real time. This was one of the unanticipated joys of CBA's bold push towards real-time 24/7 banking.

The hapless smurfs, on the other hand, were taking all the risk and being paid just $300 to $400 per day for their efforts. When police swooped, it was usually on the smurfs. Aside from the Vietnamese hotelier Thi Lan Phuong Pham, who had fallen afoul of the determined officers of Strike Force Bugam, the handlers and the kingpins were usually well out of reach.

Why would a bank get involved in the 'cash placement' phase of money laundering, carrying all the legal and reputational risks for such a fleeting benefit? Everyone in legitimate finance knew the real money (and the lower-risk, 'sticky' investments) were at the tail end of the money-laundering cycle. If a bank was going to dance with the devil of dirty money, it should at least be clever about it. Singapore and Switzerland had shown how that could be done, without losing too much face. The financial crime and risk profession was stunned. Sydney's bankers still had a lot to learn.

*

When the litigation landed, CommBank's formidable crisis communications team jumped immediately into action. In an emergency media briefing, Narev said there was no suggestion that CBA had obtained any commercial benefit as a result of the alleged breaches, including from the failure to lodge TTRs. 'There is no economic reason that would underpin the alleged activity and that is not part of the equation,' Narev assured shareholders.

Analysts questioned why the bank would risk billions in fines and endless column inches of bad publicity if there really was no commercial return. CBA was Australia's most widely held bank stock. It risked alienating the 800,000 families who owned its shares by facilitating the laundering of black money from the meth trade – and even financing terrorism.

The truth was, there was only one possible answer: hubris.

The bank's IDM strategy (coupled with the instantaneous $22 money conduit to Hong Kong) was flawed from the outset. Sources close to the bank said it never believed AUSTRAC would dare to take it on. It was a bank that had sidelined the warnings from its risk division, while its operations team failed to lodge basic financial intelligence reports for three years. The commercial units had a monopoly on the ear of senior management. The bank continually ignored warnings and pared back risk controls in pursuit of greater efficiency – and profitability.

*

The reverberations from Australia's first major bank money-laundering case shook the entire financial sector. It was clear that the industry's streak of luck with regulators had come to an end.

The problem for Australia's largest bank was that it wasn't facing just one irritated agency. An armada of Australia's most powerful federal bodies were now surrounding the bank's boardroom. Politicians expressed horror that Australia's most iconic bank had become a laundromat for organised crime. They were appalled that CBA had just delivered a record $10 billion in dividends to shareholders, juicing the bonuses for executives in the process, while turning a blind eye to the bleedingly obvious fact that a criminal element had exploited the bank.

Scott Morrison, the federal treasurer at the time, summoned the bank's chairman to Canberra for a meeting. He described the allegations as 'very, very serious'. 'I have made it very clear to the Commonwealth Bank that, in relation to these matters, the government's response is prepared to consider all options. That remains our view,' he said, with a veiled threat.

The federal regulators, meanwhile, were sending out a message of unity and force. AUSTRAC's minuscule team would not be steamrolled by CBA's political and PR might. The bank wasn't just under attack from the tiny but fearsome AUSTRAC legal division, it was facing the entire machinery of government. This was a unique moment in Australian corporate history.

The move had left the CBA board encircled, with no choice but to take evasive action.

*

Ever since the money-laundering allegations had blown up in the media, the bank's PR team had been in maximum spin mode. They had downplayed the failures, issued sincere-sounding apologies, and then punched themselves squarely in the face by calling the problems a mere 'coding error'. They were also leaking stories to journalists that questioned AUSTRAC's sincerity in working to resolve the problems.

The rear-guard campaign was terribly misguided. The cold fact that the banks needed to obey the law seemed to be lost on them. The rest of the sector watched on with horror.

Paul Jevtovic was deeply unimpressed by the suggestion that CBA's management was not given sufficient opportunities to fix their systems and culture. 'We have a saying in the AFP: you don't make an appointment to execute a search warrant,' he had once told me, on the sidelines of a terrorism financing conference in Asia. His aphorism seemed apt for this situation. After two years of broken promises and assurances, and record shareholder dividends, CBA was experiencing one of those moments.

The government and its arms of influence had determined that the bank's management was dangerous, arrogant and needed to be reminded who issued its licence to operate.

Clearly, the leadership of Australia's banks had underestimated the agencies they had crossed. They had allowed even mid-tier crime groups, such as Pham and Do's, to wash money through Australia with lucrative ease. This was no longer 'tea and Tim Tams' regulation. CommBank had become a conduit for organised crime. Through its belligerence and arrogance, the bank had become a participant in the second leg of the Australian drug trade: the safe and discreet movement of money.

As law enforcement insiders would attest, drug cartels cared a lot more about losing their money than they cared about losing their mules, smurfs, or product. To them, the product was cheap. The bag handlers were plentiful. This was simply the business of organised crime.

'Drug cartels are some of the world's most effective multinational corporations,' was the way that Martin Woods, who we will come to know later, described it. Woods would know; he blew the whistle on a multi-billion-dollar drug cartel laundering operation when he worked at Wachovia Bank in London in 2006, at enormous personal cost.

*

Back in Sydney, under pressure from the federal government, CommBank's board had spent an entire weekend in crisis talks. The first strategic move from CBA was the board's decision to cut the senior management team's bonuses for the 2017 financial year. This did little, however, to quell the public and regulatory anger. It was profoundly tone-deaf. It certainly did not defuse the demands from government agencies for management accountability over the issue.

On a Monday morning, the bank announced its second major symbolic move: chief executive Ian Narev would depart. Just days earlier, Narev had said he was committed to the role and was the right person to steer the bank through the money-laundering crisis. Now, Livingstone, the CBA chair, said it was important for the bank to 'deal with the speculation and questions' about Narev's tenure. In another fatally mixed message, though, the board allowed Narev to make a graceful departure sometime 'later in the year'.

'Today's statement provides that clarity and will ensure [Ian Narev] can continue to focus, as CEO, on successfully managing the business,' Livingstone said in an ASX filing.

For the outgoing CEO, it wasn't all bad. As consolation, Narev would leave the bank $52 million richer than when he arrived. His contract did not have any 'clawback' provisions that might allow CBA to reclaim the previous years' bonuses, which had been juiced by clipping the ticket on criminal fund flows.

As chief executive, he had accepted the bouquets; he would now have to cop the brickbats. But in accepting responsibility for the bank's misdeeds, he would never be able to escape his new reputation.

Narev would be recorded in Australian history books not as a banking prodigy but as the business world's Icarus. He was the boy who dared to dream but, in doing so, became deaf to warnings and flew too close to the sun. He had stuffed up the finest of opportunities for himself – but he had also stuffed up the finest of Aussie institutions. The Commonwealth Bank had just shredded the 'franchise benefits' of its 104-year history.

Narev would have to leave Australian banking behind, as CBA began the enormous job of rebuilding that most intangible of assets: trust.

*

CBA's mishandling of this PR crisis and its misreading of the public's fury was certain to bring down Livingstone as well as the chief executive. What the board also failed to recognise, at this stage, was that the public expected to see accountability in the form of bonus clawbacks. Shareholders did not want to be left holding the tab while their CEO sailed away with his millions. It looked an awful lot like the bankers were profiting, despite their incompetence in being played by organised crime.

For Narev, who had shown such promise as one of McKinsey's shining stars, it was an ignoble end to what had previously been a stellar banking career. As he walked down those hallowed hallways for the last time, the deep baritone of Australian history would undoubtedly have been ringing in his ears – more loudly and poignantly than ever before.

The die had been cast on his leadership. CBA was now a bank on its knees, begging for forgiveness and clemency from the very regulators it had once ruled.

FOURTEEN

A Process of Renewal

The departure of Ian Narev was the first scalp in the 'cultural renewal' at Australia's most critical financial institution. CBA's board was desperate to ensure the litigation brought by AUSTRAC was settled out of court. The regulator's leadership team held the line. Contrition and accountability, they said, would be crucial to any settlement talks.

Both parties knew that the material contained in the statement of claim would be highly damaging to CBA's brand, should it emerge in a blow-by-blow court process. The media and the public would be titillated by tales of triads, terrorists and traffickers moving billions through the bank.

To force the bank's hand, the country's leading financial regulators now linked arms in a coordinated show of force. In an unprecedented move, Philip Lowe, the RBA governor, described the case publicly as 'very serious'. He said management had to be held accountable.

Lowe was a man of unquestioned integrity, professional poise and restraint. His prognosis was damning. In addition,

ASIC revealed that it would investigate potential breaches of the *Corporations Act 2001*, including continuous disclosure obligations, in relation to the bank's handling of the money-laundering saga. ASIC chairman Greg Medcraft's move was largely symbolic in the context of the seriousness of AUSTRAC's claim, but he also made it clear that CBA was surrounded.

Even the tightly captured banking regulator APRA moved in, laying down an extra $1 billion capital charge and saying it was launching a review into risk culture.

Strategically, the key Commonwealth government agencies and regulators were reminding the banking sector who was really in charge. The banks had been running amok since the financial crisis, with what they believed was an implicit bailout guarantee, an explicit guarantee on bank deposits and a free pass on enforcement. It was truly a case of privatising the profits and socialising the losses.

The country's three other major banks watched the drama unfold like a slow-motion train wreck. None had come to CBA's defence – not even through the anonymised face of the Australian Bankers' Association. Unlike the 2008 financial maelstrom – the last time Australian regulators had joined forces in this way – CBA would be navigating this crisis alone.

*

The invisible hand behind this coordinated push, it should be noted, was the AFP. The agency had been fighting the insidious meth trade for years, citing it as Australia's most destructive illicit drug. And all the while CBA had allowed billions of dollars to move through its IDM cash conduit without basic controls that might prevent meth dealers from moving their profits abroad.

In many jurisdictions, banks that had been caught facilitating the second arm of the drug trade – moving and concealing the proceeds of crime – had been treated as complicit in the underlying criminal activity. The international drug syndicates had two main concerns: getting the drugs in and getting the money out. For years the country's largest bank had provided them with a laundering service that was cheap, fast, easy and reliable. For years, getting the loot out of Australia had not been one of the underworld's problems.

AUSTRAC's mammoth 691-page statement of claim against the Commonwealth Bank looked at only a small slice of these money flows: it detailed just $77 million worth of alleged illegal funds transfers, all of which were the subject of separate AFP criminal trials. This was just the tip of the iceberg for illicit cashflows through the 'smart ATMs'. Due to CBA's alleged failure to put controls in place, especially around its open conduit to Hong Kong, no one would ever know exactly how much of the $8.9 billion that moved through those machines was the proceeds of crime. The intel had not been lost – it had simply never been collected.

One thing was clear: AUSTRAC had made very good use of the AFP's underlying cases, prepared to a criminal standard of proof, in building its claim against the bank. For those in the know, it seemed as though Paul Jevtovic had used his deep AFP background, understanding and connections to leverage those criminal investigations into a bombshell civil AML/CTF claim.

The criminal standard of the AFP's underlying investigations left CBA with very little wriggle room in a civil trial. The bank could perhaps argue the issues around the fringes: at what point, it might ask, should suspicion have been formed? Was it appropriate for CBA to only file one SMR for each account, every 90 days, regardless of the number of suspicious transactions that occurred? But the broader claim itself, based on internal documents and damning surveillance footage of smurfs pulling up milk crates and pumping cash into ATMs until they jammed, would prove damning for the defendant.

The failure to file 53,506 TTRs over three years highlighted the iron fist that AUSTRAC was wielding beneath its velvet glove of partnerships and diplomacy. With penalties of between $17 million and $21 million per breach, the bank was theoretically facing an eye-watering fine. Under a strict reading of the AML/CTF Act, the technical breaches or 'coding errors' that CBA had acknowledged could already be grounds for a multi-billion-dollar penalty. All in all, the bank's motivation to settle with AUSTRAC was strong.

But there were risks and unknowns on both sides. Sonja Marsic was acutely aware that her client had never tested a case before a judge in full trial. The Tabcorp matter had been settled by mutual agreement, and signed off by a judge. There was also a risk that a sympathetic judge could find that all 53,506 TTRs were the result of a single 'course of conduct'. Such a finding could reduce the theoretical billion-dollar penalties to a paltry fine.

Was either party really willing to roll the dice? In the end, over a boardroom table with CBA's new Chief Executive Matt Comyn at the helm, they thrashed out a record Australian civil penalty of $700 million.

Unlike other regulators, which were hamstrung by complex laws and 'wet lettuce' enforcement penalties, AUSTRAC knew it was carrying a bazooka. Whether the country's politicians intended this when they passed the AML/CTF Act back in 2006 was another matter entirely. It's fair to say the parliament had no idea that banks might rack up tens of thousands – even millions – of technical breaches. If the parliament had twigged to this, they would never have set the penalties at millions of dollars per offence.

Regardless, Marsic and AUSTRAC's nimble legal team were happy to use every tool in their arsenal to force a fundamental shift in culture across corporate Australia. They had a shared goal: to keep communities free of crime, and to stem the flood of dark money across the country's borders.

*

More broadly, the 'smart laundromat' scandal was an inflection point for financial crime in Australia. It was the moment when money laundering was splashed across Australians' TV screens at dinner time. It was also when many Australians first discovered the depth of the criminal economy, and the extent to which illicit money had infiltrated their country's leading institutions. For the banks, it was the moment it became clear that AUSTRAC was one of Australia's most formidable regulators.

The public anger – the outrage that this could happen at an Aussie icon – was palpable. This was not the usual esoteric banking regulatory squabble. Australians made clear their contempt for any business that facilitated the illicit drug trade (particularly ice trafficking, as that drug was ripping apart families across the nation) or terrorism. Some Australians still had the small, metal money boxes, in the shape of the original CBA building, which had been handed out in schools across Australia during the 1970s. Dropping a copper coin in the narrow coin slot was a way to teach children about the value of saving, delayed gratification, forward planning and – most importantly – trust. Far from a trusty savings tin, however, the money slots on Commonwealth Bank ATMs were now being depicted in newspaper cartoons as the coin slot on a laundromat.

With the demise of Commonwealth Bank, people suddenly saw just how deeply criminal money had infiltrated the Australian economy and business community. If the country's largest and most respected bank was washing wholesale volumes of money for drug cartels and terrorists, what were the risks associated with other sectors, such as casinos, real estate, accountants and lawyers?

Paddy Oliver, one of Australia's leading anti-money-laundering lawyers, had seen this dynamic play out in other countries that had suffered from laundering scandals. Oliver is a sharp and witty Northern Irishman who moved to Australia after forging his career as an anti-money-laundering expert in the Northern Hemisphere. He loves his adopted home of Melbourne, and believes Australia's system of democracy and financial integrity is so precious as to be worth fighting for – to the death of several pints, if need be. A passionate Celt, Paddy is not one to mince words. Even against his own profession.

'The reputational damage from the Panama Papers led New Zealand to act very quickly to introduce phase two of its AML/CFT regime. Now in Australia, the involvement of CBA in a major money laundering litigation could have a similar effect. It will be very hard for the Law Council and other legal industry bodies to continue to argue against the need for reform in this climate,' Oliver said following the CBA scandal. 'The accounting and real estate peak bodies have accepted the need for the reforms. Perhaps it's time for all business sectors that are used by money launderers and the financiers of terrorism to work together for the common societal good?'

As it turned out, Oliver was overly optimistic about the appetite for fiscal integrity in his new home country. Like most proud Australians, he had underestimated the extent to which the legal, property and accounting lobbies had hobbled and bought off Canberra's leaders. Few Australians, in fact, were aware of the grip that the 'property Ponzi scheme' held over Australian politics.

Even in the wake of CBA's scandal, the proponents of reform were up against it. Like Sisyphus, the Greek cheater of death, the reformists would be burdened by the sheer gravity of the Lucky Laundry's new post-manufacturing business model, which was based on an unholy trinity of finance, real estate and washing the proceeds of international organised crime. They would spend many years rolling the boulder of reform uphill, only to see it tumble back down again, pushed by the invisible hand of political lobbying.

FIFTEEN

Known Unknowns

When Paul Jevtovic had stepped down as AUSTRAC chief in 2017, just before the CBA bombshell was dropped, it was with mixed feelings and amid the most interesting of times. The London-headquartered bank HSBC was also in the process of extracting itself from one of the world's biggest money-laundering scandals. This was perhaps a fitting development, as HSBC had been established in 1865 following the Opium Wars in Hong Kong. It had even acted as banker to the world's first multinational drug cartels, as the British used Hong Kong as a staging post to flood China with a devastating tsunami of opiates.

Fast-forward 150 years and HSBC was again banking for the drug cartels. This time, in a twist of karmic equilibrium, it was the developing world flooding the West with the weapons of mass addiction – mostly Colombian and Mexican cartels peddling processed coca leaves. In late 2012, HSBC stood on the precipice, facing the loss of its critical US banking licence. To stave off disaster, the bank forged a US$1.9 billion settlement with New York prosecutors and – the real kicker – agreed to appoint a US-nominated independent compliance monitor. This would give US officialdom a permanent team inside the bank.

The US government chose Michael Cherkasky, a former prosecutor and legend in the world of financial crime fighting, to lead the monitorship for five long years. Under Cherkasky, the bank hired Jennifer Shasky Calvery as global head of financial crime threat mitigation. Shasky Calvery was a former prosecutor herself and, conveniently, the head of the US equivalent of AUSTRAC when she accepted the role.

In another coup, Jevtovic was poached to become the Hong Kong-based head of financial crime threat mitigation for the Asia-Pacific region. For five years, the Five Eyes financial intelligence community would, by proxy, have eyes and ears inside the money launderers' favourite bank. For half a decade relationship managers would complain that they couldn't have a meeting without the risk of a monitor coming along.

Monitors in Hong Kong would share stories of being barred from a meeting with a high-net-wealth private banking client. Overnight, the banker would receive a call from New York and the terrible oversight would be corrected by morning.

HSBC had been placed on a very tight leash.

While this role in Hong Kong was an offer too good to refuse, Jevtovic had deep misgivings about leaving the team he had built over two and a half years at AUSTRAC. He had loved working within the small, nimble agency, which had been given plenty of latitude by its Perth-based minister, Michael Keenan. Around the traps in Perth, Keenan was known to be setting up a series of Jetts gym franchises in addition to running his portfolio. This was great news for AUSTRAC, as it blazed a trail of reform and took calculated risks that were unprecedented for a government agency.

In 2017, as Jevtovic prepared to leave the agency, there was one achievement that stood out above all others: the formation of the Fintel Alliance. The public launch of the alliance had attracted interest from around the globe. This was the first time – anywhere in the world – that bankers had been sworn in as public servants and physically co-located inside a financial intelligence unit. The outgoing AUSTRAC chief's initiative was described as a 'game changer' in the fight against serious and organised crime, money laundering, terrorist financing, tax evasion and drug syndicates.

AUSTRAC rolled out a physical Operations Hub, in Chatswood, with bank staff signing the secrecy charter that normally applies to sensitive government jobs. Having bank staff sitting inside a secure room, alongside police and intelligence analysts, was revolutionary. A select group of bankers were now sworn in as part of the criminal intelligence community. This was also high-risk, of course. With trust came a risk of information 'leakage'. But under Jevtovic's leadership, AUSTRAC had begun a bold attempt to bring together industry and law-enforcement expertise in a way that demolished the old dichotomy between the public and private spheres.

As it turned out, Minister Keenan's hands-off style of portfolio oversight was the best thing that could have happened to a cutting-edge financial intelligence agency like AUSTRAC.

*

Intelligence sharing is the lifeblood of the fight against financial crime, organised crime, money laundering and terrorism in the 21st century. In the digital age, criminal syndicates have access to an unprecedented array of cheap technological tools, communications equipment and information. For law-enforcement agencies, the stream of data that flows through these networks is a double-edged sword; technology is both an enabler of organised crime and the ultimate source of intelligence.

In this context, Australia's financial intelligence agency knew it was fighting a mercurial foe. AUSTRAC needed to be at the forefront of the technological and intelligence arms race between law-enforcement agencies and crime syndicates.

Dissolving the old boundaries between the private and public sectors had been a defining theme of Jevtovic's tenure at AUSTRAC. It was a vision that could only be carried out by a 35-year crime-fighting veteran with deep industry respect, boundless energy and a powerful understanding of the evolving nature of organised crime. In addition to the Operations Hub, AUSTRAC set up an Innovation Hub to encourage start-ups and entrepreneurs to develop high-tech solutions to help tackle serious financial crime. This was another example of the agency's commitment to the power of partnerships. With all of the tenacity he had learned on the football field as a youngster, Jevtovic was bringing people together and giving the 'good guys' a sporting chance.

AUSTRAC's belief that technology would be fundamental to fighting organised crime and terrorism in the 21st century was also reflected in several high-profile appointments. In 2016 it hired Gavin McCairns, the Department of Immigration's biometrics chief, as deputy chief executive, to lead the agency's digital transformation. McCairns had been instrumental in rolling out the SmartGate identity and biometrics project at the Department of Immigration.

AUSTRAC also hired Maria Milosavljevic, a former chief information officer at the Australian Crime Commission (since rebranded as the ACIC), who had been responsible for overhauling that agency's IT infrastructure. Milosavljevic had driven the establishment of the National Criminal Intelligence Fusion Capability project, where she worked closely with Jevtovic. They both believed the time was right to try something equally ambitious at AUSTRAC.

The driver behind AUSTRAC's Fintel Alliance was the urgent need to link together the expertise in government agencies, law-enforcement bodies and private-sector firms. It began with 19 domestic and international partners, including the AFP, the New South Wales Police Force, the Australian Taxation Office (ATO), the big four Australian banks, as well as Western Union and PayPal. The UK Financial Intelligence Unit also joined the alliance to provide an international perspective.

'This is the beginning of a national and global alliance that will leave nowhere for criminals to hide in the financial system,' said Justice Minister Michael Keenan in March 2017. 'Australia faces ever-increasing and changing national and international threats.'

Jevtovic's background in law enforcement had been vital to the establishment of the Operations Hub in Sydney. It was based on the 'fusion centres' he had run at the AFP, although this time government and private-sector intelligence analysts could work side-by-side.

'Organised criminals and terrorist groups do not work within the confines of the law,' Jevtovic told me during an interview in 2017. 'They're not limited by jurisdiction and they're often extremely well resourced. They're able to capitalise on the newest technologies. That makes them quite a formidable enemy for us to have to fight.

'The way to mitigate that challenge is to be the strongest that we can be. That strength is realised when industry and government agencies are actually working as one, as genuine trusted partners. It's my view that the Fintel Alliance is going to be the most powerful tool that we have in that fight, particularly in the money laundering and terrorist financing arena.'

In April 2017, however, it was time for Jevtovic to leave Sydney for the dazzling pace of Hong Kong – and to leave his team to carry on with the mission.

*

Two and a half years later, this vision – and the calculated risks the agency was prepared to take – were starting to pay off in spades. AUSTRAC had a new CEO with similar law-enforcement pedigree in Nicole Rose. The agency had concluded the CBA matter and triggered a change in culture across the financial sector. The revelations in the CBA case had been the straw that broke the camel's back, forcing the government to establish the Royal Commission into Misconduct in the Banking, Superannuation and Financial Services Industry in December 2017.

AUSTRAC was on the front foot, a nimble, agile federal government agency at its very best. With around 300 staff and a $70 million budget, they were kicking straight between the posts. New ground was being broken every week in the fight against some of the world's most heinous financial crimes. But 6 November 2019 was an extra-special day. On the seventh floor of AUSTRAC's nondescript office block in Chatswood, there was electricity in the air. The agency's financial intelligence analysts, buried in their secret world, lived for these exhilarating moments.

Deep inside the secure AUSTRAC facility was an even more secure room – a vault within a vault. The bunker was enclosed within soundproof glass and swipe-coded doors. But other than some orange banners flagging the Fintel Alliance, it looked like any other part of the financial intelligence unit's main building. The unique things about this room were that it housed members of the private sector. Most of AUSTRAC's own staff were banned from entering. On any given day there might be senior people from CBA, Westpac, the ACIC, the AFP, the ATO or a range of other government agencies. In Melbourne, a similar facility housed experts from NAB and ANZ, among others.

The alliance's top priority was now listed as 'protecting the most vulnerable from child exploitation'. And on this Wednesday morning in November, it was going public with the results of two years' worth of sensitive work. AUSTRAC was revealing that the group's intelligence reports had saved 35 children in the Philippines from sexual slavery. A total of 73 suspected offenders had been either arrested or detained with the alliance's help. The bulk of those arrests were due to 25 'intelligence products' developed within the walls of that glazed chamber in Chatswood.

It was a staggering achievement, and a world-first innovation in the use of financial intelligence. Like old Nugget Coombs and his polymer banknote, AUSTRAC was proving that Australia could be both lucky and innovative. For Australia's army of fintel experts, this was a time for quiet celebration among an elite group, and maybe even a glass of champagne or two after work.

They were winning in their interminable fight between a handful of good people and a world of unspeakable evils.

SIXTEEN

The Dark Heart of Financial Crime

More than a year earlier, in March 2018, at a discreet hotel in Sydney, two dozen senior figures from the financial intelligence community had gathered around a diplomatically square boardroom table. There was no head, no sides, no nosebleed section down the end, just a group of equals coming together with a shared vision and a common goal. They had been invited to the biannual roundtable discussion on the Fintel Alliance, the world's first genuinely co-located public-private financial intelligence partnership dedicated to fighting serious and organised financial crime.

It was a triumphant meeting, celebrating the successes of the alliance in its first 12 months of operation. This type of shoulder-to-shoulder collaboration had never happened before in the cat-and-rat world of financial intelligence. The project had broken new ground by allowing bank staff, payments companies, law-enforcement agencies and criminal intelligence experts to sit in the same room and work together on top-priority projects.

Some of the early wins demonstrated what a powerful 'triple P' (public-private partnership) model this could become. No other country had gone as far as swearing in bankers as public servants and inviting them to sit beside law-enforcement agents to discuss matters of national importance – and secrecy – in the realm of criminal intelligence. In its first year, the project team had focused on detecting and disrupting money 'muling' syndicates, analysing the financial data leak known as the 'Panama Papers', and mining data from the Australian Cyber Online Reporting Network (ACORN).

The biggest victory, however, had been a very human story. The alliance's most inspiring and successful work had been to use financial typologies, transaction monitoring, data and analytics to make new inroads into the detection of payments relating to child sexual exploitation. This had allowed banks and payment companies to file a raft of suspicious matter reports (SMRs) on the horrific 'pay per view' streaming of live child sexual abuse, primarily in vulnerable regions in the Philippines. It had been a project driven by the financial services industry. As such, it was an example of the great work that banks and payment companies do every day behind closed doors.

From AUSTRAC's perspective, this project was a top priority. It was not financial intelligence that would languish in a database waiting for a law-enforcement agency to pick up the case. The financial intelligence unit (FIU) had an assurance that child exploitation cases would be acted upon immediately by the AFP. The AFP agents, in turn, were working closely with their counterparts at the Philippine Internet Crimes Against Children Centre (PICACC) and the Philippine National Police.

The magic of the Fintel Alliance was that it allowed banks to work directly with the agencies that would make use of their intel. It meant that their knowledge, energy and resources were aligned.

In the normal world, privacy laws severely restricted the sharing of customer data. This was endlessly frustrating for financial crime teams within banks. 'I can exit a customer due to terrorism financing concerns. I can close his account and pay his balance out with a bank cheque. I can then see which bank he moved to when he cashes that cheque – but I can't ring up my friends at the bank down the road and tell them,' one senior executive told me, taking a frustrated swig from a beer, at a financial crime summit in Malaysia.

The Fintel Alliance was designed to tackle this problem.

The banks had staff sitting in the same room alongside AUSTRAC and its 'clients', giving them the ability to work together in real time. The agency could receive information from one bank, then compel information from all the other participating banks using a statutory instrument called a Section 167 notice. This allowed them to build a complex fintel picture far more quickly than had ever been possible before. By feeding that information directly to the AFP's liaison officer, they were able to save children from suffering further harm. This was nothing short of a revolution.

For the bankers working on the project, it had been harrowing work. They were not prepared, as police and criminal intelligence officers sometimes were, for the psychological toll of being exposed to acts of child abuse. To discover that their bank's money pipelines were being used to fund such acts was heartbreaking. To discover that apparently ordinary customers in the suburbs of Australia were capable of such evil acts was galling.

But the results were worth it. Every time a bank representative found a suspected paedophile in their haystacks of data, the police would investigate and swoop. The hundreds of millions that banks spend on financial crime infrastructure was working as it should. Banks and police were pooling their skills, brainstorming was happening, profiles were being created, algorithms were being set loose on vast pools of transaction data. Detailed reports were being filed to AUSTRAC. People were being arrested. Children were being saved from torture.

*

The group at the Sydney hotel that day were optimistic about the future of such public-private partnerships, not just in Australia but globally. A similar project had been attempted in the United Kingdom, through a partnership called the Joint Money Laundering Intelligence Taskforce (JMLIT), which had proven very successful. A campaign to identify human trafficking syndicates had led to more than 100 arrests. But Australia was the first country to take the concept this far, and the rest of the world was watching.

The banks had a wealth of data at their fingertips – indeed, too much data. The magic lay in learning to process and filter that information, to find the needles in these haystacks of ones and zeros. Combining and refining that knowledge was proving exponentially powerful.

The patterns of behaviour they were discovering that were indicative of child exploitation included small, regular payments of between $15 and $500, often disguised with descriptions like 'school fees' or 'uniforms'; purchases of live streaming software and VPNs, or metadata-stripping programs; travel to countries such as the Philippines; and the use of payment cards in high-risk areas.

In isolation, none of these pieces of data was inherently suspicious. A perpetual problem was how to sift out 'false positives', ensuring that the privacy of law-abiding customers was respected. But, when this had been done, the 'typologies' the team developed were incredibly powerful. In Australia, through the involvement of the AFP and ACIC, these 'red flags' could be aggregated and overlaid with other law-enforcement data sets. The banks and payment companies now had a revolutionary tool at their disposal.

Every month, as a result, children in the Philippines were being rescued from a living hell. Offenders were being brought to justice. In the 2018 financial year police had made more than 30 arrests on the back of this information. A year later, that number would continue to rise, with 73 suspects detained or arrested. Even better, those 35 children had been rescued from abusive situations with the help of financial intelligence.

Coming together to reflect and brainstorm, the financial crime community was now building the next steps for fintel, with even more ambitious hopes for what might be possible to achieve through teamwork, technology and trust.

What the participants in that room could never have known, however, was that one of the Fintel Alliance's founding members – a major Australian bank – was bluffing. It had not done the work to detect and disrupt this heinous crime typology. It had not invested in the technology it needed to apply sophisticated transaction-monitoring software to its cross-border payments. In fact, at that stage, even the bank itself had no idea it was facilitating tens of thousands of suspicious payments for at least 274 potential paedophiles.

This was a glimpse into the darkest corner of the world of dirty money. And it was happening in Australia, right under everyone's noses.

SEVENTEEN

Hartzer's Choice

As Australia's oldest and second most profitable bank, Westpac has long been a pillar when it comes to the business of living in the Lucky Country. The bank was established in Sydney in 1817 as the Bank of New South Wales, to power the growth of the fledgling British colony. It was brought into existence via a special charter inked by the governor of New South Wales, Lachlan Macquarie himself.

By 2017, the bank's various brands had been serving Australian entrepreneurs, workers, and government departments for 200 years. Westpac had weathered world wars, depressions, recessions, the Spanish flu pandemic, bushfires and droughts alongside the finest and most stoic of Aussie battlers.

In the world of prudential regulation, Westpac was also a pillar, one of Australia's most protected financial species. The government's explicit Four Pillars policy meant that a cosy banking oligopoly could exist without the destabilising pressure of continually having to fend off takeover threats. This was an arrangement that dated back to the Hawke/

Keating financial reforms of the 1980s, when Aussie banking was opened up to the world. The Wallis Inquiry in 1997 recommended that it be dissolved, but the policy lived on. At a regulators' summit in Sydney in April 2009, APRA's Laker said he believed the model had saved Australia from the worst effects of the 2008 financial crisis. Of course, this made for a much better story than the sordid Bankwest saga.

In November 2019, just two years after its bicentennial celebrations, the Westpac Banking Corporation's edifice of stability and good governance was being silently eroded by the murky subsurface currents of global money. The bank was led by Brian Hartzer, a fine man and a well-regarded leader. Hartzer had developed a concept he called the 'leadership star', which he would share enthusiastically with his staff and executives. It placed ethics, governance and integrity at the heart of everything the bank did. Hartzer was a strong supporter of the Banking and Finance Oath, a voluntary commitment that encouraged financial services workers to 'compete with honour'.

In August 2019, I was volunteering to MC the Banking and Finance Oath Conference in Sydney. Westpac supported the event by providing a stunning harbourside venue and catering at no cost to the Ethics Centre, which was arranging the event. Hartzer supported the event personally, quietly, while actively resisting any publicity. As Westpac's chief executive, he took the view that ethics was a personal matter and not something that should be shouted from rooftops. To do so would invite criticism, as well as landmining the road ahead with banana skins at best, or explosives at worst.

At the same time, ethical leadership and personal transformation was the source of that intangible entity known as 'corporate culture'. Hartzer had witnessed the cultural failures at the Commonwealth Bank and was determined to do better, without tempting fate by criticising his fallen peers.

*

Unfortunately, Hartzer's big red bank was also a creature defined by its history. Bank CEOs are captains of the ultimate slow-moving corporate vessels. Prudential regulation, alongside institutional shareholders, imposes this sensible conservatism upon them. While Ian Narev at CBA might have enjoyed basking in glory as the wunderkind of banking, the truth was that he had inherited commercial success from the leaders who came before him. Ralph Norris's tech reforms had laid the foundation for those boom years from 2012 until the money laundering disaster in 2017.

As Narev's quiet epiphany warned him that night at the Hordern Pavilion, his primary job was to not stuff up an Aussie icon. The mandate was simple: don't be complacent, don't be arrogant and don't screw things up.

The truth is bank CEOs do not truly determine their own fate. In taking the wheelhouse, they also take the ultimate leap of faith. Hartzer knew, when he took the helm in December 2014, that he would inherit the failures of his predecessors and craft a legacy for his heirs. Unfortunately for him, along with many good things at Westpac, he was also inheriting a long-term legacy of underinvestment in technology.

When Gail Kelly handed him the baton as CEO, she left on a triumphant note. The bank was roaring towards another multi-billion-dollar profit. Westpac had weathered the Global

Financial Crisis without so much as blinking. It had taken the opportunity to consume St George Bank, which had faced its own near-death experience. The tailwinds of the historic three-decades-long Australian property boom had left Westpac's shareholders enjoying record dividends.

But Kelly had also left Hartzer with a problem; he was in charge of a powerful banking brand that concealed a creaking back office. The legacy demands for tech investment were piling up. As what is essentially a massive building society, Westpac had ironically been painting the facade for years while termites dined on the roof structure.

This put Hartzer in a difficult position. He had to make major investment decisions while continuing to deliver dividends to shareholders. He also had to navigate seismic changes in the risk landscape while courting an expectant army of bank investors. He had to keep pace with the bumper profits being delivered by his peers, most notably Narev's Commonwealth Bank.

Hartzer didn't know it then, but he had just five years to make a hundred-million-dollar investment in his bank's financial crime detection and prevention infrastructure. Westpac had fallen well behind and, as voices within the bank were warning, it was highly vulnerable to criminal exploitation. Only by funding and empowering his anti-money-laundering division could Hartzer hope to turn back this tide. What Hartzer would soon discover, however, is that five years passes very quickly in the cut and thrust of steering and commandeering a systemically important Aussie icon through treacherous waters. And sometimes, a hundred million in time can save nine.

EIGHTEEN

Pulling a Swifty

Dirty money is the financial system's sewage. It infects, taints and poisons everything it encounters.

Villagers learned long ago that they needed to separate their waste from their wells. If some villagers became lazy, tipping buckets too close to their groundwater, it wouldn't be noticed at first. Over time, though, the sewage would seep into the communal well, building, accumulating. For a surprisingly long time, people's immune systems would hold up. But then, in a horrific outbreak, the entire village would become sickened with some terrible water-borne disease like cholera. The lazy ones, who believed no one would notice if they didn't play by the village rules, would bring misery to their entire community.

So it was with Westpac. For many, many years, the bank thought it was being clever. It was facilitating multinational tax crimes so complex and obscure that no regulator, it was sure, would ever discover them. And even if it did, the bank took a punt that the risk of litigation was low.

But behind the scenes, the Westpac disaster was another tragic case study in how turning a blind eye to criminality would inevitably come back to haunt an institution. A major bank – or any organisation, for that matter – could not facilitate financial crime and expect to maintain a healthy internal culture. Like polluting society's groundwater, the day of reckoning would surely arrive. Westpac would soon be facing its own existential crisis, as it became embroiled in the world of tax evasion … and worse.

*

Banks, like their partners in the major accountancy firms, have a front-row view of the global tax evasion industry. This is a system so craven and shameless that it would make a hardworking 'pay as you go' taxpayer cry. This is a system where the major accounting firms consult to governments around the world on law reform, seed policy with their secret loopholes, only to market those loopholes to wealthy clients.

Only rarely do punters get a dizzying glimpse into the sinkholes that disappear tax dollars into the abyss of the hidden offshore world. The Panama Papers, Project Wickenby, the Paradise Papers and the Pandora Papers have all exposed an arcane world where complex accounting structures are given comical names like the 'Double Irish, Dutch Sandwich'. It's a world of SWIFT payments and even swifter money-hiding schemes. It's a magician's shell game with the world's tax dollars.

In case you haven't met it, SWIFT is the Brussels-based quango that maintains the architecture for the world's cross-border payments. It sets standards for a range of things, including the messages that must accompany international money transfers. You see, money doesn't actually move around the world when interbank payments are made. Only *information* moves, and account balances are credited or debited accordingly. One of the things SWIFT needs to manage, when setting standards, is the risk of payments being used to avoid taxes or bring down governments through more immediate and violent means.

In 2009, SWIFT introduced a new rule called the MT202 COV obligations. Essentially, this was a payment instruction to ensure that information about both the sender and the beneficiary always moves with a payment as the money sluices between the world's banks. This was one of a range of global financial controls introduced after 11 September 2001, both to combat the financing of terrorism and to facilitate data sharing on cross-border funds transfers. This information was crucial to AUSTRAC and its international chums.

Prior to the introduction of the MT202 COV format, the banks that processed these transactions had little visibility over the funds they were handling on behalf of their overseas correspondent banks. The older MT202 messaging format didn't require financial institutions to provide any information on the sender and recipient of cross-border payments. This was particularly dangerous with cover payments, where a combination of the older (and less detailed) MT103 and MT202 messaging formats was being used.

The global banking sector holds many dark secrets. One is that many institutions around the world put complex systems in place following the 2009 SWIFT reporting changes to ensure that they could continue to facilitate lucrative transactions in the shadows.

The US Department of Treasury's litigation against UniCredit in 2019, for example, found that the Italian-headquartered bank had sought specific advice from consultants on how it might circumvent the SWIFT-reporting obligations. Incredibly, as soon as the ink had dried on the new standard, the same consulting firms that had helped devise the MT202 COV reforms had begun selling their lucrative workarounds. It was an egregious scheme manufactured by criminals in pinstriped suits.

The US prosecutors in this case said UniCredit had engaged a German consulting firm, which had helped it to 'construct the evasive process by which UniCredit AG carried out this illegal conduct'. In internal emails, UniCredit staff made it clear this was designed to mask payments to 'sensitive' countries, such as Sudan, Syria, Iran, Cuba, Myanmar, Belarus and North Korea. The aim was to ensure there was no data in field 72 of the SWIFT messages for transactions involving any US bank. They were gaming the system put in place to combat terrorism and nuclear programs such as those in Iran and North Korea.

UniCredit was busted trying to outwit the fearsome US Office of Foreign Assets Control (OFAC), which oversees trade sanctions. The Italian bank was locked out of US-dollar clearing and eventually paid US$1.3 billion to atone for its sins.

*

What few people knew, however, was that some banks had developed an even simpler way to avoid submitting this SWIFT data. Australia's Westpac was one of them. With its LitePay and Australasian Cash Management (ACM) products for international cross-border payments, Westpac could bypass the SWIFT rails completely.

An AUSTRAC investigation revealed the horrifying extent of this skulduggery. Westpac had helped its clients hide evidence of cross-border payments moving to and from sanctioned countries such as Sudan, Cuba and Iran. The Australian authorities discovered that several major international banks had taken advantage of this service. Not only was this facilitating billions of dollars in tax evasion every year, it was also having a devastating impact on financial intelligence gathering.

'Westpac considered that the SWIFT payment network was costly and not an efficient means of sending low-value, large-volume payments for clients of global banks that need to make and receive payments around the world,' AUSTRAC discovered. 'For this reason, under a number of the ACM arrangements, the correspondent banks "batch" funds transfer instructions from multiple payers to multiple payees and send the instructions to Westpac in a single structured data file, via non-SWIFT channels.'

Essentially, the banks would 'net off' transactions and bypass SWIFT entirely. The irony was that this was precisely the model that *hawaladars* had been using for hundreds of years to move money quickly, cheaply and invisibly across borders. Australia's oldest bank had become a *hawaladar* itself, that pariah of the banking community. In doing so, it had failed to collect data on tens of billions of dollars' worth of international transactions. The quantum of taxpayer losses through this wholesale multinational tax evasion would never be known.

The cost savings Westpac was seeking were not in the avoidance of microscopic payments to SWIFT. They were in the circumvention of compliance, reporting and data collection. There was a steady line of correspondent banks and their customers who wanted to avail themselves of low-cost services such as ACM and LitePay. Most of them, however, were seeking lite-visibility.

As a service to its most prized customers – the banking equivalent of a pass to the Qantas Chairman's Lounge – Westpac would even go one step further. Major multinationals could secure an Australian BSB number, for their own use, that would direct local payments straight into their overseas accounts – for example, into a nice low-tax jurisdiction such as Singapore.

To a payer, these BSB numbers looked like they belonged to a local Westpac branch. To the multinational holder of this magical six-digit number, however, Australian revenue disappeared beneath the murky waters of Barangaroo and into the banking system's Bermuda Triangle. As far as the ATO was concerned, the money could never be found again. The cost to Australian taxpayers was, quite literally, incalculable.

The SWIFT-avoidance system that the German consultants (and others) were marketing to banks was ingenious in its simplicity. All around the world it was near-impossible to unravel. Regulators and tax authorities simply had no mechanism to unfurl this Gordian knot.

*

The tripwire for banks that used these strategies in Australia was, as it turns out, equally simple yet ingenious. It was safe to say that the consultants who pitched these schemes were unaware of a curiosity in Australia's AML regime called the

International Funds Transfer Instructions (IFTI) reporting rules. Australia was the first country to introduce these 'wire reporting' obligations under pressure from AUSTRAC official Neil Jensen way back in 1989.

Jensen is a legend of the Australian AML community. He's a mild-mannered man, humble, with a razor-sharp pair of eyes and a neatly trimmed moustache. Jensen is universally liked and was at AUSTRAC from its first day of operation, under the old *Financial Transaction Reports Act 1988*. He later rose to the position of chief executive. Crucially, Jensen was there when the agency came of age with the Aussie parliament's comprehensive 2006 legislative overhaul, bringing in the AML/CTF Act.

'Over the past 20 years I have been concerned that not enough is being done to readily identify cross-border funds transfers, whether the funds arise from corrupt practices, drugs, fraud, people smuggling and trafficking, or any other serious crime,' Jensen once told me. 'I have made it a point to highlight in many speeches around the world since the early 1990s that we have "left the door open" to sophisticated criminals to launder money through the global financial system and that we need to start to close that door by having ready access to these transactions in real time.'

The solution, Jensen believed, was to require every transaction that passed through Australia to be reported to AUSTRAC. The government could then use its banks of supercomputers to crunch that data, seeking out hidden patterns like a mathematician chasing fractals in nature.

'I did something about it back in 1989, and subsequently the Australian government implemented legislation in 1991 to enable AUSTRAC, the Australian FIU, to receive reports of inbound and outbound international funds transfer instructions [wire transfers] from financial institutions and other remitters,' Jensen explained.

Jensen would eventually receive the Public Service Medal for his vision in helping to introduce IFTI reporting 30 years ago. The senior executives and board members at Westpac, would eventually come to use his name in a less complimentary manner. Because when it came to Westpac's cunning scheme, there was one small hitch. Every time the bank aggregated these bundles of cross-border payments into a batch, to avoid reporting, it was breaching the IFTI laws. Every time it gave a client a fake Australian BSB, to whisk funds abroad, it needed to file a report. Failing to do so could rack up millions of breaches, all of which would carry a theoretical $21 million fine.

The Australian approach, Jensen said, offered a very simple answer to this global problem, by forcing the data to flow to FIUs regardless of whether it is a SWIFT payment or a correspondent banking inter-bank transfer. 'Put all of the information in one place so that it can be monitored effectively, where it can be readily linked to other highly relevant financial intelligence and from where appropriate investigative action can be quickly commenced. One of the major benefits of the reporting of cross-border funds transfers to AUSTRAC has been the ability of its analysts to identify criminals not previously identified by law enforcement agencies,' he said. 'The results in Australia speak for themselves.'

What Jensen couldn't know was that his laws had also ensnared some of the global tax laundromat's biggest players. AUSTRAC, it seems, had once again outsmarted the smartest guys in the room.

NINETEEN

The Day of Reckoning

There's an old saying in the criminal underworld: never give a copper an excuse to be 'lawfully on premises'. Once the fuzz are in the house, they can bag anything they reasonably suspect was used in connection with an offence.

Many a crime has been uncovered in the course of investigating something more trivial. Trafficable quantities of drugs and bags of cash have been picked up in cars during routine traffic stops. In one case in Sydney, a pair of police officers pulled over a driver only to discover his hands were shaking so much that he couldn't get the car into 'park'. When they searched the vehicle, they found freezer bags full of unexplained cash. The driver was in the country on a tourist visa, moonlighting as a smurf.

The same principle applies with bank visits from the anti-money-laundering unit. When AUSTRAC started requesting evidence from Westpac about its IFTI reporting, it knew pretty quickly that it had struck a rich vein of enforcement gold. The Section 167 notices – a legal mechanism for the agency to make 'requests for information' – whirled around like confetti. Of course, once an intelligence agency has access to the vehicle, there's no guessing what it might find in the boot, under the hood, or stashed inside the spare tyre. Banks are highly complex creatures; in many cases they've grown both too big to fail and too big to manage. Westpac knew it had a catastrophic problem with IFTI reporting, and it was fairly certain that this was going to explode in a very public manner.

AUSTRAC also had a challenge. Multinational tax evasion was highly complex, technical and difficult to explain to stakeholders among the Australian public. Politicians and taxpayers might not really appreciate the significance of an accounting trick with a name that sounded like a Subway special. 'SWIFT avoidance' lacked the lapel-grabbing impact of the types of crimes that the Commonwealth Bank had been facilitating: drugs, illegal firearms, terrorism. With civil enforcements, a government agency always needs to satisfy a number of tests. Chief among these is that the action is in the public interest. Another less explicit test is that the public understands, and supports, any use of these onerous enforcement powers.

AUSTRAC's enforcement team had been poring over thousands of documents. This was highly complex material involving the minutiae of internal bank mechanics. It might be riveting stuff to a chartered accountant, but multinational tax evasion was hard for the evening news to capture.

Then one day, with 12 filings, everything changed.

*

The AFP had been making huge inroads into targeting the pay-per-view streaming of child abuse. This was a crime type where international viewers would connect on darkweb forums and agree to pay for a child to be tortured for their own gratification. Within the police, it was regarded as one of the worst crime types imaginable. The Fintel Alliance had given the AFP incredibly valuable financial intelligence to assist with a wave of arrests across Australia. Unusually, a disproportionately high number of the customers being arrested held accounts with Westpac. As yet, though, no one had connected those dots.

As part of its enforcement work, AUSTRAC asked the bank to run a 'lookback' on its transactions. It suspected that Westpac's cunning multinational tax evasion service may have triggered around 23 million alleged reporting breaches. At a theoretical maximum of $21 million per offence, the bank could be facing a $483 trillion fine. This was a staggering figure, equivalent to 250 times Australia's entire annual GDP.

To put that in context, a year earlier Westpac had been fined a measly $3.3 million over its attempts to manipulate Australia's version of LIBOR, the Bank Bill Swap Rate. These 'benchmark rates' are used to set interest rates across the lending markets. If they're rigged, it can cause millions of customers to pay too much in interest. To put the fine in context, in the Northern Hemisphere the six largest banks were fined a collective US$5.8 billion for rate rigging. In Australia, Justice Jonathan Beach said the penalty of $3.3 million was clearly inadequate but his hands were tied. It was the maximum he could impose under the *Corporations Act 2001*, which was overseen by ASIC. This corporate regulator, hopelessly muzzled and neutered, was meant to be Australia's most feared financial watchdog.

The theoretical AUSTRAC penalty proved two things: firstly, that when the Australian parliament passed the AML/CTF Act in 2006, it had no idea what it was unleashing; and secondly, that the Australian banks had a new gamekeeper in town. Fresh from the Commonwealth Bank litigation, AUSTRAC was now considering adding another shrunken head to its belt. These were banks that had seemed untouchable just two years earlier.

As it considered its options, AUSTRAC ordered Westpac to do a retrospective review of a sample of its cross-border payment channels. This was a process known in the industry as a dreaded 'lookback'. These types of reviews were never pleasant. Westpac had been forced to do one of these in the United States several years earlier, when it discovered it was not monitoring transactions through its institutional banking arm in New York. In that case, with a huge sigh of relief, the bank found that it was not underreporting, and it was let off with a warning by the feared US regulators, including OFAC, which was known to hand down monster penalties. For instance, in 2014, the French bank BNP Paribas had been fined US$8.9 billion for stripping information from its SWIFT messages.

This time, the results of Westpac's lookback were terrifying. The bank's financial crime team watched in horror as the reports lined up in its multi-million-dollar Norkom transaction-monitoring software. How had these all been missed? The team discovered they had not been monitoring these overseas channels, including payments to high-risk countries such as the Philippines. Worse still, it had not been applying the child exploitation typologies that it had helped to generate within the Fintel Alliance.

The bank ran the filters and discovered it had 12 customers who matched the profile of a purchaser of live-streamed 'child exploitation material', or CEM. Many of these should have been flagged as 'suspicious' and reported to AUSTRAC as far back as 2013. Some were linked to AFP child exploitation investigations. None had been reported. The realisation of what this meant made the bank's AML experts physically sick.

One customer had opened an account in November 2013 and was using Westpac's remittance services, including LitePay, to send regular, small amounts of money to the Philippines. Over five years the customer had moved $136,000 in 625 separate transactions. He was sending around two transactions every week, averaging $217 each time. The regulator examined the transactions: the location, the payment narratives, the recipients. All were consistent with the child exploitation typologies. Yet Westpac had failed to notice.

The terrible truth was that, despite its promises, Westpac had not been screening its remittance channels for suspicious transaction patterns. Its most sinister customers had been moving money in the dark. Even worse, Westpac's failure to screen its cross-border transactions meant it had inadvertently become the bank of choice for these types of customers. As other banks used the typologies, closed the accounts and reported their suspicions, Westpac was welcoming these customers into its ecosystem and maintaining their business relationships.

Westpac was about to learn two of the toughest lessons in banking: never let a regulator like AUSTRAC get 'lawfully on premises'. And when you don't know what's going on inside your bank, *anything* could be going on inside your bank.

As the chief executive, Brian Hartzer's day of reckoning had arrived.

TWENTY

Into the Heart of Darkness

On 20 November 2019, AUSTRAC staged another of its so-called 'ambush' attacks. A statement of claim against Westpac was filed in the Federal Court detailing a staggering 23 million breaches of the anti-money-laundering laws. The headlines were dominated, however, by a relative handful of those transactions: the ones linked to the 12 most abhorrent customers Australian banking had yet encountered.

The case sent shockwaves ricocheting around the country. Once again, the nation's households were disgusted to discover what was going on within the rarefied air of our largest financial institutions.

'As a board and as individuals, we are devastated that anyone may have been exposed to the risk of harm, as a result of a failing by Westpac. For this, we are truly sorry,' said chairman Lindsay Maxsted, who would bring forward his retirement in light of the scandal. This was the most terrible way to leave.

Likewise, chief executive Hartzer, a parent himself and a fundamentally good man, was horrified. Shattered. Until the claim was lodged in court, Hartzer had no idea the bank had been failing at such a basic level. Straightaway, he said that the bank admitted to charges of breaching money-laundering-laws, but he denied the allegations that its compliance failures had allowed children in the Philippines to be abused. That was, quite simply, a bridge too far.

Hartzer, as the face of the bank, said the failure to report international transfers was due to a mix of technology and human errors, going back more than a decade. The bank blamed 'faults of omission' and 'not intentional wrongdoing' for the millions of breaches. It all reeked of CBA's disastrous 'coding errors' defence.

AUSTRAC's 48-page statement of claim, drafted once again by the quiet legal phenom Sonja Marsic, argued differently. It said that Westpac had serious and systemic deficiencies in its AML/CTF program, its risk assessment and its systems and controls. This was basic, fundamental stuff that a Four Pillars bank needed to get right as part of its privileged legal and social licence to operate.

'These contraventions are the result of systemic failures in [Westpac's] control environment, indifference by senior management and inadequate oversight by the board,' AUSTRAC's legal team wrote in one excoriating passage. 'They stemmed from Westpac's failure to properly resource the AML/CTF function, to invest in appropriate IT systems and automated solutions and to remediate known compliance issues in a timely manner. They have occurred because Westpac adopted an ad hoc approach to [money laundering and terrorism financing] risk management and compliance.'

The IFTI reporting failures detailed in the claim involved a total of $11 billion of dark money. This was 72 per cent of all the IFTIs the bank had processed between November 2013 and September 2018. The bank was only screening one-quarter of its crucial cross-border money flows.

The case quickly attracted top-level political attention, given the systemic importance of the country's second-largest bank. Any financial settlement on AUSTRAC's side would first need to be signed off by Federal Treasurer Josh Frydenberg, and then by Attorney-General Christian Porter and Home Affairs Minister Peter Dutton. The case had reached into the highest echelons of Australian political power. Once again, Westpac was not just sizing up against a 300-strong agency. It was shaping up against the entire Australian federal government.

Despite some heavy condemnation from Canberra, Westpac decided it would need to go to war. It had a long track record of taking on complex cases against ASIC and winning. The bank lined up an array of its finest legal advisers and barristers, including the law firm Allens and leading silks John Sheahan QC and Dr Ruth Higgins SC. Sheahan was an old hand at this: he had acted for the Commonwealth Bank in its AML court case in 2018. Peter Haig was brought in as the Allens partner to advise Westpac. His team included many of the lawyers who had defected to Allens from Herbert Smith Freehills, which had overseen the civil litigation defences of both CBA and Tabcorp. This was an armada of lethal legal force.

For its part, Westpac hired an additional 200 full-time staff to work on the 'uplift program' and threw hundreds of millions at consultants. The savings the bank had made on basic compliance over a period of years would now need to be paid back – with punitive interest.

On the other side was the small team from the Australian Government Solicitor, working alongside AUSTRAC's enforcement unit, led by Shane Campbell. With a possible trial looming, they briefed leading barrister Wendy Harris QC to prepare for battle in court. And standing behind them was an intangible yet crucial ally: the first tranche of the AML/CTF Act, the most onerous civil laws in Australian corporate history. As the US regulators had repeatedly proven, nuclear force was often the only way governments could bring rogue banks to heel.

In the background, AUSTRAC's team began working on an amended statement of claim to keep the pressure on Westpac. This was the same tactic that AUSTRAC and its lawyers had deployed to devastating effect in the case against CBA. They also pressured Westpac to continue with the 'lookback' project.

In another major blow to the bank's defence, Westpac discovered that its failures weren't limited to Australia. The breaches meant it also had problems with its worldwide tax reporting compliance obligations. This included issues with its Foreign Account Tax Compliance Act (FATCA) obligations in the United States, and its Common Reporting Standards (CRS) tax compliance framework.

International banks were also watching the case closely, as many major overseas banks had exploited the same service. A fuse had been lit and no one was sure how far the blast radius would reach if this particular disaster zone was raked over in court. Bankers around the world were praying the case would settle; financial crime boffins wanted to see it teased out in court. Some very public legal bloodshed would be entertaining, but – more importantly – a trial would bring with it some binding legal precedents. As yet, these nuclear-powered laws had still not been tested before a judge

Dirk Feinauer, director of a boutique law firm in Perth, predicted the case would settle before trial. He had some sobering words for those in the AML community who were looking forward to full litigation. 'Where the law is not clear it is brave to try and create a precedent,' he said. 'The key questions to ask are: can we afford to litigate? And can we afford not to litigate? Much like a war, despite the bravado, no one wants to be on the losing side.'

*

One thing was for certain: Hartzer's leadership was untenable. Despite his lack of knowledge of the exact nature of the breaches, there had to be accountability. Both he and chairman Lindsay Maxsted would perform the career equivalent of public *seppuku*. As a man of principle, Hartzer knew he had to own this disaster. He would not cling on out of pride, like Narev had done at CBA.

The bank's board also made the unprecedented move of penalising senior executives by clawing back $20 million in bonuses. It said a 'range of remuneration consequences' had been imposed on 38 senior staff, including recovering some of the long-term remuneration issued in previous years. On average, each executive lost more than $520,000 as a result of the clawbacks.

The case marked the first time an Australian bank had used medium- and longer-term remuneration to penalise bank employees for organisational risk and compliance failures. Although this symbolic gesture was welcomed, the near-unanimous feeling (which went well beyond Australia's shores) was that it was still too little to drive real change.

Dr Nicholas Gilmour, a former police officer and financial crime consultant in Auckland, said there were some fundamental industry-wide problems to address. When banks profited from financial crime by ignoring their basic obligations under the law, where were the orange jumpsuits? 'There are still many opportunities for criminals and financers of terrorism to exploit services, systems and processes,' he said. 'I feel until there is the clicking of handcuffs in the boardroom, the options for exploitation will continue.'

*

As the case dragged on, lawyers for Westpac continued playing hardball. Banking stalwart John McFarlane was brought in as chairman, a steady hand to right the tiller and lead the big red steamer out of these treacherous waters. McFarlane would be no pushover; and, as a cleanskin, he certainly wouldn't be paying with shareholders' money to cover up the sins of the departed. He wanted to make it clear to AUSTRAC that the bank would not simply roll over and settle. At the same time, Westpac's board knew they were in for a massive penalty. They set aside a record $900 million for a potential settlement, which was still significantly short of the more than $1.5 billion that AUSTRAC was seeking.

As part of its remediation work, Westpac was ordered to run more retrospective transaction monitoring lookbacks across more of its accounts. The bank looked specifically at accounts in South-East Asia and Mexico. Just when it seemed things couldn't get any worse, the unthinkable happened. To their horror, the bank's financial crime team found an additional 262 customer accounts that matched the profile of a child sex offender. This was the bank's worst nightmare. It was so galling that some staff left their jobs in disgust. Westpac could no longer argue that the 12 evil customers were simply isolated cases. This was a systemic problem.

One of these 262 accounts was held in the name of Drew Shobbrook, an Australian national living in the Philippines. In February 2018, he had been convicted and jailed after 15 child victims came forward to report horrific sexual abuse. When the Philippines National Bureau of Investigations searched Shobbrook's home, they found hundreds of photographs and videos he had recorded and distributed online. The 15 victims were rescued, but many would never recover from their trauma.

The criminal trial heard that Shobbrook and his 'recruiter' would lure vulnerable children to his house with the promise of work, gifts or the chance to go to school. 'These promises took a dark turn when Shobbrook forced them to perform sexual acts on camera, which he then distributed online,' said members of human rights group International Justice Mission, who had supported the victims and were in Cebu City, Philippines, for the trial. 'The girls – who were as young as 12 years old – also testified that he would arrange for other foreigners to sexually abuse them.'

Shobbrook was sentenced to life in prison. The sentence reflected the fact that his debt to society was, to put it bluntly, unpayable. Somehow Westpac's adverse media screening, which monitors customers who appear in the news, had missed this fact. The accounts were never identified, they were never flagged, they were never closed. Incredibly, when Westpac's financial crime team conducted a review, they discovered that payments from Shobbrook's Australian accounts had continued to flow even *after* he was locked away in jail.

This was just one of the 262 newly identified customers Westpac had lurking within its database. Westpac's failures hadn't just become a systemic problem, they had inadvertently made Australia's oldest financial institution the bank of choice for the very worst types of customers.

*

Sonja Marsic and her legal team at the AGS were gobsmacked. This was beyond belief. She sharpened her quill and worked even more furiously than usual to prepare a revised statement of claim. As it turned out, they wouldn't need to. When these revelations came to light, Westpac's senior management and board were equally disgusted, horrified and shattered. Within 72 hours, both parties were ready to bury the hatchet.

It was time for Australia's oldest bank to learn the lessons from the past and move forward to a better future. It was, after all, a partner with AUSTRAC in the fight against financial crime. No one had more interest in a strong and stable financial system than Australia's banks.

After months of playing chicken, Westpac and AUSTRAC quickly agreed on a fine of $1.3 billion. The money would be paid straight into the federal government's consolidated revenue account, to avoid the risk of 'empire building' at AUSTRAC. This was by far the largest civil penalty in Australian history, for any offence, ever. Incredibly, it was also the largest AML fine anywhere in the world outside the United States. Westpac's shareholders would pay a huge price for their chosen management team's failures.

*

The $1.3 billion settlement was another historic moment for the Aussie financial intelligence agency. Its chief executive, Nicole Rose, said the figure reflected the bank's recognition of the 'seriousness and magnitude of [its] compliance failings'.

Justice Jonathan Beach approved the penalty, which avoided a trial, but he didn't pass up the opportunity to denounce the bank in his written decision. He said Westpac had undermined the integrity of the entire Australian payments system when it failed to monitor cross-border payment channels.

'The Australian banking industry processes many billions of transactions each year and financial institutions are an important line of defence in protecting the community and the financial system from the risks associated with money laundering and terrorism financing,' Justice Beach wrote.

The judge also criticised the actions of the foreign banks that had abused the weaknesses in Westpac's controls to facilitate serious crimes such as multinational tax evasion. The Australian payments system had been 'contaminated', he noted, by the 'suspect practices' of foreign correspondent banks and their customers. By pooling the funds into 'batches' Australian authorities would never be able to unbundle the transfers to reveal the individual customers and transactions. Corporate tax evaders could simply hide their money from the prying eyes of Australian tax authorities within these opaque conduits.

Westpac's oversight had cost taxpayers billions in lost revenue. This was money that should have been funding Australia's hospitals, schools and infrastructure. Instead, the money for those public services would need to be sourced from more humble and 'captive' taxpayers who didn't have the benefit of top-tier accounting tricks.

Westpac's new chief executive, Peter King, said he wanted to 'apologise sincerely' to all stakeholders for the bank's failings. He said the bank was truly committed to rebuilding its internal risk culture. 'We are committed to fixing the issues to ensure that these mistakes do not happen again,' he said in a statement. 'This has been my number one priority. We have also closed down relevant products and reported all relevant historical transactions.'

With the admission of catastrophic wrongdoing and the settlement of the country's largest ever money-laundering case, Australia's oldest bank had reached the lowest point in its proud 200-year history. From a brand perspective, this was even more catastrophic than the near-death experience the bank had in 1992 with the failure of its finance subsidiary, AGC. For a long time, families across Australia would associate Westpac's red logo with unspeakable acts of evil.

Surely, things for Australia's financial system – and for the economy in general – would have to improve from here?

TWENTY-ONE

The Circuit Breaker

Barangaroo, Sydney 2018

It's the afternoon of 30 April 2018. Australia's most highly regarded prudential tsar is hunched over his computer in a tower at Barangaroo. Behind him, Sydney Harbour sparkles in the afternoon light. Green and yellow ferries work their way across the silvery water like toys in a bath.

Dr John Laker doesn't ponder the scene for long. He is down in the weeds, tinkering obsessively with the wording of one of the most important publications of his career.

Laker has just spent nine months buried in APRA's inquiry into the culture at Australia's largest, most iconic and most commercially successful financial institution, the Commonwealth Bank. Along with industry heavyweights Jillian Broadbent and Graeme Samuel, he has led a team of 30 people who raked over the ashes of the bank's reputational inferno. Once the country's great central bank, it's now the engine room of shareholder dividends that powers millions of Australian superannuation accounts.

Bankwest, institutional money laundering, charging fees to dead customers, financial advice scandals, the non-payment of life insurance claims — the list of reputational scandals and parliamentary inquiries is long. And now it has single-handedly triggered the Hayne Royal Commission after being busted laundering money for terrorists and drug cartels. At that point no politician could stand and defend the banking sector against the cries for a judicial inquiry. Australia's proudest financial institution has suffered a string of damaging and very public regulatory and reputational failures. The big questions for Laker are how and why.

APRA had harboured concerns about the culture at CBA for some time. Even before the AUSTRAC action, APRA was worried that the bank's success had made it arrogant, dismissive of and tone-deaf to community and political expectations. The supervisors responsible for overseeing the bank on a day-to-day basis found it very difficult to challenge an institution that was so commercially strong.

When it all came crashing down, APRA knew it needed to act. It also needed to show support to the tiny legal team at AUSTRAC as they attempted to bring this banking Goliath to heel. And that's how John Laker found himself sitting in a tower in Barangaroo nine months later, finessing a report on a banking behemoth that had gone rogue on his watch.

*

What only a handful of people in Australia knew, at that stage, was the extent of the cosy and complex relationship between APRA and the country's largest bank. Only those in the room with the Council of Financial Regulators in 2008, as they pulled together an emergency bailout of Bankwest, knew the full extent of the truth. The Commonwealth Bank had grown arrogant, dismissive and tone-deaf because it had good reason to do so: it had saved Bankwest, and with it saved Australia from the financial crisis that had ravaged the Northern Hemisphere.

The Commonwealth Bank had been acting like an addict, drunk on money and power. APRA knew it needed to stage a strategic intervention. But it needed to do so in a manner that addressed the prudential regulator's own failings, and the fragility of the Australian banking system, which had become one of the most highly leveraged in the world. Australia's households could only have become the second-most indebted on the planet – after Switzerland – with the support of an aggressive banking system and supine banking gamekeepers.

APRA had realised that CBA's cultural failures were not just damaging the bank's reputation. They were putting the entire financial sector's standing at risk. APRA needed to force CBA's management to look squarely in the mirror.

The best person to construct that mirror, APRA decided, was its own former chairman, John Laker. After all, he was there leading the prudential regulator when the financial crisis hit and the Bankwest bailout took place. Laker's brief was to throw a metaphorical bucket of cold water over the board and senior executives at an institution that had become deaf to criticism. At the same time, he would also be conducting a delicate post-mortem on the extent of APRA's own 'regulatory capture'.

The report also needed to be honest and clear enough to resonate with the public. It needed to eschew 'regulator speak' in favour of language that ordinary Australians could understand

and believe. Public confidence in the entire Australian financial system was at stake. This mission was so important that Laker decided he needed to write the report's executive summary himself. From scratch. It was 1450 words, and every one of them needed to carry a punch. It may also have been a way for Laker to exorcise his own demons over the Bankwest crisis.

The report was due to be released on the morning of 1 May. At 4.35 pm on 30 April, Laker was still tinkering with the wording. His trusted lieutenant, Stuart Bingham, decided he needed to be prised away from his computer. 'I went up to him and said, "John, it's time. We've got to send it to them,"' recalls Bingham, general manager of the Diversified Institutions Division at APRA. 'He said, "Stop, everyone" and that was it. We were done.

'We got the final report and we released it at 8 am the next day.

'We had a lot of trepidation,' Bingham acknowledges. 'We didn't know how the report was going to be received. We thought it was a very good report, we thought it was insightful, we thought people would get a lot of benefit out of it. But you never know.'

The report pulled no punches. Laker wrote that CBA's continued financial success had 'dulled the senses of the institution'. This complacency was particularly apparent in CBA's management of its non-financial risks. Operational, compliance and conduct risks were not clearly understood and not properly owned. The bank had failed in its core duties.

'CBA turned a tin ear to external voices and community expectations about fair treatment,' Laker concluded.

*

APRA's inquiry into CBA had three focus areas: culture, governance, and accountability. These were the main areas where APRA believed the bank had fallen down.

'We were concerned about the trust within the public around the banking sector,' Bingham says, 'and what could we do to help restore that trust. We also thought it would provide CBA with a good roadmap to fix up some of the issues that were becoming apparent.'

The decision to take control of the process was an important one for APRA. As the Hayne Royal Commission had shown, so-called 'independent reports' from law firms and consultants were often anything but. The public read them (if they read them at all) with a pinch of salt.

According to Bingham, the process of researching the report had been nothing short of 'intense'. APRA had pulled together a team of 30 experts, including external advisers from management consulting firm Oliver Wyman. 'The key thing ... was to make sure that we didn't just rely on one piece of evidence when we made a recommendation. The panel themselves interviewed every director of CBA – both past and present – and they interviewed the key senior executives. The team as a whole interviewed a range of executives and they were all done one-on-one.'

In total, 90 executives had to front up for two-hour face-to-face interviews. This was a direct and not-so-subtle reminder to executives as to who was in charge. There were no Tim Tams this time. The reviewers also surveyed 6000 of the bank's staff, those working at the coalface, as part of a 'cultural assessment'. They pored over between 10,000 and 20,000 internal documents – so many no one could keep count – which turned up some insightful statistics.

The review looked at chief executive Ian Narev's internal messaging and tone. More than 50 per cent of the chief executive's company-wide emails, it emerged, celebrated success. There was little focus on how things could be done better, or where problems or landmines might lie. The idea that the bank might have become a wash-house for international organised criminals was simply anathema. No one reading those emails would have ever believed it was true.

Laker's team also scrutinised the agendas of executive committees. Only 2 per cent of the items on these 'exco' agendas dealt with non-financial risks, such as money laundering. The assessors thought that this was indicative of a culture that downplayed and disregarded non-financial risks. This was a bank, APRA said, that took its public mantra of 'We can' to extremes.

The overarching finding was that CBA's continued financial success became its Achilles heel. In the absence of criticism and self-reflection, the bank's strengths had become its weaknesses.

'Because they were so successful, they dulled their senses and turned a tin ear to what was happening,' Bingham explains. 'I guess one of the ways I think about this, and I think it's a warning for all of us, is that CBA's strength actually turned into a weakness.'

This is an ever-present danger for powerful institutions in all sectors. 'Taking a strength to an extreme is always detrimental to performance, but even a mild tendency to overdo it can be harmful,' wrote leadership experts Robert Kaplan and Bob Kaiser in the influential *Harvard Business Review*.

For the regulatory supervisors charged with overseeing such a powerful and at times arrogant institution, this was always a challenge. APRA was the country's most powerful financial regulator – and yet its own report acknowledged that the supervisors simply could not bring the bank to heel. As Bingham explains: 'If we say to them, "Perhaps you're not doing as well as you could be in this space," the response would be, "Well, we make more profit than anyone else so we must know what we're doing."'

*

Behind the scenes at APRA, CBA's failure had also driven a lot of soul searching and internal self-criticism. Though the report was focusing on the bank, it could just as easily have been written about the performance of its key regulators. Laker and his team had created a mirror that reflected both ways.

'Internally, we have had a lot of discussions about what the inquiry report tells us about the way we have performed,' Bingham said. The problem of 'regulatory capture' – including the merry-go-round between government and private-sector jobs – was open for all to see. This was really a chance for APRA to transform its own internal culture and make amends for the failures of the past.

'As a supervisor, it's very challenging,' Bingham says. 'It's really the art of supervision. How do I convince an entity that they need to improve processes in certain areas and frameworks and the way they do things when they are extremely successful organisations? That's the challenge that we have at APRA, as supervisors.'

The subtext of the Laker inquiry was that Australia's most celebrated prudential regulator had also become inwardly focused and complacent. The suggestion that CBA was insular and tone-deaf to criticism could equally apply to APRA, one of Australia's most opaque regulatory agencies.

The regulatory capture at APRA had led the Commonwealth Bank to believe that the financial intelligence agency was a mere mosquito trying to pierce the hide of an elephant. In truth, this strength had become the bank's own weakness.

*

Barangaroo, Sydney, 2018

At 4.35 pm on 30 April, Laker presses 'send' on the final report. The job is done.

He looks up to see Sydney laid out in front of him. The entire expanse appears miniaturised, like a scene from a tilt-shift movie. The city still sparkles, perfect and toy-like. The green and yellow ferries are still working their way across the silvery water like toys in a bath.

But as every Sydneysider knows, it's a different story at ground level.

As Laker leaves the air-conditioned building he slams into a wall of peak hour noise. Traffic, energy and organised chaos is everywhere. A typical Monday afternoon in Sydney, in all its gritty and vibrant brilliance.

Somewhere in the city, someone is handing over a freezer bag full of powder-coated banknotes, bundled into neat bricks. Somewhere a person is making their last ever mortgage payment. Somewhere else, a new couple has settled on their first loan and are moving into a new home. They hold dreams of pets and children and growing old together. In their excitement the couple probably don't realise that the mortgage, not the house itself, will be the largest purchase of their lives.

Laker buzzes with achievement, relief and post-project catharsis. It's a good report. And it has given him a unique opportunity to consider his own successes — and failures — as the head of the most important regulatory agency that many Australians don't even know exists.

Laker knows better than anyone that models and risk assessments and capital projections are worthwhile tools. But this, down here at street level — this is the real picture. And when banks turn bad, this is where the pain will be felt.

TWENTY-TWO

Money Moves Back Underground

In the wake of these massive legal wins, AUSTRAC was starting to become a victim of its own success. The agency now had a new problem: enforcement 'blowback'. The impact of its merciless litigation against the country's two largest banks had kicked off a wave of risk aversion. Banks across Australia were shuttering high-risk personal and business accounts in droves. Boards that had been indifferent to the money-laundering risk just a few years earlier had experienced their 'road to Damascus' moment. Now they didn't want anything to do with dangerous lines of business – not even remitters, cryptocurrency firms or payday lenders.

Members of the criminal intelligence and policing community were alarmed. They already knew that Australian banks' closure of accounts linked to remitters, under the guise of 'de-risking', had led some criminal operators to resort to underground money transfers. This in turn had made their transactions invisible. The anti-money-laundering community was losing sight of these transfers as they moved outside the formal, regulated economy.

The outcome was proving to be the exact opposite of what the financial crime regime was trying to achieve. Informal *hawala*-style illegal money transfers were once again surging, and the fintel community needed to respond.

*

AUSTRAC had been warning banks for years that de-risking the accounts of registered remitters would lead to a loss of financial intelligence, and could drive remitters and their customers into the black economy.

In August 2019 the agency issued a stark warning: 'Money transfer dealers that have not registered with AUSTRAC and are operating illegally are at a high risk of having their services abused by criminal groups and do not have the same level of risk protections in place as registered money transfer businesses.'

The truth was that, behind the scenes, the banks were playing passive aggressive. AUSTRAC had dared to take them on and now they were retaliating. It was the same with the AFP; banks were closing accounts that were under active police surveillance. This was alerting criminals that they were being watched, and they were disappearing into the shadows.

Remittances were a huge business, and a lifeline for many people in countries across the Pacific. In the 2018/19 financial year, customers made 17.3 million transactions coming to or from Australia. The value of these remittances exceeded $60 billion. Now, an increasing number of these, were moving underground. A meeting was held in Canberra to discuss growing use of *hawala*-style illegal money remittances.

Nicole Rose, AUSTRAC's chief executive, said unregistered money transfers were being exploited as a conduit for criminals to move money to fund their criminal activities. As more people moved legitimate money through those illegal channels, it was becoming harder for FIUs to detect and disrupt the illicit funds.

Rose said AUSTRAC had identified money linked to heinous crimes, including human trafficking, child exploitation, firearm sales and illegal drugs. 'Supporting unregistered money transfer dealers can potentially attract criminals into a community,' Rose warned. AUSTRAC also tried to educate the communities that typically used *hawala*-style services. Officials met with ethnic groups and businesses across Australia to talk about the threat that *hawala* dealers posed. They also discussed how people could anonymously dob them in. They were, after all, undercutting legitimate money-transfer businesses.

The government urged all unregistered remitters to approach the regulator and go through the process of registering as a reporting entity. Running unregistered money transfers risked fines of up to $420,000 and seven years' jail.

'Dealers who are providing an unregistered money transfer service must stop now,' Rose warned.

*

For years, AUSTRAC had struggled with the complexities of the money transfer sector. Now that the two largest banks were offside, its task was getting even harder. Westpac, after its enforcement action, spat the dummy and withdrew from the

Pacific remittance corridor entirely. This created havoc for island communities that were reliant on inbound remittances for things like food and school fees.

In Samoa, one-quarter of the country's GDP comes from inbound remittances from the Samoan diaspora working abroad. In Tonga, the figure is a staggering 43 per cent of GDP. Organisations like the Asian Development Bank (ADB) were growing extremely concerned about the impact Westpac's withdrawal would have on these fragile economies.

An additional complexity was that when countries in the Pacific could not access funding, they were more likely to succumb to overtures from China, which was using this as an opportunity to project 'soft power' across the Indo-Pacific. Once again, Australian failures in financial crime and terrorism financing were having flow-on impacts upon matters of national security.

Remitters complained, in turn, that by registering they were being placed on a public database to enable members of the public to confirm that they were dealing with a lawful remitter. The banks were then using this for a wave of 'de-risking'.

Behind the scenes, the banks were going even further. Word got out that they could download a spreadsheet on the confidential AUSTRAC Online platform, which listed more than 5000 registered remitters. AUSTRAC was making it available as a reference to help 14,000 'reporting entities' verify that they were dealing with legitimate remitters. The banks used this, unofficially, as a 'de-risking' database. They were eliminating entire classes of customers that might expose them to regulatory enforcement. Many remitters found themselves losing access to banking services as a result of registering with AUSTRAC.

Remitters who had been locked out of the banks were resorting to desperate measures. Some of them were maintaining a database of more than 30 bank accounts, registered under the guise of personal and business names, which they used to maintain access to the banking system. When accounts were closed, they simply used a new identity and a false premise and opened more. 'As soon as one account is closed, we have to migrate our customers to a new BSB and account number,' one remitter said.

Digital currency exchanges, trading cryptocurrencies such as bitcoin, were also finding themselves in the banks' crosshairs. Australia was one of the first countries in the world to register digital currency providers. The sector welcomed this in the mistaken belief that it would secure their access to banking services. Some of them were advertising this as an 'endorsement' from AUSTRAC, even though they had been warned against doing so.

'Businesses must not use their registration status in any way that suggests AUSTRAC or the Commonwealth Government endorses you or any of your services or products. Words including "endorsed", "approved" or "licensed" are examples of inappropriate wording,' AUSTRAC warned.

The payment wars were heating up. And in the background, criminal syndicates were once again running amok, finding new loopholes and vulnerabilities within the complexity of the financial system. But they weren't the only ones harmed by the banks' new 'de-risking' strategies.

TWENTY-THREE

Pulling in the Remittance Lifeline

When he thinks back to 2010, Ramanthan Karuppiah remembers a time of halcyon days in the Lucky Country. His memory floats back to an era when he was bristling with optimism. As a first-generation migrant to Australia, he was living his dream, despite life's inevitable challenges. Karuppiah's wife had health issues and was now receiving top-tier care; his young children were being educated in Australia's amazing public-education system, and he was working hard and funding their good fortune through his taxes as an Aussie entrepreneur. Life in sunny Brisbane was simply the icing on the cake.

Not only that, his remittances and money exchange business, Remox, was going from strength to strength. There was a large expat community in Australia, and Karuppiah was helping them to send money cheaply to their children, parents and extended family overseas. The Filipino and Pacific Islander communities were prolific and ever-reliable customers, sending small amounts of money without fail to pay for things like school supplies, food and rent. Many of their home communities were dependent on these regular payments.

Remitters like Karuppiah relied on their relationships with the larger banks, which gave them the ability to transfer funds abroad via correspondent banks. The remitters would aggregate their customers' payments into a single batch, and then transfer that at a wholesale price, which allowed them to pick up the retail margin from their customers and a few basis points on the forex spread. The recipients would collect the funds from another remitter in their home country.

Those who sent money were often the hardworking migrants who powered Australia's fruit-growing and farming sector, who cleaned offices, or who did tough jobs in construction or hospitality. They were working to support their families, villages and communities. And as senders of small but regular payments, a few hundred dollars at a time, keeping down the cost of the remittances was crucial to these workers.

In 2010, Karuppiah was feeling jubilant, opening his first outlet in Darwin. There was a dearth of remittance providers in the Northern Territory, and he saw this as a huge untapped opportunity. This was the next stage in his dream of building a nationwide network of remittance outlets. Ram was a real example of the Aussie Dream and he felt a huge debt of gratitude for the opportunities that Australia had given his young migrant family.

When his store opened, though, Karuppiah was surprised to discover that customers were reluctant to use his service. Contrary to what he had believed, they were already sending money quickly and cheaply outside the formal banking system.

What Karuppiah had inadvertently stumbled upon was a hotbed of illegal *hawala* activity.

Darwin hosted a significant Filipino community, many of whom were sending thousands of dollars home each year using the cheap, fast and unregulated *hawala* transfer channel. They didn't know or care that it was illegal. It was simply what everyone did.

Darwin had a thriving 'sea cargo' industry at the time, which was operating largely as a front for illicit money transfer businesses. In addition, grocery stores and other retail outlets were servicing the black market demand for cost-effective ways to transfer funds abroad in small, regular instalments.

'I was really surprised to come across this,' Karuppiah recalls. 'In the early stages of setting up my Darwin office I had to convince these people, one by one, to use a legitimate remittance agency to transfer their funds legally. I was literally putting a hand on their shoulder, explaining the situation to new customers for 45 minutes. That was what it took to win their trust. One customer at a time.'

For the following nine years, Karuppiah, the founder and part-owner of Remox, was at the coalface of the Australian government's quest to move migrant communities away from underground money transfer agents. He witnessed the sea cargo outlets slowly closing down as customers moved to remittance as a legal, yet still cost-effective, way to send funds home to their families.

Karuppiah observed huge changes in the remittance sector since he first began working for a business that provided money transfers in 2004. During that time he experienced the introduction of the *Anti-Money Laundering and Counter-Terrorism Financing Act 2006*, he'd become qualified as a

Certified Anti-Money-Laundering Specialist (CAMS), and he'd registered with AUSTRAC as an AML/CTF auditor.

Karuppiah had also been a strong advocate for the introduction of the national Remittance Sector Register, which took effect in November 2012. He believed a transparent and regulated remittance sector was crucial to help the Australian government fight terrorism and money laundering.

*

Considering the way that Karuppiah had embraced AML/CTF compliance, it was ironic that this register would quickly facilitate the destruction of his business.

Behind the scenes, Australian banks were closing the accounts of their remittance sector customers. Without these accounts and the ability to make aggregated overseas payments, the remittance firms were doomed.

Over a period of five years, Remox, like many other remittance providers, had been progressively 'de-risked'. This was the term that banks developed for the closure of high-risk accounts under the guise of targeting money laundering. First Remox was de-banked by the Commonwealth Bank in 2010, then by ANZ in 2012, then by Westpac in 2015. His final refuge, NAB, announced plans to close his accounts in January 2016. By then Karuppiah had a national retail network, with leases and salaries to service. It was all secured by personal guarantees on his family home. For Karuppiah, the great Aussie dream had morphed into his own private nightmare.

When the first letters came streaming in, Karuppiah was baffled. He said his business had never been involved in any laundering-related incidents. On the contrary, his commercial model was to lure people away from illegal *hawala* trade and into the formal economy.

He wasn't the only one. An entire industry was being de-banked.

The banks would not offer Karuppiah and his ilk an explanation. Behind the scenes, though, they told me that it was to satisfy their correspondent banks in New York. Industry sources said many banks had de-risked remitters across the board under pressure from their US-based counterparts. Without these relationships, the Australian banks would be unable to clear US dollars, which means death for any major bank with international ties.

In reality, this was only part of the picture. The banks were also covering for the fact that their outdated and broken AML systems were not up to the task. It was safer and more lucrative to push the remitters out – and then steal their customers with competing products.

This was the dark side of the anti-money-laundering project, the unintended consequences of well-intentioned regulation at play. Law-abiding businesses were being destroyed, while 99 per cent of criminal funds were sailing through the gaping holes in the government's financial crime net.

Karuppiah was getting increasingly distraught, more desperate. His leases were locked in for years and he was facing ruin. In addition, he said the banks were sending marketing material to his customers offering their own competing services.

Banking sources told me that the remittance sector was notorious for triggering high numbers of suspicious matter reports (SMRs). Some banks, such as Westpac, had a secret policy of closing the accounts of any customer that triggered three or more SMRs. This was despite the fact that an SMR merely means the reporting entity has 'formed a suspicion' – it does not necessarily mean there is any substance to that suspicion.

For Karuppiah, the consequences of his de-banking were catastrophic. When NAB announced plans to close Remox's accounts on 23 January 2016, it marked the end of Remox as a going concern. It also threatened to trigger personal bankruptcy for Karuppiah.

He was desperate. He felt betrayed by the Australia he loved and called home. He wrote to politicians all over the Lucky Country. He had tried to negotiate with the banks, but the reality is that no one has the right to banking services in Australia. If you have a bad track record or are in a high-risk sector, you can find yourself completely cut off from a financial system that is increasingly demonising cold hard cash.

'After moving to Australia, I lost my job as the only breadwinner in June 2007. I applied for many jobs and did not get any interviews. I had a very brief engagement in a practising accounting firm but was made redundant,' Karuppiah recalled, looking back on his experience since arriving in Australia on a skilled migrant visa in 2000.

'My wife and my close friends suggested that we start a currency exchange and remittance provision firm. This sounded good and we incorporated a company and started one branch in March 2008. With our ethical pricing, face-to-face customer service and compliance practices we had instituted one branch every year and reached seven branches,' he said.

'We had then transformed from job seekers to job providers for over 50 people, with 20 employees at any point in time.'

But Karuppiah refused to let his business die quietly. He took his fight against what he termed a 'regulatory injustice' to the highest levels. At AUSTRAC conferences he was often in the crowd asking questions. He also received significant support from two high-profile federal politicians from Queensland, Labor's Bernie Ripoll and Liberal's Ross Vasta.

Vasta sympathised with Karuppiah's situation, particularly in light of the significant time and money he had spent complying with AML/CTF legislation. Vasta made representations to the Minister for Finance, the Minister for Justice, the Assistant Treasurer, the Attorney-General, the Treasurer and the Minister for Small Business. All these efforts were ultimately in vain.

By then, Ram Karuppiah was broken. He told me he was having dark thoughts. He was thinking of setting himself alight on the steps of Parliament House in protest against what he saw as an unspeakable injustice.

'My family and I, we have nothing left after this,' he told me, his voice breaking.

The Australian government is not in a position to dictate to banks how they should assess their risks – or to whom they should provide accounts. Nor does it have any influence over the behaviour of the US-based correspondent banks that, arguably, were driving much of the de-risking activity in relation to remitters. The issue needed to be tackled at an international level.

As he fought to save his business, Karuppiah was encouraged in a letter from the Department of the Prime Minister and Cabinet to seek out other banks that would provide services to his industry. Karuppiah says this advice was out of touch; there were none left.

Justice Minister Michael Keenan said in a letter to Karuppiah that the government was involved in ongoing talks with banks and remitters to seek a solution. 'A working group has been formed to facilitate liaison between financial institutions and remitters and to consider possible market-led solutions to this issue,' Keenan wrote.

For Karuppiah, however, these efforts came too late. He was forced to sell his interest in Remox in return for the new owner taking over the business's liabilities. After a decade of work, his only reward was to avoid bankruptcy. The company that bought the Remox business had access to bank accounts due to existing relationships with some of the country's major financial institutions.

Karuppiah had done a great service to the AML/CTF cause in Australia by convincing migrant workers to stop using *hawala*. His only reward was to avoid bankruptcy. In Darwin, in particular, the success of his business was due to the success of this campaign. He warned that the decimation of the legal remittance sector in Australia at the hands of the country's banks may turn the tide back towards the use of *hawala* networks, a concern, we have seen, that is shared by officials at AUSTRAC and the Attorney-General's Department.

As the end of the line came for Ram Karuppiah, he made a silent promise to his family never to quit. He would use the strength he learned as a migrant and lift himself up from despair.

After the loss of his business, Ram Karuppiah assured me he was doing okay. He still had his family and his faith. He was still an Australian, though he didn't celebrate that fact as naively as he perhaps once had. His striking facial features, once warm and lifted upwards by optimism, looked drawn. His spirit seemed weighed down. A darkness dwelled in the ridges and valleys under his eyes. He'd aged noticeably in the space of the two years we had known each other.

Ram pulled a sheet of paper out and read to me from a last-ditch appeal he had written to the federal government. As the clock had counted down on the closure of his business he'd pled for justice, an intervention, some compassion.

'The suffering I am going through is not small, nor short ended. I am socially and economically assassinated. I am not seeing a light at the end of the tunnel. It could take my lifetime to come out of this. I need comfort and my family needs to be safe,' he had written in a final letter to the government and banking officials.

His appeal, of course, fell on deaf ears. Ram Karuppiah became a victim of Australia's war on dark money. And all the while, with a relentless background hum, the multi-trillion-dollar global laundromat kept spinning away, unperturbed and unobstructed.

TWENTY-FOUR

Flying Under the Radar

The art of money laundering – the financial origami of the underworld – shares more than a few similarities with martial arts. 'Be like water making its way through cracks,' said the legendary Bruce Lee. 'Do not be assertive, but adjust to the object, and you shall find a way around or through it.' The truly successful launderers, too, cannot be aggressive or assertive. They don't rush into battle when obstacles arise. After all, these are the black belts of black money. They think first and fight only when their enemy is weak, distracted, sleeping.

Both the launderer and the warrior must be shapeless, malleable, adaptable, invisible. When a foe appears, the smart warrior will simply disappear back into the shadows. The clever launderer, like the skilled warrior, eschews conflict and attention. They strike from under a veil of darkness, slipping through the city walls unnoticed, perhaps dressed as a merchant. Better still, a launderer will simply wait to be invited inside the castle walls; like a great warrior, he may come bearing irresistible gifts, never relying solely on the hubris of force.

These are truisms that I've observed over two decades following the path of dirty money. I've seen the ones that get caught, and I've seen many others that simply evade detection. I've seen first-hand the fact that police tend to catch the foolish, the impulsive and the desperate. They also catch those who become too big, too arrogant, too visible, as Bill Majcher did at the height of his undercover game.

Fort Lauderdale, United States, 2002

This is the moment Bill Majcher's whole career — 12 long years — has worked towards. Sharp, well-dressed, well educated, and the representative of a major Colombian drug cartel, Bill 'MacDonald' is a character he has cultivated through years of covert training.

Bill is operating out of a yacht in Fort Lauderdale. The FBI seized the boat in another case and it is his to use — the proceeds of crime — for the rest of the operation. It is rigged up like a TV studio, with hidden cameras and mics, and it is Bill's job to invite the best lawyers and accountants in North America onto 'his' boat to see what they can do for his clients.

This includes a two-hour recorded meeting with a representative of a major offshore law firm, who offers to arrange money-laundering services for Bill's clients. The cost is very reasonable, they say, at 7 per cent of funds laundered. Of course, there are other professional fees for setting up a foundation and the offshore vehicles that any successful criminal organisation requires.

But today ... today is the big one. Martin Chambers, a high-profile Canadian businessman, is coming down. Bill is about to hit a grand slam — the biggest criminal in Western Canada.

A criminal genius. And he will ask Chambers, on camera, to launder drug money.

By now, Bill knows MacDonald's character backwards. 'My boss, Ricardo, he has a cashflow problem,' he tells the targets. 'Too much cash, not enough flow.' It works every time.

Operation Bermuda Short is already one of the US's biggest white-collar crime stings. So far they've had over 60 of North America's and the Caribbean's finest launderers on the boat, expressing no problem with washing CA$500,000 a week and moving up from there.

But today they are after one of Canada's biggest money-laundering targets.

When Chambers arrives, Bill can't believe it. He has butterflies. Chambers looks comfortable, relaxed, and waltzes breezily onto the boat. The guy is even wearing Bermuda shorts, paired with deck shoes and a white T-shirt. He could be any other holidaymaker on the marina.

This is it. Game on, Bill thinks. Within 30 minutes, over a glass of wine, he is going to hand Chambers two bags with CA$500,000 stacked in bricks of $5s, $10s and $20s. This will look like street-level cocaine sales. Bill's team will get Chambers on video acknowledging that he knows it's the proceeds of Bill's boss's coke business.

When Chambers arrives, the first thing he asks Bill for is a money counter — no serial number, no history. 'I don't mind the small bills, I can deal with it,' Chambers says.

Game on.

*

Operation Bermuda Short turned out to be one of the major law-enforcement stings of its era. The FBI started out hoping to take down some of the pump 'n' dump stock frauds that had continued from the Wolf of Wall Street era. What few people realise is that the Stratton Oakmont scam was, unwittingly, the tail end of a massive mafia laundering scheme. Russian and Italian mafia groups had used the 'pink slip' stocks to ramp prices pre-IPO. They could then trade these over-priced shares in full public view, transferring hundreds of millions of dirty dollars via worthless paper through shell companies in offshore banking hubs. The masterstroke was that at the end of this wealth transfer scheme they had over-priced stocks to sell to credulous investors. That was where Belfort and his ilk came in, finding suckers to buy the worthless scrip.

Similarly, Bermuda Short started out chasing 'penny stock frauds' and then morphed into a major money-laundering operation. They had a veritable who's who of the Miami legal and finance set lining up to wash the money of Bill MacDonald's non-existent Colombian boss. Majcher eventually got more than 130 people on his yacht, on tape and camera offering to wash cocaine money through the financial markets.

But these successes are rare. They might occasionally catch the Altaf Khananis, the Sam Gors, the Martin Chambers, but the truth is, 99 per cent of the money that fuels the dark economy slips through undetected, shrouded like a ninja in the night. Is it any surprise, then, that the Asian 'triad' organised-crime gangs, steeped in traditions of martial discipline and Sun Tzu's *The Art of War*, have proven to be such formidable opponents in Australia's war against profit-motivated crime?

Behind the scenes, and against incredible challenges, the

AFP had long known that the only way to target this scourge was through partnerships. They needed to build trust and cooperation with their counterparts in the Golden Triangle, in Vietnam and particularly in China. They needed to outsmart the smartest of criminals, building a net that would fan out across Asia. They needed to understand their enemy. They needed to wait and watch as the big koi swam in, growing brash and careless, and then cast their net with the alacrity of an ancient Chinese fisherman.

The AFP, AUSTRAC and their Australian law enforcement partners were continuing to work valiantly on their mutual cooperation channels. It was slow going, building alliances through trust and gentle persuasion. In late 2018, AUSTRAC expanded its network of overseas posts to include Guangzhou, in the crucial southern province of Guangdong. This was a huge development that would allow Australia's financial intelligence agency to work closely with China's financial intelligence unit (FIU).

They had a symbiotic relationship. Australia was absolutely dependent on Chinese authorities to stem the flow of lab-created drugs, including methamphetamine and ecstasy, from the bustling chemical factories and ports of Guangzhou. The relationship with Beijing was the result of years of work. In 2017, the AFP had convinced the Chinese Ministry of Public Security (MPS) to stop running covert law-enforcement operations within Australia. This agreement followed worrying cases of Chinese spooks harassing Australian residents or nationals who had fled justice on the mainland. The agreement was part of a deal signed in Beijing to improve cooperation on economic crimes.

Australia had flagged its 'deep concerns' in April 2015, when Chinese police started harassing a suspected corrupt official based in Melbourne. China took the view that Australia was harbouring both the kleptocrats and their ill-gotten loot. The AFP agreed to target the assets of these corrupt officials. In return, it asked the Chinese police to assist it in tackling drug trafficking out of Guangzhou, the bustling southern province where methamphetamines and precursor chemicals began their seabound journey to Australian ports.

They agreed to work together on financial crimes such as fraud and money laundering. Corruption offences, however, were excluded from the deal. One of the challenges was that Australia could not extradite individuals to China while it still had the death penalty for corruption.

*

In late 2018, the AFP-led Criminal Assets Confiscation Taskforce (CACT) prepared to show Beijing it was serious. It swooped on a group of people suspected of laundering the proceeds of economic crimes in China. The CACT seized more than $15 million in assets linked to mainland Chinese scams and investment frauds. In televised raids, AFP officers led pixelated suspects out in handcuffs. The assets they seized included jewellery, real estate, cars and cases of Grange wines. In another raid, police seized real estate, jewellery and cars worth $8.5 million in an operation that spanned all the way from Melbourne to the Gold Coast.

The AFP investigations proved that Chinese nationals were setting up Australian shell companies to launder the proceeds of crime, buy property and evade tax. In October 2018, it seized three residential properties and two bank accounts worth $2 million.

Next, luxury houses worth $5.2 million in Glen Waverley and Southbank, Victoria, were seized. A commercial property was nabbed in Oakleigh South. The proceeds of major Chinese scams, many of which centred around property investment, had been washed in Australia. They were funding the lifestyles of foreign nationals living the good life on the eastern seaboard.

The Chinese authorities said these raids showed how easy it was for criminals to move illicit funds into Australian housing and commercial property. Despite the cooperation, they were sending a diplomatic shot across Australia's bow. Pressure was building on the Australian government to push ahead with changes to its AML/CTF regime, as another wave of hot money poured into real estate and high-value goods. Now the Chinese government was joining the Australian families who resented being forced to bid at auction against these foreign criminals, who were snapping up some of the best homes in their own neighbourhoods.

The raids also showed how easily dirty loot diverts itself to the path of least resistance. Criminals could negotiate with lawyers, real estate agents, accountants, jewellers and other dealers of high-value goods in Australia, safe in the knowledge that these 'gatekeepers' would not rat them out to AUSTRAC.

Commander Bruce Hill, the AFP's Acting National Head of Organised Crime, said these cases underscored the social justice issues at stake when criminality penetrates and subverts the Australian economy. 'This kind of activity, where significant criminal proceeds are moved into Australian assets, can erode the level playing field for Australian homebuyers and small business owners,' he said. 'The ripple effect impacts our whole community. It is far from a victimless crime.'

Paddy Oliver, a financial crime lawyer based in Melbourne, said the cases proved how urgently Australia needed to close its money-laundering loopholes. Paddy's home city had become a leading location for Chinese crooks and organised criminals, with its leafy streets, good schools, multicultural character and – perhaps most appealingly – some gaping loopholes in the country's extradition laws. 'The government cannot expect the banks to spot these suspicious inflows into trust accounts,' Oliver said. The banks, he noted, had no visibility of the underlying customers. Without better regulation, it was all just a mass of anonymous payments.

In one raid, the AFP and AUSTRAC managed to detect dirty cash that had moved through a solicitor's trust account to buy property. The bank reported the cash transaction as suspicious and the agencies were able to link the deposit directly to a cash property purchase. This success was only possible, however, because the launderer made the mistake of dumping the loot in a single suspicious transaction. Had the deposits been structured into smaller amounts, the authorities would have been none the wiser. Without cooperation from the law firm, it would have been near-impossible to unravel.

The AFP's successful raids, of course, were just the tip of the great illicit money iceberg. The agency said the lack of regulation of gatekeepers meant the transactions that ran through those professions were 'largely invisible' and there was an inability to 'create a complete picture of Australia's money-laundering and terrorism financing risks'.

On the plus side, AUSTRAC was doing wonders with the tools it had and in the sectors it was empowered to oversee. The posting of an AUSTRAC analyst to Guangzhou to work side-by-side with China's financial intelligence teams, had been a coup. It would prove to be another game changer, particularly in the fight against meth, synthetic drugs and precursor chemical trafficking.

This was such a significant win that Peter Dutton, Australia's home affairs minister, decided to fly to a regional terrorism financing summit in Bangkok to break the news in person.

TWENTY-FIVE

When Crime and Terror Connect

The Regional Counter-Terrorism Financing (CTF) Summit was another of Paul Jevtovic's bold ventures at AUSTRAC. It kicked off in 2015 with a joint event in Sydney, delivered by Indonesia's Financial Transaction Reports and Analysis Centre (PPATK) and its Aussie counterpart. Jevtovic had forged close personal ties with Indonesia after working on the AFP's investigations into the 2002 Bali bombings. He had deep respect and affection for his colleagues to the north, and held onto many old friendships.

Although the first CTF Summit was an Australian event, Jevtovic didn't miss the opportunity to build partnerships. If AUSTRAC carried 100 per cent of the cost and did 90 per cent of the work, and their friends from Indonesia could celebrate half of the success back home, it would be a win for everyone. Even better, the success of the first event could be used as a springboard to encourage Indonesia to pick up the baton in 2016. The plan worked. The second CTF Summit would be held in Nusa Dua in 2016, and other regional partners were vying to host the following year's event. By 2018 the summit had grown into the largest gathering of its kind anywhere in the world, with more than 350 counter-terrorism experts flying in to participate.

The old AUSTRAC chief was canny enough to realise that countries would often pursue their own self-interest when it came to money laundering. Australia had proven it was no exception to that rule. On the subject of terrorism, however, the entire region was aligned. As a national security issue, combating terrorism had attracted support at the highest levels of political power across the entire Indo-Pacific region. This was the ultimate platform from which to build closer regional ties through the wonders of teamwork, technology and trust.

Australia was co-hosting the fourth summit, in November 2018 in Bangkok, with the Thai government. The event was held at the Royal Orchid Sheraton, a luxury hotel that was teeming with security. The mood was tense. On Tuesday, the night before the political dignitaries arrived, including the Thai Deputy Prime Minister, men in black were sweeping every corner of the hotel lobby for unusual electronic signatures. Every elevator had a guy with an earpiece standing in the back corner, watching incoming passengers intently.

On the morning of the event, Thai military police took over the venue. In the lobby, soldiers deputising as police lounged about on couches nursing machine guns and military helmets. These were the feared agents of the ruling Thai military junta. Since the coup d'état of 2014, members of the Royal Thai Armed Forces had been given brutal powers to suppress insurrection. They could arrest anyone without a warrant, hold them for a week in terrible conditions without charge, freeze their assets and ban them from travelling. This was one way to tackle the twin scourges of organised crime and violent extremism. Unfortunately, it had also been criticised as a brutally effective way to suppress political opposition.

The atmosphere at the 2018 summit was nothing like the previous years' in Sydney, Bali and Kuala Lumpur. The levity was missing. There was tension in the air that suggested the Thai counter-terrorism squad may have got wind of a credible threat. Rumours were swirling. In the conference room at the back of the hotel, seasoned counter-terrorism experts made macabre jokes about their table's lack of proximity to the exits.

When Dutton came to the podium, he spoke with gravitas. Silence prevailed, broken only by the machine-gun rattle of camera shutters. Dutton thanked the Thai deputy prime minister, Wissanu Krea-ngam, for his hospitality. He thanked Captain Surasunt Kongsiri, who had been in charge of keeping the Australian delegation safe. He made special mention of Indonesia's security minister, Wiranto, a strong supporter of the summit since that first year in 2015. (In a tragic sign of what was at stake, Wiranto would be knifed in the stomach, less than a year later, in Western Java, in an attempted assassination by a radicalised militant with links to ISIS. Combating terrorism in this climate was no laughing matter.)

Dutton told the summit that Australia was working closely with its regional partners to tackle the funding lifelines that supported terrorism. The backdrop was an attack on Marawi, in the Philippines, where ISIS had established its first Asian 'caliphate'. After the Siege of Marawi ended, and the Philippine military took control of the island of Mindanao, ISIS-linked extremists had fanned out across the region, launching attacks in Surabaya and Sumatra. In response to this new threat, Australia had posted financial intelligence agents to Indonesia, Malaysia and the Philippines. They would work alongside partners from the AFP and other agencies to track militants through their indelible financial signatures.

'No region is immune, as ISIS-affiliated organisations have demonstrated with terrorist attacks in our region within the past two years,' Dutton said. 'Targeting the financing of these organisations is absolutely essential to the disruption and ultimately the prosecution of terrorism. That involves collaboration with the private sector, relationships with NGOs, with financial institutions.'

*

In the wake of the Marawi catastrophe, things were moving fast. Two days before the summit, several FIUs had unveiled a working prototype of a secure cross-border information-sharing platform to hook up the region's fintel agencies. The project was based on distributed ledger technology, the same fabric that powered bitcoin and other cryptocurrencies. The summit delegates explored the 'double-edged sword' of technology, including the threats and opportunities posed by military-grade personal digital encryption, cryptocurrencies and ongoing radicalisation through social media. Australian counter-terrorism experts revealed that 90 per cent of their top-tier targets were using some form of encrypted communications. The tech landscape had shifted and they had to move with it; tapping phone lines was becoming a thing of the past.

The conference also heard that extremist groups like ISIS had become, essentially, politically motivated organised-crime gangs. In the case of the Siege of Marawi, which began in May 2017, the 'seed capital' was just US$1.5 million in proceeds from ISIS's activities in the Middle East. Four months earlier, Abu Bakr al-Baghdadi, the Islamic State leader, had started authorising discreet payments to a group of militants in the southern Philippines. The transactions went undetected and, over a series of weeks, US$1.5 million weaved its way from the Middle Eastern ISIS strongholds to the colourful, peaceful, mosque-dotted island of Mindanao.

In the Middle East, ISIS had become a highly successful criminal enterprise, controlling oilfields, taxing citizens, trafficking drugs and running extortion rackets. This was a new kind of cartel terrorism and, like all successful organised-crime groups, ISIS believed it had the formula to expand. The caliphate model being executed in Mosul and Raqqa would soon be expanded to a franchise in South-East Asia.

Baghdadi believed the Philippines, Malaysia and parts of Indonesia would all provide fertile ground for his brand of vertically – and brutally – integrated cartel terrorism. On 23 May the bloody and destructive Siege of Marawi kicked off. Five months and hundreds of lives later, the battle was still raging. It was a regional crisis. Australian special forces operatives had joined the fight, although the government didn't explicitly acknowledge this fact. The ISIS Inc franchise in Marawi was eventually crushed, along with the once-bustling city itself.

It was a Pyrrhic victory for the 300,000 former townspeople of this colourful village, now reduced to a mass of grey ruins. For them the psychological wounds would run deep; still reflected in the rubble covering the streets, the mosques ripped apart, the Islamic domes lying cracked open like shattered concrete skulls, buildings pockmarked with bullet holes. Even after the international rebuilding campaign, this city would never be the same.

With the demolition of ISIS's stronghold in Marawi in October 2017, the surviving militants disappeared like wisps. For counter-terrorism experts, the island chains across South-East Asia became an area of strategic concern, as militants attempted to infiltrate local communities and slip into mainland Malaysia and Indonesia.

The Marawi case study had acted as a bloody example of the threat that terrorism posed in the Indo-Pacific region. Counter-terrorism experts were concerned that ISIS would attempt to regroup using old and new funding channels. There was a danger that militants could re-establish the caliphate model, taking control of sympathetic areas and then looting and extorting the population to finance their growth. This was the business of terrorism.

Police Major General Preecha Jaroensahayanon, acting secretary-general of the Thailand Anti-Money Laundering Office (AMLO), said countries were working more closely than ever before to battle this common foe. 'To properly deal with terrorism threats, we need to change. More innovative countermeasures need to be created and developed,' he said.

Nicole Rose, AUSTRAC's chief executive, told delegates at the CTF Summit that choking off the funding to extremist groups was a common priority for FIUs across the region. 'Terrorism is one of the most significant threats we face,' she told a packed room of international delegates.

Back home, the Australian federal government was backing this talk with action. It invested $4.6 million in November 2017 to tackle terrorism financing in South-East Asia, primarily to counter the ISIS threat post-Marawi. AUSTRAC quietly used this money to place Australian fintel experts in strategic locations across Asia, as well as in the United Kingdom and the United States. Their brief was to build stronger alliances to target terrorist financing.

Rahman Abu Bakar, head of financial intelligence at Bank Negara Malaysia, said one of the main aims of the fintel community should be to prevent another ISIS stronghold from forming in the Asia-Pacific region. 'All of us need to make sure that doesn't happen again,' he said. 'But I think one thing we recognise as a group is that whatever happens in one country will affect other countries. Thanks to the Philippines Army, Marawi is done. They are no longer there. But I think everyone in the region needs to be vigilant about the possibility of that happening in other countries.'

*

At the CTF Summit in Bangkok, home affairs minister Peter Dutton said ISIS-inspired attacks were likely to be an ongoing threat in the wake of Marawi and the destruction of the Middle Eastern caliphates. 'Financing is an important aspect [of terrorism] for us to truly understand,' he said. 'We need to get to money flows, we need to understand where money is coming from to buy equipment, to buy product and to buy contraband that can contribute to facilitating a terrorist attack.'

The approach was working. Despite the high-profile violence, there had been a far greater number of disrupted attacks across

Australia. The Department of Home Affairs said 14 terrorist-linked acts of violence had been thwarted in Australia by the end of 2019. In total, 90 individuals were charged with terrorism offences as a result of 40 counter-terrorism operations.

From a fintel perspective, transaction data had been used in some cases to pre-empt attacks and prevent 'foreign fighters' from leaving the country. Australia had also charged and convicted 11 people on terrorism financing charges, with a further six cases before the courts. In one instance, a partnership between Australia, Thailand, Indonesia and others allowed Australian authorities to build a complete picture of a domestic terrorist cell that was funding itself as an organised-crime syndicate.

On the sidelines of the summit in Bangkok, Dutton said the AML/CTF community was pushing new boundaries in bringing together the skills from the public and private sectors to fight a common scourge: terrorism financing and organised crime. As a former copper himself, Dutton was well aware that the lines between the two camps had grown increasingly blurred.

'I think this is world's best practice,' he told me. 'I think it's a credit to the FIUs and their leadership. But most importantly to the front-line staff; the analysts and the people who are involved in the analysis of the transactions and dissemination of the information. That is incredibly important. Those information flows are open and they result in lives being saved and people being taken off the streets who would otherwise cause harm in our respective countries.'

*

The summit wrapped up on 9 November 2018. Despite the heightened risk level, everything had gone to plan and everyone was heading home safely, thanks to the efforts of the Thai hosts.

On Friday, 9 November, delegates were waiting at the airport getting ready to return to Australia. It had been an exhausting but exhilarating couple of days. New friendships had been forged across borders, and others had been rekindled. While waiting for the airline call up, the Australian delegation's phones started to light up with messages. A news flash from Melbourne broke across tiny mobile screens. At 4.20 pm there had been an Islamic State–inspired attack in Melbourne's central business district, leaving one victim and the perpetrator dead.

A bearded, bald-headed man had driven a ute into a cafe in Bourke Street, and then set it alight. The cabin was filled with gas bottles. As bystanders ran to help, they were attacked by a crazed, knife-wielding Hassan Khalif Shire Ali. Two people were injured and a 72-year-old man died from his wounds. Shire Ali was shot dead. Thankfully, the gas cylinders he'd packed into his ute didn't explode into a shower of shrapnel across Melbourne's bustling Friday afternoon business district.

For the Australian officials who had participated in the CTF Summit, the irony that an attack would take place on home soil that week was staggering.

Australia had a well-established protocol for dealing with live terrorism incidents. The Centre for Counter-Terrorism Coordination (CCTC), within the Department of Home Affairs, was responsible for the immediate 'response and recovery' operations in the event of a physical attack. On that Friday afternoon it kicked into action.

Following a suspected terrorist incident, banks' financial crime teams were often called upon to scan a suspect's accounts to find any evidence of suspicious transactions or potential funding pipelines. This real-time financial intelligence could play a role in the immediate response to the attack, including building a picture of the terrorist's network and access to resources. It could also help authorities to work out whether there might be other attacks, involving accomplices, or establish the presence of unknown explosive devices.

During the 2014 Lindt Cafe siege, in which three people were killed in Sydney's CBD, the banks were scanning the suspect's accounts for evidence as the crisis unfolded. The authorities wanted to verify – immediately – whether there was any truth to the offender's claims that he had links to ISIS and was ready to detonate ballistics around the city if attacked. The culprit, Man Haron Monis, had also asked for an ISIS flag, raising concerns that he may have been part of a wider network. If the police were going to move in, these possibilities needed to be excluded.

During the siege, in coordination with the CCTC, Westpac's financial crime team found a match. In real time, their best analysts pored over Monis's transaction history. They provided financial data that suggested he was not part of a broader gang, and had likely not purchased materials to build explosive devices, as he had claimed.

This immediate information played a part in the authorities' decisions about how they would handle the siege. These were the quiet victories Australia's reporting entities were, unfortunately, never allowed to share with the public. Under the 'tipping off' rules, even disclosing to an outsider that a 'suspicious matter report' had been filed could see a bank officer charged with a criminal offence.

Unlike the Lindt Cafe siege, which rolled on for 16 hours, the attack in Melbourne was over in a matter of minutes. After news broke, it only took a few hours for ISIS to claim responsibility. 'The one who executed the ramming and stabbing operation in Melbourne ... is one of the fighters of the Islamic State and he executed the operation in response to [a call] to target the citizens of the coalition,' the ISIS propaganda arm Amaq said.

A few months earlier, Abu Bakr al-Baghdadi, the Islamic State leader, had called on militants to use 'bombs, knives or cars to carry out attacks' in countries taking part in the US-led coalition to destroy the caliphates in Iraq, Syria and Marawi. Australia was named as a target.

Financial intelligence again came to the fore. Officials quickly determined that the perpetrator, 30-year-old Shire Ali, had no formal ties to a militant extremist group such as ISIS, and had not received funding. The government had revoked Shire Ali's passport in 2015, however, amid fears that he was preparing to move to Syria to become a foreign fighter for ISIS, an offence under Australian law. ASIO did not have Shire Ali on heightened monitoring, as he was not deemed to pose a significant risk of launching a domestic attack. It is highly likely his financial data and access to funding would have played a role in making that assessment. The ASIO prediction turned out to be correct, as the offender's crude attack fizzled out with far less impact than he had intended. The vehicle he had brought in did not explode, the gas bottles did not ignite and the offender was shot after killing one innocent bystander.

It would be near-impossible, and cost prohibitive, to run around-the-clock surveillance on every individual in Australia who met that profile. To do so, Australia would become a surveillance state, and ASIO would need a billion-dollar budget to manage its 400-plus high-risk targets. Physically and digitally monitoring one suspect, on a 24/7 basis, requires at least 20 full-time staff working around-the-clock shifts.

'The assessment was made that while [Shire Ali] held radicalised views, he did not pose a threat in relation to the national security environment,' an AFP official said. 'Obviously, the circumstances of how and when he moved from having those radicalised views to carrying out this attack ... will be a key focus of the investigation. We're not saying there was direct contact [between Shire Ali and ISIS]. We're saying it's from an inspiration perspective.'

In essence, they decided, this was a disturbed individual, possibly with mental health issues, launching a 'lone wolf' copycat attack. For the authorities, the goal was to respond quickly, contain the harm, build a picture of any networks and learn valuable lessons for the future.

TWENTY-SIX

Tranche Too Hard

In 2019, the entire facade of the Australian economy was teetering on the brink of recession. A year later, the country would enter its first technical recession – defined by two successive quarters of negative growth – in 29 years. An entire generation of working Australians had only known economic growth. This was a world-beating record. Even the Netherlands, the home of 'Dutch disease', couldn't keep up with Australia's credit-fuelled miracle. But economists warned the bull run was coming to an end; the engine of the economy was starting to splutter.

The truth was that Australia was no longer just suffering from Dutch disease. It also had a chronic case of 'Netherlands Antilles disease': an economic dependence upon the facilitation of foreign tax evasion and the processing of criminal funds. The scandals involving Australia's two largest banks had left no one in any doubt about the extent of the problems in the financial services sector. What was arguably worse, however, was the lack of visibility into the professional services and property markets. How much of the epic national property boom was due to

Australia having the world's most accommodating environment for washing dirty money through realty?

Those in the financial crime game simply couldn't comprehend how Australia could continue to protect the housing market's professional facilitators: lawyers, accountants, real estate agents. As the former undercover agent Bill Majcher said, these sectors were at the core of almost every major money-laundering operation that had ever been broken apart. It went without saying that professional facilitators would be involved in the great majority of money-laundering schemes the cops weren't managing to bust.

As the May 2019 federal election approached, a Labor win seemed inevitable. Bill Shorten's opposition was campaigning with an aggressive reform agenda based on big-ticket social justice issues such as housing equity, ending negative gearing and reforming franking credits.

Buoyed by the Commonwealth Bank revelations, the reform of Australia's anti-money-laundering laws became a pre-election policy hotspot. In response to public pressure, shadow treasurer Chris Bowen committed to 'push ahead' with new laws for real estate agents, lawyers and accountants if his Labor Party won the election. A Labor government would also reverse funding cuts to the AFP and ASIC, so they could better tackle serious and cross-border financial crime. Behind the scenes, those in the fintel community, along with the financial crime teams of the country's 14,000 businesses, were celebrating this policy commitment. They knew Australia had one of the most effective anti-money-laundering frameworks in the world, but a decade and a half after the original laws were introduced, the dam wall was still only half built. The truly smart dark money could flow around this elaborate structure, finding refuge in the willing embrace of Australia's booming property sector.

The Morrison government, fresh from scalping Prime Minister Malcolm Turnbull, said it would begin to move on the issue 'as soon as the parliamentary timetable allows'. Turnbull had aggregated all the major national security agencies (including ASIO, the AFP, ACIC and AUSTRAC) and handed them on a platter to Home Affairs Minister Peter Dutton. It was a thinly veiled attempt to keep the hard right, represented by Dutton and its chief pugilist Tony Abbott, content and non-combative. In the end, it didn't work. After making his own tilt at the prime ministership, Turnbull was dragged down and Dutton retained his super-portfolio. Turnbull left parliament and began work on his six-centimetre-thick retaliatory memoir.

In truth, Dutton was never going to move on the long-promised Tranche 2 reforms to the AML/CTF Act. The lobbyists from the Law Council, the accounting firms and the all-pervasive tentacles from the property sector were too powerful. These bodies were even more influential, as it turned out, than the well-heeled banking lobby, which was pestering Canberra for urgent reform. The banking sector was particularly annoyed that it was facing more than $2 billion in money-laundering penalties, which was going straight into federal government coffers, yet the banks were getting no support from the gatekeeper professions. Canberra was holding the banks to a very high standard, yet the politicians were failing comprehensively to meet their own commitments.

Dutton was playing coy. He said the government could not set a 'firm timetable' for laws to introduce the second tranche of the anti-money-laundering regime. This was despite the laws being an all-too-rare example of bipartisan federal policy since 2006.

Bowen railed against this sheer disregard for national security – from a sitting minister for home affairs, no less. He cited evidence about the 'bounty hunters' who were operating in Australia, working to recoup assets on behalf of the Chinese government. He pointed to the lessons from the Commonwealth Bank scandal. More often than not, he said, these dirty assets had been sluiced through Australian real estate with the aid of professionals.

'The government has completely dropped the ball on money-laundering reform,' Bowen said in March 2019. 'According to the government's own work plan, real estate agents should already be covered by our money-laundering laws. The Liberals have done nothing to progress this.

'The Liberals aren't interested in prosecuting serious financial crime. They cut funding to ASIC, they planned to cut funding to the Serious Financial Crime Taskforce and they ripped hundreds of millions of dollars out of the AFP, who work with our partners abroad to disrupt transnational organised crime,' the shadow treasurer had told me before Labor's ill-fated 2019 election.

Bowen conveniently overlooked the fact that Labor had done the same thing during its six years of rule (2007–13), the period in which the Global Financial Crisis ravaged the world economy. The inconvenient truth for Labor was that the sheer weight of money had bought off Australia's voters – and with them onside, it had captured the entire political system.

What the public didn't realise was that the 'property industrial complex' had more influence over the Australian government than the so-called threat of Chinese influence in Australia. The government had defied its own international commitments for over a decade under pressure from the property lobby, which fed Canberra nonsensical 'Chicken Little' threats. The lobbyists said that blocking criminal funds from flowing into Aussie property would crash the real estate market. They convinced the newly minted Morrison government that this would be political suicide.

As it turned out, they weren't wrong about the latter. Leading up to the 2019 election, Newspoll showed Labor benefiting from a 2.5 per cent swing away from the Coalition. The cooling economy was working in Labor's favour, as it usually did.

On 18 May, the day of the election, I flew to Canberra, seated by chance alongside a veteran Labor 'numbers man'. I watched as he scribbled high-profile names and exit-polling numbers on spreadsheets that looked like hieroglyphics. At midday, as the plane took off, he was jubilant. By the time we landed and our phones beeped back to life, he looked crestfallen.

The exit polls would show that Aussies were voting, above all, for the protection of their franking credits and their high house prices. The Lucky Country had rolled the dice. Faced with the prospect of some difficult reforms – in the name of both intergenerational equity and economic integrity – they had voted instead for self-interest. Although the margin was slim, Australians had chosen to keep the punchbowl topped up and drag out the band for another round of national musical chairs.

*

And so, in 2019, the band came out for an encore performance. The Lucky Laundry's morally bereft business model was back in business, like an old rocker squeezing into last-decade's spandex. As with climate change, Australia would defy the rest of the world and stick with its comfy, familiar, path-of-least-resistance economic model until there was no other option left. It was a mutually destructive relationship, similar to the co-dependency between a wino and his favourite bottle shop. The nation's leaders in Canberra had proved they would not take away the punchbowl as long as voters were still willing to view the world through rosé-coloured glasses. Behind a proud veil of public integrity, Australia's failure to crack down on laundering through real estate and the gatekeeper professions would attract another wave of flight capital to the country's shores. Did anyone actually care?

Over the past two decades, Australia had taken a tough stance on border control, declaring it was closed to humanity's most unfortunate. But it wasn't entirely without compassion. We were sending a message to the world that Australia was still willing to offer safe passage and refuge to the world's tired, poor, huddled masses of wretched lucre. We were willing to accommodate – quite literally – the world's kleptocrats and their precious assets, as they fled crime scenes from all over the world to build new lives of freedom and opportunity in Australia. Unlike in the post-war period, these migrants would not arrive on ocean liners, bringing with them only a suitcase filled with hope. They would fly in on private jets, on gambling junkets, with suitcases full of cash and off-duty police moonlighting as their security guards.

Launderers are like tax evaders. They love nothing more than a country with a good reputation, the pretence of tight controls and a buffet of loopholes to gorge themselves upon. Sitting down near the geographical South Pole, Australia is like a nether land to the global economy. The world's dirty money moves through its major financial centres – London, New York, Frankfurt, Singapore and Hong Kong – and a large reservoir of murky loot rests there permanently. But illicit money is restless, footloose. It's always avoiding detection and seizure, so it's not wise to stay anywhere too long. Inevitably, some of this lucre seeps its way down to settle in supposedly squeaky-clean Australia and New Zealand. Like water building up in a dyke, this relentless, determined liquidity finds any cracks and weaknesses. Before too long it becomes a flood, sometimes threatening to dissolve the entire barricade that stands in its path.

And so it was with the Lucky Country. By late 2019, there was a growing diplomatic disquiet between Beijing and Canberra. President Xi Jinping had vowed to crack down on corruption, which was leeching vital development funds from the roaring Asian tiger economy. Beijing believed that Australia was not doing enough to bring that money, and its owners, to justice.

The AFP, meanwhile, stressed to its Chinese counterparts in the MPS that, under domestic law, Canberra couldn't seize assets without proper evidence or an underlying prosecution in China. Conveniently for some of Asia's biggest kleptocrats, the Chinese police did not prosecute corruption charges in absentia. This loophole created fertile soil for an array of crooks to flee the country and apply for Significant Investor Visas (SIVs) in Australia, for the small inconvenience of a $5 million local investment. The perverse result was that, all too often, Chinese kleptocrats were laundering their ill-gotten fortunes through Australian government bonds as part of their SIV commitments.

Government agencies, of course, were not AML/CTF reporting entities. They didn't need to have attentive financial crime compliance teams on the case looking for anomalies.

Behind the scenes, Beijing was livid – although not enough to tighten up their own laws. This was one of the reasons the MPS had resorted to the use of private-sector 'bounty hunters' like Bill Majcher.

Neil Jeans, one of Australia's most experienced financial crime gurus, describes the civil recovery agents as 'operating in a very grey area of what is legal and what is illegal in Australia'. 'I think the bounty hunters need to tread carefully,' he says. 'They need to walk a very, very narrow line, or they could find themselves on the wrong side of the criminal law very easily.'

In Hong Kong, Majcher views it slightly differently. Money, he tells me, is the real criminal game. The people hanging out in dirty bars? The mules moving contraband across borders? The muscle enforcing debts and executing hits? They are just serfs in this grubby world. The real power sits at the top of the chain. The 1 per cent of the 1 per cent. Those who control the money control the game. Majcher says that 'tens of billions' of dollars have moved to Australia from China, as corrupt officials seek to park their funds in a safe, rule-of-law, non-extradition country. As corruption carries a potential death penalty in China, these former government officials feel very safe. They can comfortably deflect the southern sun's rays from the comfort of their deckchairs, behind dark sunglasses, in some of Australia's finest waterfront properties in Sydney, the Gold Coast or Melbourne.

Majcher believes real estate agents, lawyers and accountants have become central to major laundering activities in Australia. The former undercover agent for the Canadian Mounties says it is well known that illicit funds are flowing to the path of least resistance. 'Australia is a very attractive destination for Chinese kleptocrats,' he once told me, from that bar in central Hong Kong.

'China is also concerned about a tsunami of money flowing back into the country after being washed abroad,' Majcher says. This is a big concern for the increasingly autocratic President Xi, as the returning proceeds of corruption undermine the authority of the Chinese state. 'That money ... fuels further corruption and criminality,' Majcher says. 'So it's a two-way street.'

TWENTY-SEVEN

The Forever Wars

There are myriad sources of the criminal loot that sloshes its way through the darkest corners of the global economy. But there's only one primary reason why Australia's economy has become so burdened by criminal money: the war on drugs. Over the past two decades, the Australian synthetic drug trade has exploded like a poorly run meth lab. The popularity of lab-created drugs such as ice and fentanyl has transformed the US$400 billion global drug trade. It's no longer necessary to control poppy fields across Asia and coca plantations in Latin America, along with the complex supply chains that allow for processing and distribution. Instead, clandestine labs can produce A-grade recreational drugs, engineer new pharmacological highs and deliver them directly to consumers via darkweb marketplaces.

Australia's hard borders and extreme appetite for these social lubricants has made it one of the world's most lucrative drug markets. If criminal syndicates can get large volumes of chemicals across our sea and air borders, they've struck it rich. Australia has some of the world's highest prices for illicit drugs, making it a victim of its own good fortune in having these hard borders.

History has shown that illicit substances will always find their way into a lucrative market. Prohibition does little to restrict supply when the demand is constant. Addicts are good customers like that, as is the steady stream of recreational users hoovering up lines of home-delivered dopamine at private parties across Australia's affluent suburbs. Recreational users are gaming their brain's hardwired reward circuits. Putting hype and antiquated morality aside, drugs such as cocaine, fentanyl and meth are simply a set of chemical instructions that tweak the brain's delicate system of neurotransmitter homeostasis, which has evolved over millions of years to keep us motivated – and alive.

*

Martin Woods, the Wachovia bank whistleblower, is fascinated by the dynamics of illicit markets. He views drug markets as some of the most responsive to supply and demand pressures. Woods has worked at the coalface of London's law enforcement, anti-money laundering and financial markets for decades. He has watched as society's pretend puritanism about drugs has allowed a class of people to emerge that have access to limitless funds – all for the economic contribution of moving contraband across artificial borders.

Woods has seen the harm from illicit drugs spread, imperceptibly, like the cloud of red in a junkie's aspirated syringe. The destruction has diffused, as would a cutting agent being injected into the arm of an addict. Over decades, the suffering has spread from an army of addicts to the point where it has thoroughly infected the body of society. Woods has witnessed with horror the abuse of the immense financial power that this criminal industry has generated. As a former organised-crime cop, he has seen this weight of money give underworld figures the incentive and the means to corrupt our institutions – from banks, to regulators, to police, to the pillars of democracy itself.

*

To trace the global laundromat back to Australia, I needed to go to the source. Naturally I jumped on a flight and, on a cold, moody Sunday in London, met up with Woods to talk crime. We agreed to meet outside the gleaming silver Canary Wharf tube station, a marvel of good ol' British engineering. Above me the ticker tape on the Thomson Reuters building rolled off the day's financial headlines. For a financial crime writer this, right here in the heart of London, was hallowed ground.

The minute the big Liverpudlian arrived, it was as though the temperature and fog lifted. He was draped in a colourful knitted scarf – looking like a slightly dishevelled Doctor Who – and the deadpan gags were flying fast. Like many cops who have worked at the coalface of organised crime, Woodsy had developed a wicked, razor-sharp wit to go with his armoury of 'war stories'. I suspected it was part charisma, part pressure-release valve, and partly a psychological survival instinct.

'Sorry I'm late,' he said, huffing. 'Just had to drop past and check on Dad. You know, he's so old now, I do worry about him. A scarlet lady came to the door the other day – a setup from one of his friends at the nursing home – and asked if he wanted "super sex". All poor Dad could say was, "I'll take the soup thanks".'

Classic Woodsism.

With that we set off on a walk from London's newest financial epicentre in Canary Wharf, down the road from the original Square Mile. 'You know that's the capital of London, don't you?' Woods said, pointing at a major bank's tower, crowned with its proud red-and-black logo.

I looked at him quizzically.

'The money-laundering capital,' he replied.

With umbrellas hoisted, we walked along the Thames Path, through Wapping, and finally down to the Prospect of Whitby, a 500-year-old watering hole overlooking the muddy Thames.

Woods ducked under a beam as we entered the historic pub. 'There's been a pub here since the days of Henry the VIII,' he said. 'Which might explain why there's only ever blokes at the bar.'

Outside was a swinging replica of the old hangman's noose. Fittingly, the noose pointed directly at the Canary Wharf financial centre of London. It's a nod to Chief Justice George Jeffreys, known as the original Hanging Judge, who condemned more than 320 men to the gallows following the Bloody Assizes of 1685. The rope is also a reminder of the days of high-seas piracy, when the lifeless bodies of vagabonds and ne'er-do-wells were left to swing from the gallows for three tides – a macabre reminder to others to tread the narrow path. Were pirates the first transnational organised-crime gangs? I wondered.

'Nah, that was the British East India Company,' Woods quipped, deadpan.

As we settled into this up-market part of London, the history was palpable. The table we were resting on was older than my home country. Even better, I was receiving a live running commentary from one of the greatest criminal raconteurs in Blighty. Woods had been on the National Crime Squad supergrass program, spending months with informants, building their trust, and extracting their criminal testimonies. It was a job that required every ounce of his wit, charisma and ability to empathise without passing judgement.

'You know, they become your friends in a strange way,' he said, nostalgically. On one job he spent every working day for six months with a Jamaican gangster in a secure 'supergrass' unit, at a secret location in South London. That prisoner was eventually linked to more than 50 murders back in the Caribbean. Every two weeks Woods had to switch hire cars. He would take a circuitous route to and from work, just to be safe. As the months rolled on, they formed a bond. Woods could empathise with how this criminal's options in life had led him there. Eventually, he won the supergrass's trust. The prisoner became an informant and blew the whistle on the Jamaican gangs' transcontinental violence and drug business, which reached right into the heart of London.

In front of us, Woods pointed to banks of beautiful two-storey townhouses that were built of reclaimed brick. Some of these houses were owned by oligarchs. 'Just a tidy £3,500,000 for one of those,' he said, pointing to a four-bedroom penthouse with glimpses of St Katharine Docks. 'Many of them just sit empty. You come here at night and guess what? The lights are all off,' he lamented. 'Perhaps we need a return to good ol' squatter's rights? There's so many people in the world with so much illicit wealth that they don't know where to park it. Why not stash it in a nice safe place like London, where you can be protected by the best justice system that money can buy?'

Over a second tepid beer, Woods directed his attention southwards. He wanted to issue a warning to Australia. He said the Lucky Country had become a prime target for international criminals, just like the UK and Canada had before it. He said these were among the most favoured jurisdictions for gangsters and international politicians who wanted to convert the polymer proceeds of the drug trade into physical property.

'Until you start jailing some of the criminal underworld's bankers, none of this will change,' Woods said. 'Money is the lubricant of the criminal economy. The objective of the drug trade isn't to get people high. It's simply to generate profit by exploiting our border controls.'

Behind him, the water rippled to suggest the Thames tide was turning. The sluice coming in the other direction seemed murky and the skies were still grey. Boats moved up and down the river, a postcard image. Next to a great old skiff the hangman's noose swung loose in the wind.

Woods couldn't resist one last jape. 'I've got the answer. P'raps we need to get old Judge Jeffreys back? Fire up that thing again?'

TWENTY-EIGHT

Turning the Tide on the Parasite Economy

Woods's warnings about the scale and impact of the drug trade, and the way that it infiltrates and corrupts the economy, had huge lessons for Australia. He had a strong affection for the country and its people. He loved coming Down Under – especially when the Brits had just claimed the Ashes. I had toured with Woods around the east coast of Australia in April 2018, on a 'Whistleblower's Whistlestop Tour', where we did a live Q&A on his time with Wachovia Bank. I played the serious interviewer and the deadpan foil to Woods's classic British humour. He came armed with an endless supply of jokes about the Australian Test Cricket cheating scandal, which had blown up weeks earlier. He wasn't going to miss an opportunity to mock our national penchant for ball-tampering.

On one night, during the Q&A, I'd made the rookie error of asking: 'So, Martin, what do you see in Australia when you look into your financial crime crystal ball?'

'Well, being Australia, the first thing I see is that it's sandpapered on one side,' came his lightning response.

He regaled the audience with his yarns, gags and incredible anecdotes from life in the field. But the trip also had a serious side. Australia was debating federal legislation to protect whistleblowers and Woods wanted to gently nudge the policy needle in the right direction. His tour would generate a pile of media coverage, exploring why it was so important for civil societies like Australia to protect their whistleblowers.

Woods spoke of the trauma he suffered after speaking out when he discovered that Mexican drug cartels were washing billions of dollars through his employer's global operations. We asked the audience to ask themselves: what would you do, in his situation? For Woods, it was simple. He carried on and did his job as the money-laundering reporting officer, feeding information on the suspicious transactions to the British financial intelligence unit. For his efforts, he came face to face with the bank's criminal subculture and was driven to the brink of a nervous breakdown. He was threatened and harassed. Woods eventually became a whistleblower and provided evidence to US authorities that contributed to the bank's US$160 million fine in 2010. Woods's courage had helped investigators to uncover hundreds of billions of dollars worth of suspicious wire transfers, US$4 billion in bulk cash smuggling, cartel aeroplanes and more than 20 tonnes of cocaine.

The Wachovia case was a stark reminder of the sheer scale of the global drug trade, and the crucial role that banks play as the collective recipients of more than US$400 billion each year in drug money.

If the goal of the Australian 'drug wars' is to reduce the supply of and demand for mind-altering drugs, then it's not working. On the other hand, if the goal is to waste police resources, undermine democracy, foster corruption and enrich the underworld, it's been a roaring success.

*

The techniques the cartels use are ingenious. Their motivation is relentless, unfailing. In some cases, Australian officials have tracked ships with illicit cargo – known by law enforcement as 'parasite tubes' – strapped to the hull under the waterline. Divers will secure parasite cargos in the ship's 'sea chest', which is an opening in the hull where seawater is pumped in to fill the ballast tanks.

The ship's crew may have no idea they are carrying additional cargo beneath the surface. Once the ship arrives in port, divers on rebreathers, which do not release air bubbles, are sent to collect the missile-shaped cargo.

In one case, a drug syndicate organised a cocaine shipment to be attached to a ship carrying fruit juice from Brazil to Australia. But the authorities were onto them and, during a stopover in Ghent, Belgium, sent down a team of specialised divers from the neighbouring Dutch customs agency. The divers found three black canvas bags strapped together with ropes and secured to the ship's sea chest with ratchet straps. Back on shore, they sliced open the parasite bags. Bingo. Out tumbled bricks of the purest cocaine, wrapped tightly in red or yellow waterproof tape. The ship's captain and crew had no idea they were running a complimentary drug courier service.

This was big business with an incredible markup. In Brazil, the retail street price for cocaine is around US$12 a gram. When sold at $300 a gram – the going rate in Sydney – the cargo of 216 kilograms would have been worth a tidy $64 million. Had this bust not been successful, the drugs would have been sold on the streets of Australia. The proceeds would then have been laundered through the usual channels: banks, casinos, pokies or property. Could the income from this massive haul have ended up being washed through the booming, lightly regulated Aussie property market?

For Australian families seeking to buy a home in their own country, this was the 64-million-dollar question.

*

The sheer scale and ingenuity of these drug importations, and the profits at stake, make Australia an attractive target for the drug tsars. The illicit drug trade siphons at least $11 billion from Australian wallets each year. But the harm and volume of one particularly nasty drug – methamphetamine, ice – makes the cocaine cowboys flooding Australia's wealthier communities with 'blow' look like choirboys.

Each year, Australians ingest more than 11 tonnes of meth, twice as much as the second-most popular drug, cocaine. The nation's ice addiction costs a staggering $7 billion annually. It's the most common drug due both to its highly addictive nature and its affordability relative to coke. The more expensive and fashionable cocaine trade is more like 5.6 tonnes, according to the ACIC's figures from wastewater analysis.

Other lab-made drugs, such as fentanyl and ketamine, which have legitimate uses, are also on the increase as recreational drugs.

The port city of Guangzhou, in China's southern Guangdong Province, is perfectly positioned to take advantage of this trading opportunity. There are tens of thousands of chemical suppliers in China, operating hundreds of thousands of production facilities. The bustling Guangzhou port, with its containers stacked to the horizon, is the perfect place to export both legal and illicit drugs and precursor chemicals.

Conveniently for triads and other Asian organised-crime groups, China also has capital controls, which limit outflows of yuan to US$50,000 per citizen each year. This creates a voracious appetite for foreign currency in China – matched only by Australians' hunger for illicit chemical compounds. When syndicates deliver wholesale quantities of drugs to Australia, the proceeds, after distribution to consumers, are held mostly in $50 and $100 banknotes – the RBA's pineapples and Melbas. These cash proceeds of the black economy then need to be washed, pressed, folded and placed like starched serviettes into the Australian financial system.

This is where the *hawala* laundering process we looked at in chapter three kicks in. In a country like China, with hard currency controls, the triads run a roaring underground economy that provides hard currency to Chinese and Vietnamese investors, in particular. Currency controls in those countries mean that otherwise law-abiding citizens with legitimate savings are forced to engage with the shadow economy to move their assets overseas. When a Chinese family borrows in yuan to purchase an Australian property through an underground lender, they have no idea that the money that's used in Australia is the proceeds of the drug trade or other crimes. The real estate agent simply sees an unconditional offer from a wealthy Chinese 'cash buyer', the best type of client. The cash that is placed into the real estate agent's trust account, often in multiple large deposits, could well be the proceeds of those meth or fentanyl sales.

In 'cuckoo smurfing', the foreign property buyer has no idea their house has been purchased using the proceeds of crime as part of the foreign currency exchange. Nevertheless, in multiple cases, the AFP has seized the incoming funds as the proceeds of drug crime, leaving the hapless buyer in China or Vietnam hundreds of thousands of dollars out of pocket. By the time the funds are seized, the drug syndicate and the triad have disappeared into the ether, leaving the unknowing purchaser tied up in the Australian courts as they try to secure the release of 'their' hard-earned funds.

This parallel economy of illicit substances and illicit money movements works brilliantly for the criminal gangs. Unfortunately, it doesn't work so well for Australians. In essence, it means that every year Australia swaps billions of dollars of our best green-title property for cheap chemicals from overseas labs. These are chemicals that are only made valuable through the magic and madness of prohibition.

*

As with the fentanyl and ice trade, Australia has been a target destination for the proceeds of mainland Chinese corruption for many years. The problem has worsened significantly in recent years, as Chinese kleptocrats seek to move assets to safe havens amid a crackdown from Beijing on so-called 'flight capital'. Tens of billions of dollars have moved to Australia as corrupt officials attempt to park their funds in a safe jurisdiction.

The existence of strict Chinese capital controls has made it even harder for the Australian fintel community to spot dirty money. Money-laundering teams at banks and agencies like AUSTRAC find it particularly difficult when dealing with funds flowing from Hong Kong and Macau. The evasion of Chinese capital controls is not a predicate offence (or precursor to laundering) under Australia's money-laundering laws. 'It's very hard for Australian authorities to differentiate between what we view as a legal movement of funds and money laundering. The challenge is finding out the source of funds in China, which can take up a lot of time and law-enforcement resources,' says money-laundering expert Neil Jeans.

Jeans has had an unprecedented insight into the world of black money, working for the elite National Crime Squad in the United Kingdom, as well as many of the world's leading banks. He says that identifying illicit funds flowing within the vast majority of legitimate transactions is extremely challenging, for both banks and for law-enforcement agencies. And the cross-border nature of modern organised crime aims to exploit this complexity. 'Cross-border investigations are time-consuming and require significant cooperation between agencies,' Jeans says. 'This is compounded by the fact that many of the gatekeeper professions sit outside the purview of Australian financial intelligence agents.'

The challenges are compounded when there are vastly different legal systems in countries that need to cooperate on investigations. Despite some big wins, issues of trust, privacy and judicial fairness can often hamper major international AML operations between China and Australia.

The leakage of funds from China doesn't just happen through the black-market lenders, who secure their loans with kneecaps more often than land titles. For more conservative clients, Chinese banks with branches in Hong Kong often use back-to-back loans to allow Chinese nationals to invest in real estate abroad – in direct breach of capital controls.

According to investigator Bill Majcher, Aussie lenders often give collateralised loans to Chinese customers. 'They show up in Australia without any jobs or declared income, but they can show blocked funds of unknown ownership or origin sitting in a bank in China. The Australian bank accepts the Chinese funds as collateral to secure loans to buy property in Oz,' he says.

Casinos, travel junket operators, high-value goods dealers, remittance agents, education providers and trade-based finance are all popular with mainland Chinese money movers. Traditional banks are also playing a key role by inadvertently facilitating trade-based money laundering.

The sheer volume of these money flows makes it very difficult for Australian authorities and banks to identify bad actors.

The failure to regulate lawyers, accountants and real estate agents makes the entire process doomed to fail.

Australian lawmakers have effectively built half a dam wall to stop the Yangtze-sized deluge of illicit funds that is flowing Down Under, relentlessly, as if by gravity. Canberra then feigns shock when the water simply flows around it – much like the Manchurian hordes that went around the Great Wall. Even more absurdly, when the murky water continues to flow south, politicians of all colours wag their fingers at the banks and casinos, issue billion-dollar fines and promise voters they will build that half-sized dam wall a little higher.

According to Majcher, ordinary Aussies are the ultimate victims. 'This tsunami of unexplained wealth has had a corrosive effect on the average law-abiding Australian, who is playing by the rules and yet falling further behind,' Majcher says.

TWENTY-NINE

A Few Beers ... and the Best of Ideas

Most cops enjoy two simple things after wrapping up a major operation: blowing the froth off a frosty schooner and spinning a couple of yarns with their mates, the people who share their knowledge of this secret world. They invariably have a dark sense of humour. It's a form of therapy, and a way of making sense of their high-pressure existence. They must walk through life carrying secrets, bearing things they've sworn to hide from even their most trusted partners in the surface world.

The release of those secrets can sometimes carry as much jubilation as the successful job itself. It's a heady mix of excitement, achievement and the rush of air that comes when a valve blows open. On a Tuesday in June 2021, AFP Commissioner Reece Kershaw wasn't just beaming, he looked like the cat who'd scored the first creamy pint from the post-operation vat.

The head of the AFP shuffled some papers as he fronted a media conference that was being broadcast around Australia.

Kershaw was about to announce the results of Operation Ironside, one of the biggest global stings in history. And in doing so he was about to detonate a bombshell that would reverberate throughout the criminal underworld. This one would deliver a body blow to serious and organised criminals in more than 100 countries around the world.

'Now, as you know, some of the best ideas come up over a couple of beers,' he said.

The beers that Commissioner Kershaw was referring to were imbibed at a clandestine meeting in 2018 between a tight bunch of Australian police investigators and their colleagues from the FBI's Australian attaché.

In March that year, US police had taken down the encrypted Phantom Secure BlackBerry network. The Canadian-based encrypted platform serviced more than 20,000 users, giving them the ability to communicate securely and to wipe their devices remotely if they were ever captured. Users had handles such as 'the.killa', 'the.cartel', 'narco' and 'knecapper9'.

The takedown was the talk of the global criminal intelligence community. But these operatives knew that whenever there was a takedown, there was a vacuum. And like our atmosphere, the underworld abhors a vacuum. The AFP and the FBI knew that criminals would be looking for an alternative to Phantom Secure. And within the rush of that vacuum lay their opportunity.

What if the authorities themselves could create a secure, encrypted device and release it on the underworld market? That would give them a backdoor into the communications of some of the world's most high-profile criminals. It would create a honeypot for intelligence, allowing them to eavesdrop on real-time conversations as drug syndicates organised deliveries, criminal groups laundered money and hits were arranged on people's lives.

It was an audacious scheme, one that perhaps could only be contemplated with the benefit of a little Dutch courage. To pull it off, the authorities would need three things: funding; permission from their superiors; and access to a coder and criminal insider who could seed the devices into the underground world. As it turned out, the FBI had their hands on precisely the man for the job.

*

The FBI and the AFP had a history of working together in ambitious covert operations. Their takedown of international money launderer Altaf Khanani, one of the world's most wanted men, went down in policing folklore. It's even been immortalised in the ABC's documentary *The Billion Dollar Bust*.

In that case Australian authorities had stumped up US$1 million as bait to lure Khanani away from his secure base in Pakistan to Panama, where the US authorities pounced. There was a significant risk that Khanani would get wind of the scheme and humiliate the fuzz by absconding with their bag of bait. It would have been a policing PR nightmare with headlines like 'Cops gift launderer a million of your tax dollars' plastered over the redtop dailies. The ultimate middle-finger from a Teflon-coated crim.

Sources in the US said their law-enforcement agencies simply wouldn't agree to finance such a scheme. The Aussies, however, were willing to take a reputational risk to lure such a high-level target. Working together, the FBI and AFP allies achieved what many thought was impossible. In the end, Khanani got caught but also got lucky. He argued some technicalities, wangled a deal and pled guilty to just one charge, serving 68 months in prison and copping a measly US$250,000 fine.

In this case, with Operation Ironside (or Trojan Shield, as it was called on the US side), the working capital was much smaller. And yet the yield was massive. The AFP happily stumped up a mere US$120,000 plus expenses. The Americans, on the other hand, would contribute something far more valuable: a deeply connected human informant who had found himself ensnared in the FBI's net following the Phantom Secure takedown.

The FBI informant had blown a lot of time and filthy lucre developing a next-generation encrypted communications device for the underworld. It was called AN0M, and had a stripped-back functionality. It would run on standard Android devices, but with a modified operating system that locked down all features aside from an encrypted chat app. This hidden program would appear after the user punched a few magic numbers into the calculator app. The device couldn't make calls or receive messages using traditional mobile communication platforms – this was designed to reassure users that the cops couldn't eavesdrop. Customers were only able to send encrypted messages to other users via a server operated in an offshore jurisdiction. To the criminal user, it looked secure and legit.

The informant who created AN0M had been arrested by the FBI's San Diego field office and was facing a long stint in jail. In a bid to cut a deal with authorities, he made them an offer: he would agree to keep working on the project – but this time he'd be working on behalf of the FBI. He would essentially be paid with US$120,000 and his freedom.

The audacious offer turned out to be both a stroke of genius and very fortuitous for the Aussies. The developer-turned-informant agreed to tap his network, which primarily targeted the Australian market. His Aussie clients secured the rights to distribute the product via an Australian soft launch in October 2018. The cost of the devices – US$1700 for the handset and US$1250 for an annual subscription to use the service – meant these Aussie intermediaries stood to reap a windfall if the platform became the next Phantom Secure.

The land Down Under would be the test case for an incredible digital, covert law-enforcement operation.

*

To work, the scheme would have to grow slowly and organically, through underworld referrals. If they rushed to market, authorities knew the criminals would get suspicious. Initially, the FBI's informant released just 50 devices to the Aussie market. The distributors were happy to drip-feed these 'secure' handsets into the underworld.

As the devices started to be used, the magic happened. A tight group of trusted AFP agents were able to monitor real-time communications between some of the country's most sought-after criminal figures. The police were in on their most secret conversations. The criminals felt so secure that they even dispensed with their usual coded language and spoke openly of drugs, cash, guns, murders. The AFP's technical staff were able to intercept the server traffic. They also had the encryption keys, allowing them to trace the planning of international crimes in real time. This was giving law enforcement an edge it had never had before.

The AFP analysts watched as photos of weapons and drugs were encrypted and sent around the country to other users of AN0M handsets.

During the test phase, the authorities found that '100% of AN0M users ... used AN0M to engage in criminal activity'. The high cost of the phones and the distributor's links to the underworld meant that no civilians would take advantage of the platform for legitimate use. The law-enforcement agencies now had a honeypot that would act as a beacon for criminal activity. This was investigative gold. The AFP soon had visibility over the antics of Italian organised criminals, major Asian triads, outlaw motorcycle gangs, Albanian organised-crime groups and other transnational drug syndicates.

Soon the devices started popping up in other countries as overseas criminals looked for a new tool to evade phone intercepts. The recent demise of Phantom Secure meant that take-up was rapid. Commissioner Kershaw said the scheme was a greater success than they could have ever imagined. Soon, the Aussies and Americans would share this intelligence with their trusted partners in other countries. Other encrypted phone service takedowns, involving the Encrochat and Sky ECC platforms that were popular in Europe, saw user numbers surge. The AN0M user base tripled in a matter of months from 3000 to 9000 users.

Images shared on the devices showed mountains of drugs and illegal firearms shipments, and revealed intricate details about how consignments would be delivered. Hundreds of tonnes of cocaine were concealed in shipments of fruit. A French diplomatic pouch was used to transport cocaine directly from Colombia. The net also ensnared many corrupt government officials who were facilitating the global drug trade.

As the authorities feared, there was also evidence that insiders were tipping off criminals about imminent busts and other enforcement actions. For police, AN0M was ratting out the rats in the ranks.

By the middle of 2021, monitoring the volume of traffic on the AN0M network was becoming unwieldy. The FBI and AFP had now disseminated 12,000 devices, giving them a porthole into 300 major criminal groups operating in more than 100 countries. International police forces were now in the unusual position of having an intercept that was so successful they couldn't keep up with what it was revealing. They made the decision to swoop, in internationally coordinated raids, on 7 June 2021.

An operations centre was set up. Before daylight broke in Australia, police fanned out across the country. This was no longer a tightly held secret. But the crooks didn't have long enough to get wind of it. Black-clad police in paramilitary gear busted open doors, waking the inhabitants from a dreamy slumber with repetitive shouts of: 'Police, we have a search warrant!' For them the game was over. The evidence collected from the encrypted phone chats would prove to be prosecutorial dynamite.

Worldwide, the results were staggering: more than 800 suspects were arrested. The Aussie police confiscated 30 tonnes of drugs, weapons, cash, Harley-Davidson motorcycles and luxury cars – the usual perks of the criminal life. They also seized 104 firearms, including a military-grade sniper rifle. Australian authorities claimed they had disrupted 21 murder plots, including the contract killing of an entire family over a drug debt. This was invaluable intelligence.

The Australian and US police described it as 'one of the biggest infiltrations and takeovers of a specialised encrypted network' ever conducted by law enforcement.

Suzanne Turner, the special agent in charge of the San Diego FBI field office, had been deeply involved since the original arrest of the informant-coder. She said the bust represented 'more than five years of strategic, innovative, complex investigative work'.

Kershaw, the Aussie, put it more bluntly: 'We've been in the back pockets of organised crime ... All they talk about is drugs, violence, hits on each other and innocent people who are going to be murdered.'

Of course, the police also found dirty cash. Polymer notes of dubious provenance. They seized bricks of Melbas – some $45 million of the billions that the more credulous RBA believed were being hoarded in homes around the country in case of an ATM outage or for a grandchild's birthday. In one case, they found $7 million in a safe buried under a backyard shed – indeed, beneath a concrete slab – in a suburban home in Sydney. It was almost as Aussie as the money launderers sitting on milk crates outside Commonwealth Bank ATMs.

The staggering volumes of cash confirmed what money-laundering experts believed: the COVID-19 pandemic had disrupted the criminal underworld's black money pipeline, particularly for cash placement. With businesses in lockdown, it had been much harder than usual for gangsters to sluice their illicit funds through the legitimate system. As Canadian ex-undercover operative Bill Majcher would put it, 'These guys had a cashflow problem: too much cash, not enough flow.'

But it wasn't just in Australia and the United States, of course, where Operation Ironside/Trojan Shield bore criminal fruit. Ironside also proved that modern crime is an inherently international game. Criminal cartels are some of the most effectively governed multinational organisations on the planet. They don't fire their recalcitrant or troublesome employees, they just shoot them.

Across Europe, there were vast numbers of arrests: 49 in the Netherlands, 75 in Sweden and over 60 in Germany. Authorities seized hundreds of kilograms of drugs, more than 20 weapons and over 30 luxury cars and cash. In Finland, meanwhile, police arrested 100 suspects and seized the usual stashes of drugs. They also raided a warehouse full of 3D printers that were being used to manufacture illicit – and anonymous – gun parts.

It was one of the largest and most well-coordinated criminal takedowns in policing history. More than 9000 officers from law-enforcement agencies around the world took part in the arrests.

The stench of dirty money was never far away from the action. Most of the schemes unearthed in Ironside were profit-motivated crime. These types of criminals were washing a collective US$2 trillion, at a minimum, through the global economy every year. This money was being moved, washed, scrubbed, hung out to dry, wrapped and bagged with all the efficiency of a busy laundromat.

The AN0M handsets had given police a fresh insight into the frightening efficiency of the dark side of the 'financial services' industry. In Australia, the AN0M takedown showed that waves of illicit cash were sloshing around the country like floodwaters. The movement of criminal money was relentless, fluid, responsive, eroding the foundations of the Australian economy – and also the pillars of civil society. In Perth, a lawyer was nabbed for assisting criminals to structure their empires and wash their loot.

Commissioner Kershaw stressed the critical importance not only of following the money to assist with intelligence and prosecutions, but also of separating criminals from the proceeds of their crimes. 'They are almost certainly using those encrypted platforms to flood Australia with drugs, guns and undermine our economy by laundering billions of dollars of illicit profit,' he said.

Of course, the prohibition of drugs and Australia's good fortune to have a fringing reef of hard borders was turbo-charging the demand. The better cops got at busting the US$400 billion-a-year global drug market, the higher the prices.

'Organised-crime syndicates target Australia because, sadly, the drug market is so lucrative,' Kershaw acknowledged. As already noted, illicit markets are some of the most capitalistic on Earth. There is no oversight, no invisible stabilising hand of regulation. An army of addicts and dependent users want their hit regardless of seizures, meaning prices react sharply to any supply issues.

Of course, the invisible networks behind these markets would regroup. Some would collapse. Others would prosper from the loss of competition. And the poisonous dollars from the world's dark economy would continue to flow Down Under, relentlessly but ever discreetly weathering away the sandstone foundations that uphold a great democracy and one of the world's most civil, liveable societies.

THIRTY

March of the Cartels

In January 2019, chatter on the AN0M network led US and Australian police to a massive drug haul. A deluge of cross-border messages indicated that three shipping containers full of car audio equipment were on their way from Mexico to Melbourne, via California. One of them was a decoy, two of them would contain drugs. The members of this cross-border task force, dubbed Operation Hoth, were certain the containers would be loaded with meth.

Australian intelligence led an American multi-agency task force, Homeland Security Investigations' Border Enforcement Security Taskforce (HSI BEST), to intercept the three containers. When they opened them, they found pallets of sealed car audio components – speakers, amplifiers, capacitors. The equipment was branded as Audiobahn and Alphasonik, companies run by a smooth Californian living in Melbourne named Nasser Abo Abdo. It all looked good. The US authorities opened the first container and used angle grinders to cut open the components, which had been welded shut during manufacturing. It took them eight painstaking hours to get through the first container. To their amazement nothing showed up. This could have been the end of the operation, but the intel was so good they didn't give up. They moved on to the next container.

In the middle of the night, AFP agent Mandy Sutherland's phone pinged. It was her American friends; they'd hit paydirt. The packages of drugs – lots of them – were concealed deep inside the car stereo capacitors. The Americans would keep cutting them open for several days, finding hundreds of foil-wrapped bags of white crystals. The professionalism of the concealment suggested the Mexican manufacturers of the components were in on the deal. In all, the authorities seized a record 1.7 tonnes of ice worth $1.3 billion on Australian streets. They also picked up 25 kilograms of cocaine and 5 kilograms of heroin for good measure.

Sutherland and her joint taskforce team were beyond jubilant. Seven people from the state and federal police had worked on this case for half a year. 'It was amazing briefing the team,' she later said. 'The outcome was recognition for many long hours on the job.' The haul was six times bigger than the AFP had been expecting.

After extracting the cargo, the Americans repacked the containers and sent them on their way to Melbourne. The surveillance and the intelligence gathering would continue for another month as the cartel began to panic about their precious cargo. Finally, the AFP used the information they had gleaned from their ANOM intercepts to arrest and charge six suspects across New South Wales and Victoria. During their raids, they found half a million dollars in cash – money that was waiting to be placed, washed and moved.

The meth shipment was the largest ever seized in the mainland United States, reflecting the Mexican cartels' huge appetite to make inroads into the lucrative Australian drug market. The same cartels had already flooded the American markets with their industrial-scale meth production from south of the border. As an ever-expanding empire, they were now looking further abroad. In this case they had teamed up with Australian bikie gangs to get the product through border security and into the hands of the country's not-so-lucky ice addicts

Assistant Commissioner Bruce Hill, of the AFP, said the cartel behind this shipment was 'one of the most powerful and violent drug trafficking syndicates in the world ... We now believe the Mexican cartels are actively targeting Australia. They have been sending smaller amounts over the years. This is now flagging the intent that Australia is now being targeted.'

The AFP's partnership with the Americans had also expanded to include the Royal Canadian Mounted Police. A year earlier, a gentle 70-year-old man named Rolando Guajardo had travelled from Canada to Australia to visit Abo Abdo. The Mounties were watching. As he left the country, they checked Guajardo's phone. One particularly interesting photo they found showed a brick of a white powdery substance in a vacuum-sealed bag.

The Mounties were brought into the circle of trust and agreed to wait for coordinated raids. On 8 February 2019, as temperatures in Canada dropped to minus 6 degrees Celsius, members of the Mounties' organised crime unit waited in a car outside a grey, timber-clad apartment building. When they received the all-clear from their colleagues in Australia, they pounced. A heavily armoured team raided Guajardo's nondescript townhouse in the suburb of Burnaby, British

Columbia. It was loaded with cash. A Walmart shopping bag was crammed with C$188,000; a Nike backpack held C$390,000; more money was quite literally stashed under a mattress. Even the kitchen teapot was stuffed with tightly rolled Canadian banknotes. Guajardo's low-income subsidised apartment was, ironically, becoming uncomfortably crowded with unexplained cash. Once again, it was a case of too much cash, not enough flow.

The Mounties counted a total of C$3.2 million yet to be laundered cash, allegedly the proceeds of crime, which police said reflected the sheer scale of the Mexican drug cartel's international money-laundering operation.

In the police intercepts Guajardo was nicknamed 'The Old Man' or 'Tio' — Spanish for 'Uncle'. He was tight with Abo Abdo, even dating his sister-in-law. He was also serious about personal security. Stashed throughout the house were guns and another $20,000 in greenbacks and $6,300 in Aussie polymer banknotes.

*

According to the AFP, the cartels had formed alliances with Australian outlaw motorcycle gangs, combining the Mexicans' highly addictive product with the bikie gangs' covert distribution chains.

Some of Australia's bikies did not appreciate this slur upon their reputation. In an unusual development, the Bandidos motorcycle gang took umbrage at the Feds' suggestion that their members were involved in the importing of a drug as odious as methamphetamine. They even went as far as issuing a formal media statement.

'We, like most Australians, shared a sigh of relief that these drugs never reached our shores,' the Bandidos' PR team said following the 1.7-tonne seizure. 'The Bandido Motorcycle Club vehemently distance ourselves from this insidious scourge on humanity, in every way, shape and form. We categorically refute any suggestion of involvement whatsoever, in this or any other matter concerning ice.'

It was a sign of the sheer wretchedness of the meth trade that the Bandidos didn't want to be associated with it. Either that, or they had shared a sigh of relief as one of their major competitors had just been whacked.

In fact, the Bandidos weren't the only ones sighing with relief when Operation Hoth seized almost two tonnes of meth from the Mexican-linked syndicate. That volume of drugs would have had a significant impact on the price and availability of drugs in Australia. It would have kept four-fifths of Melbourne's meth users high for an entire year. It could have flooded the market for a time. As the US drug syndicates had already discovered, it's hard to compete with the sheer professionalism of the Mexican cartels.

The truth is, of course, there were many other 'import/export' businesses competing to satisfy Australians' voracious appetite for stimulants, in return for those precious polymer notes. And they had some even more ingenious ways of getting their lucrative cargo into the country.

Wastewater analysis by the ACIC showed that getting contraband into the country wasn't proving to be too much of a problem. And, as we have seen, getting the resulting billions of dollars in cash out of the country wasn't all that difficult either.

THIRTY-ONE

Amman of Conviction

Contacts had told me that an investigation into the netherworld of Australia's black economy wouldn't be complete without a trip to the front lines of the war against violent extremism. As usual, they were absolutely right.

The vast majority of the money that flows through the world's fiscal laundromats is the proceeds of crime. This is evil money that carries an indelible karmic stench. It's a permanent taint that diminishes anyone who touches it, even the money handlers. But while they might pile up bad juju, and draw down their finite lines of spiritual credit, too often these money handlers get a free pass from the laws of man.

If someone handles the getaway car following a drug deal or provides refuge to the gangster, they can be jailed as an accomplice. Throughout my global travels, coppers would repeatedly express frustration that dirty money moving through the hands of 'professionals' was all too often treated differently. Why should the accountant or banker who recklessly handled the proceeds, for a share of the profit, be treated any differently to the bloke who drove the getaway car? Was this money truly separate from the predicate crime in any meaningful way? Or were the bankers, lawyers and accountants playing essential roles in the modern criminal economy? Were those cries of plausible deniability enough, given the scale of the threat that Aussie society was facing?

These were deep questions that I would ponder during a lengthy flight on Qatar Airways, from Australia, via Doha, to Jordan's Queen Alia International Airport.

My aim was to get closer to the actual lived experience of terrorism financing. I wanted to see it up close, share the experiences of the people who lived every day under the shadow of this human scourge. As with those philosophical questions about handling criminal money, there was a similar challenge with terrorism financing. Sitting in Australia, inside a bank, looking for patterns indicative of a foreign fighter who was getting ready to leave the country was very noble work. Lives had been saved as a result of Australian banks, and the country's financial intelligence agents, working diligently to 'follow the money'.

Terrorism financing, as it turned out, was an even greater challenge for the world's financial intelligence community.

*

I walk slowly through the streets of central Amman, Jordan, alongside our host, Danyelle Gerges, who is the regional director for the Financial Services Volunteer Corps (FSVC). We're with the man I've come to see: former Drug Enforcement Administration (DEA) special agent turned fintel consultant Michael Messier.

There's a tension in the air that bristles like the arc of a guard dog's spine. Jordan has seen more than five million war refugees surge in relentless, landlocked waves across the border from Syria. This continual flow of desperate refugees has overwhelmed the population, to the point where King Abdullah II has pleaded with the world to help spread the burden of this cascading humanitarian crisis.

In spite of the difficulties, Jordanians have continued to show compassion to their neighbours. 'It's because we're Bedouins,' a senior female official from the country's financial intelligence unit told me once over tea. 'In the desert, if someone stumbled upon your camp you had a human duty to feed and warm and protect them for two days before allowing them to continue on their journey. We still think this way today.' Rather than build breakwalls, the citizens have formed bridges.

The Jordanian intelligence service, the GID, is acutely aware that with the influx of millions there will also be some war-hardened violent extremists. Yet Jordan has remained compassionate. As King Abdullah II told the international community, 'How are you going to turn back women, children, the wounded? It's not the Jordanian way.'

Danyelle, originally from Lebanon, has lived in Amman for years. She speaks Arabic like a poet, knows history like a scholar. She also knows every corner, every nook, every alley in this network of streets and shops and adventure.

On the main street of downtown Amman, the tension is visceral. Someone from the US embassy told me over a beer that it's one of the most surveilled — and ironically safest — places in the region. Eyes and ears are everywhere. 'Look at the street cleaners,' he told me. 'They walk around, pick up a can, put it down again. These are the GID's eyes and ears. There hasn't been a single terrorist attack in Amman yet, despite the millions of refugees streaming across the border.'

These assurances are encouraging but I still remain on heightened alert. Two Westerners and a Lebanese lady walking through central Amman isn't exactly subtle. Messier, my tall, muscular companion, stands a head above the crowd. He's as discreet as the Starbucks cup he's holding, but he isn't concerned. In truth, he's totally comfortable with it. His walk has the air of someone who has been well trained in the dark arts of counter-intelligence and self-defence, and after a life mainlining adrenaline on the front line of the Latin American drug wars, he still feels most at home 'out in the field'. Mike once showed me a photo of his early days in Mexico City, pounding a heavy bag in a sweaty boxing gym.

'You were a weapon,' I said, shocked by his Sly Stallone physique.

'Yeah, I kinda had some anger management issues,' he replied with a Rhode Island drawl, which I learned combines the accents from Boston and New York. Mike came to Jordan as a volunteer, part of an FSVC–funded capacity-building trip to help the Jordanian Financial Intelligence Unit (FIU) detect and disrupt terrorism financing, particularly through the securities markets.

After his decades in law enforcement, Messier moved to the private sector. He was given an opportunity to apply his knowledge on international financial crime — to lead Bank of America's Latin American region for Financial Crimes and Compliance.

In addition to his six-foot-two height, Messier has a ticker the size of Phar Lap's. He also has a strong commitment to assisting developing countries to harden their financial system, driven largely by his experiences in Latin America. Now here he is, giving his time and knowledge freely in Amman to help a country that is groaning under the weight of millions of war refugees — along with the ever-present risks of terrorism.

*

Amman is a truly captivating city. It beguiles you, lures you in. Jordan lacks the 'curse of resources' that has been experienced by its neighbours, Iraq and Syria. Both of those countries are bloody, broken battle zones in the wake of the great petrodollar wars. In Jordan, there is no free ride on the back of serendipitous underground reservoirs of hydrocarbons. But there's not much for other countries to covet, either. There's barely even enough water to go around.

But what Jordan lacks in natural bounty it has made up for with its culture, its spiritual richness, its history, its tolerance, its generosity and its people.

Jordan's education system is the envy of the Middle East. You're just as likely to find a woman in a top-tier government or private sector role here as you are a man. The historical treasures are otherworldly and the Jordanians have a sense of culture and identity and stoicism that is remarkable in view of the difficulties they face on a daily basis.

As I walked through central bustling Amman on a Friday afternoon alongside Messier and Danyelle, there was an electricity in the air. We craned our necks down the Byzantine alleys, past gold shops, windows displaying delectable sweets and pastries, bazaars and restaurants serving simple ancient fare that was fresh and available at all hours of the day.

Messier wanted another Starbucks (yes, they're there too) but Danyelle wouldn't hear of it. She led us through a nondescript doorway, up some creaking wooden stairs, into a bustling tea and tobacco shop. The sun was already turning warm and colourful as it fell behind the skyline of Jordanian rooftops.

We took a seat on the edge of the balcony and watched the drama and energy playing out below. People and cars flowed, erratically. The waiter offered a smile as she brought tea to our table.

I rested a teacup in my hand and gazed across the ordered chaos below us as Messier started to talk. He was willing to tell me his story about life as a soldier on the front lines in the war against dark money.

*

When Messier started out in law enforcement, he looked like he'd walked out of a Hollywood casting call for a DEA agent, but he wasn't your average cop. He'd studied economics at a private university in Washington DC and went on to spend his first 10 years on Wall Street. It was this background in finance, coupled with his magnetic draw towards investigations and intrigue, that led him to the murky world of dirty money.

Messier is in his 60s now. Still ropey and hard-jawed. But decades ago, back in his prime, Messier spent 15 years as a DEA Special Agent. For six of those years he was in Mexico City specialising in cartels, the bloody drug wars, and the dirty money that both fuelled and funded it. Messier didn't need to be told by a financial intelligence officer to 'follow the money', he knew it was always about dirty lucre. In the underworld, money was a proxy for power, survival and greed.

'Money is the lifeblood of organised crime. The global financial network is its arteries. If you cut off the blood flow, the body will die,' Messier said.

On the bloody streets of Mexico City, where honest citizens tried to live and love another day, it was all gangster capitalism – profit-motivated crime. Messier hated it with a righteous fury.

'It's almost filmstrip stuff, but it was also a great experience, especially my time in Mexico City working with the DEA,' Messier said, bringing a handmade cup to his bristled chin.

Of course, the work wasn't always easy to stomach.

Back in October 2005, Messier was on the cusp of breaking open one of the biggest ever money-laundering investigations in Mexico City. It was one of the first cases where they wanted to get bankers – the money men – on the hook for facilitating murderous drug crimes. He had a crucial informant who was willing to flip. This guy's testimony, as the bag man, would be crucial to building a water-tight case. Prosecutors needed witnesses. It was tracking well. But in the Latin American drug wars, nothing ever goes as planned.

'For about 18 months we'd been dealing with the Colombian drug traffickers. We'd received information the previous year about Colombians moving cocaine from Mexico and South America to Europe, primarily through Spain. We received information that they were using Mexican currency exchange services, known as *casas de cambio*. The person who ran the primary *casa de cambio* that they used to launder their funds, we were looking to flip this guy. We were hoping he would work with us as a possible informant, to give us more information on the financial side.'

Messier took another pensive sip of the warm, slightly bitter-edged tea.

'In October 2005, we found out that he was murdered in a suburb of Mexico City. He was badly beaten. He had three or four bullet holes in him. He was found in the back of a car with his hands tied behind his back.' He told me about the blood all over the seats and pooling on the floor, fingers blackened from what could have been a blowtorch. When cartels murder someone, their torture techniques usually send a message. The singed fingers meant this guy was either 'skimming from the top', a fatally dangerous game, or the murderers were covering for an inside police informant. Had they somehow learned he was a potential target for the DEA to flip? 'So that was a little disheartening, for many people.'

Messier finished in his understated, fact-based manner. Civilians in a coffee shop will usually compete with theatrics to make their dull anecdotes interesting. Organised crime infiltrators, I've found, tend to compete to be the most casually understated.

We were silent, encouraging him to swim deeper.

'When you're down in Mexico or any place in Latin America, and you're dealing with drugs and money laundering, it's a violent culture. And it's not just in Mexico. Wherever you are in the world, when you're dealing with this type of element and then you throw the money there on top of the whole thing, it creates a tremendous amount of aggressiveness.

'It's a business. But in this type of business they don't report to boards of directors. They just make quick changes. If they believe that you're short-changing them, they'll take action. Swift action.

'Mexico has come a long way in combating money laundering and financial crimes,' Messier told me. 'But during those days, when the military or the police went in and did an enforcement operation on certain traffickers, their lives and their families' lives were in jeopardy. They would find out who they were and come after them.'

The laundromat they had developed was a spin on the black-market peso exchange. It took advantage of the strong demand that legitimate Mexican importers had for hard foreign currency – particularly dollars and euros.

Both Danyelle and I were captivated by the images he painted with his words. Pallets full of drug cash being loaded onto private jets. We were being invited into a world where money was no object. Or perhaps it *was* just an object; a tool to subvert society and enrich the world's most ruthless criminals beyond comprehension.

As if on cue, the sound of an explosion ricocheted across the pocked faces of concrete Jordanian buildings, rattled down the main thoroughfare and sliced through the crowds. In a split-second, Michael reacted, placing his arms around us and lowering our heads with a pair of hands like baseball mitts. Before Danyelle or I could blink, he was surveying the streetscape. We looked at each other in a combination of shock, bemusement and confusion. We tensed for the follow-up. Thankfully it didn't arrive. We stood up, unsteady, and leant on the railing overlooking the bustling arcade below. There was no blast radius, no chaos, no bloodshed. All three of us burst out laughing. A car exhaust backfire. That's all it was.

We tried to look cool but, in reality, it made me realise I was completely unprepared for that type of situation.

If it had been a real explosion, Danyelle and I would have been observing our shredded flesh from above, in the process of transitioning to the afterlife. Messier, on the other hand, would have emerged from the rubble and, without thinking, ripped his shirt and started wrapping tourniquets around gushing limbs. He'd trained for this and he'd been here before, witnessing the cat-scratch-thin veneer that separated the souls of the living from the eulogies of the dead.

With adrenaline still coursing through our veins, we retreated to humour, relentlessly mocking each other. Messier rightly accused us of being as green as bamboo shoots and entirely unprepared for life on the front line, while we chastised him for being an overly paranoid ex-DEA agent with clear signs of PTSD.

'If you're trying to look like a tourist, you ain't doing a very good job, Mike,' I prodded, in the most laconic Aussie accent I could muster. 'Perhaps take a leaf out of our playbook.'

Messier laughed. 'Actually, y'know what?' he drawled right back, looking me straight in the eye. 'You Aussies oughta take a leaf out of our playbook. These war stories about the Mexican drug trade, the money laundering, they're still happening today. These cartels are no joke. They're stronger and more ruthless now than ever before. They're expanding. Australia needs to watch out. They're spreading their tentacles across the Pacific. And when they arrive, trust me, they'll bring with them a whole new world of misery and destruction.'

The tragic experience of Mexico stands as a warning for Australians. There, the drug cartels' bloodshed and tyranny over humble citizens are gut-turning. Every year in Mexico, more than 36,600 people are murdered. Cartel violence has saturated and undermined the political system. The profits from the drug trade ensure that politicians, police and government workers are usually given two choices: *plata o plomo*, silver or lead. During the 2021 elections, more than 90 politicians were murdered. The country is experiencing a reign of terror at the hands of the drug cartels that's up there with anything wrought by a 'designated terrorist group'.

Australia's two favourite illicit drugs – methamphetamines and cocaine – are the Mexican cartels' leading export products, so Australia's market is increasingly attractive. If the cartels get their product here, it will retail for up to $350,000 per kilogram. The same brick in the United States will fetch one-tenth of that, possibly less. With those price dynamics, the Mexican cartels are heavily incentivised to expand their supply chains into Australia.

Dirty money has the same effect on a society that dirty drugs have on an individual. Any country that turns a blind eye to the all-pervasive rot of criminal money eventually pays a price. Accepting the easy income from organised crime would always prove to be a Faustian pact, Messier warned. And he was speaking with the authority that comes from witnessing drugs, death and destruction first-hand in the field.

THIRTY-TWO

The Palestinian Connection

Mike Messier's anecdotes from life inside the Mexican drug wars – and his warning to Australia – had shocked me more than the acoustic blast from that car backfiring in central Amman. Australia's hard borders had always given us a sense of security, a protection from the scourges of the wider world around us. Those sea borders were part of the Lucky Country's great fortune. With no land borders we had been spared the inevitable geopolitical flare-ups that other countries faced over disputed territory or ancient land quarrels – issues of colonisation notwithstanding. We also had a greater chance of controlling what came across those dotted lines in the sea, whether it be contraband, cash or radicalised militants. This good fortune, however, had fostered a sense of complacency.

I had travelled to Amman with Messier to help train the Jordanian financial intelligence community, and their financial regulators, ahead of a FATF international assessment. We were part of an international effort to ensure that the country did not suffer the economic equivalent of purgatory, getting relegated to the FATF's 'grey list' of non-cooperative countries. This had happened to many other developing countries and it had proved to be economically devastating. As always, the poor and the vulnerable ended up shouldering most of the burden.

Pakistan, for example, had been on the FATF grey list for extended periods of time since 2008. The international body was particularly concerned about its inability to detect and disrupt the financing of terrorism and other forms of radical extremism. Researchers based in Islamabad, the country's capital, estimated that this had cost Pakistan US$38 billion over the past 13 years. This was money that was desperately needed for economic development in a country where the average household survived on little more than US$10 per week.

We had also hoped to get an insight into the links between terrorism financing in the Middle East and potential donor countries like the US and Australia. Capacity-building projects such as the one we were part of were always a two-way street. If wealthy countries such as Australia and the US could harden their system against terrorism financing, this would have flow-on benefits for the countries where these transactions fuel extremist violence.

We had heard incredible tales about the sluice gates that moved money around the planet to fund groups like ISIS. And it wasn't just money that moved into these conflict zones. Australia had been aware for years that citizens were disappearing to the front lines of the jihad in Syria and Iraq. Aspiring combatants would usually leave Australia with maxed-out credit cards, empty self-managed superannuation funds and overdrawn bank accounts. These were individuals who would have no further use for a good credit rating. Radicalised Australians were hoping to find the caliphate they had been promised over social media, or in professional-quality recruitment videos. In reality, they would be greeted with lies, extreme danger and a one-way ticket to either a detention facility or Jannah.

*

In the law-enforcement world, terrorism financing is sometimes referred to as 'laundering in reverse'. This generalisation relates to the fact that there's often legitimate money involved, which is moved and disguised and then used to fund violent acts. This was common with militant ethnic groups, such as the Tamil Tigers, who put pressure on the Tamil diaspora abroad to fund the resistance back home in Sri Lanka. The same model was used to fund the Irish Republican Army (IRA) during the Troubles in Northern Ireland.

Thankfully both of those threats have largely subsided with ceasefires. But there are many organisations still using these funding techniques: persuasion, radicalisation, threats, violence, extortion. Australians with family or ethnic ties to conflict zones are not immune from the pressure to fund overseas resistance movements.

Even if the money is moving outwards, to finance violence abroad, it's still an enormous national security concern to Australia.

The 'foreign fighter' phenomenon surged in Australia during the Syrian conflict and with the establishment of a caliphate in Mosul, in Iraq. One of AUSTRAC's major priorities at this time was to help banks recognise the financial fingerprints of potential foreign fighters. This type of work had been done, very successfully, to prevent radicalised Australians from travelling into conflict zones abroad.

But, as we have seen, the banks weren't always at the top of their terrorism-financing game. The story of Hayssam Melhem is a good case in point. Melhem was a Lebanese-Australian who left the country in 1999 and moved to Lebanon. According to media reports, he was convicted in Beirut on terrorism-related charges and jailed for three years. He had never returned to Australia. Despite this, in May 2017 Melhem was able to open a bank account – from abroad – with the Commonwealth Bank. Ignoring his convictions, which were listed in the World-Check intelligence database, CBA opened an account under an Australian address. An 'associate' turned up at the branch to do the paperwork. The bank recorded Melhem's occupation as 'unemployed'. Days later, an unknown individual started making cash deposits through CommBank's infamous IDMs in Bankstown. First $2250 went in. Then $9000. Then $5000. To an astute financial crime analyst, this would look like classic 'penetration testing' of the bank's terrorism-financing defences.

In June 2017, Melhem logged on to the CBA online banking platform, with a tell-tale IP address in Lebanon, and tried to transfer $5000 to a bank account in Beirut. CommBank's sanctions team were immediately on the ball. An automated 'red flag' was raised, given that this was a high-risk region. An astute staff member did a search in World-Check and discovered that, sure enough, Melhem was listed as having links to terrorism. Bingo! The AML team member blocked the transaction and a report was lodged with AUSTRAC.

But this expat Aussie, who according to his bank was living simultaneously in Sydney and Beirut, wasn't to be so easily dissuaded. Another $9000 was deposited into the account through an anonymous donor in Bankstown. Then a second $5000 international transfer request was made, via Melhem's overseas login. Again, the outgoing payment was flagged on CommBank's system, and the analyst decided to block the payment. She wrote in a report that 'the customer was identified as allegedly raising funds in Australia to support terrorism and had been convicted in 2005 for terrorism-related activities'. Even so, Melhem's CBA account stayed open.

On the third occasion, the money slipped through and went all the way to a correspondent bank in Beirut for processing. The AML team clawed the money back just before the funds cleared. When AUSTRAC discovered these transactions, it was livid that the bank's commercial arm was undermining the work that was happening inside the sanctions and AML/CTF teams.

In July 2017, CBA's financial crime team asked that Melhem's account be frozen due to his suspected links to the funding of terrorism. Instead, Melhem's associate in Australia, who had opened the account on his behalf, received a polite bank letter giving him 30 days to withdraw the mysterious funds.

What's worse, AUSTRAC discovered during an investigation that CBA had failed to undertake any due diligence on Melhem, as he was deemed a 'pre-commencement customer' – indicating the account holder was 'grandfathered in' when the AML laws were introduced in 2006. This, the bank said, was because he had opened an account with CBA back in 1995.

The Melhem case was one of many examples of Australia's vulnerability to the scourge of terrorism financing. While the attacks might not take place here, the generation of funds often did. Were these cash deposits part of an attempted scheme to wash the proceeds of crime in Australia to fund violent extremism in the Middle East? Or was it legitimate money being diverted to fund the illegitimate purpose of terrorism? Was the depositor using IDMs because these were an easy and anonymous way to break the money chain and transfer cash to a terrorism hotspot?

*

These are the challenges Australian banks face every day, as they try to support the national security agencies in hardening the financial system against violent and organised crime. The broader situation in the Middle East reflects just how difficult it is becoming for banks to support the national security agencies as they seek to prevent Australian citizens from funding terrorist groups. They are often torn between competing policy objectives – such as avoiding the 'de-risking' of customers while also preventing the funding of terrorism.

The victory of Hamas in the Palestinian legislative election of 2006 highlighted the tightrope that regional banks were walking in the geopolitically complex Middle East. Hamas was designated in the United States as a terrorist group, yet, following elections backed by the United States Agency for International Development (USAID), it unexpectedly became the official leader of the Palestinian Legislative Council (PLC). The US$2.3 million in funding that USAID had donated, via Jordan's Arab Bank, had failed to secure a win for President Mahmoud Abbas and his more moderate Fatah leadership.

For Arab Bank, the largest and most active international bank in the Palestinian territories, this had created an impossible bind. On one hand, it needed to continue banking for the

Palestinian government, and to funnel international aid to prevent a simmering humanitarian disaster. On the other hand, a year earlier, Arab Bank had come close to losing its crucial New York banking licence as a result of money-laundering and terrorism-financing breaches.

In a bid to maintain its presence on US soil and retain its critical access to US-dollar clearing, Arab Bank had appointed a silver-haired legal expert from America as its head of compliance. Michael Matossian had worked across an array of star-spangled American banks, as well as with the Comptroller of the Currency in New York the 1970s. His genealogy traced back to Armenian ancestry. If anyone could walk the tenuous tightrope between US interests and the difficult realities on the ground in the Middle East, it was him.

By 2016, Matossian had moved permanently to Arab Bank's headquarters in Jordan. This turned into an unexpected reconnection with his roots; he was being drawn by what felt like the currents of fate. Matossian had already determined that he would leverage his strong ties with the United States for the benefit of people in the Middle East. He held a number of high-level meetings with the US ambassador in Amman, where his institution was headquartered. One of his big concerns was how the bank could continue to process USAID's humanitarian payments. Now that Hamas had taken control of the PLC, his bank would technically be financing terrorism on behalf of the US government's main foreign aid arm, in breach of that government's own sanctions. This was a banking riddle wrapped up in a geopolitical conundrum if ever there was one.

Matossian asked for guidance in a letter to the US Department of the Treasury's financial intelligence unit, the feared Financial

Crimes Enforcement Network (FinCEN). He explained that Arab Bank had 22 branches in the West Bank and Gaza, and they processed the payroll for the Palestinian National Authority and local governments. Without those funds, most of which came from foreign aid, the desperate people of the Palestinian territories would be facing another crisis.

He met with the US ambassador. The diplomatic cable on their meeting was blunt. 'Specifically, Arab Bank requests clarity on US law governing financial relationships with a governing body that includes members of, or is connected to, a Specially Designated Global Terrorist and Foreign Terrorist Organization. Does such affiliation require that Arab Bank cease all payments to the government agency as a whole?' the US ambassador asked his government.

It didn't help that, a year earlier, Arab Bank had paid US$24 million in civil penalties to keep a toehold on US soil.

The ambassador went away from the meeting convinced that Arab Bank was 'demonstrating the extent of its continued, keen desire to strengthen its regulatory compliance regime for countering terrorism financing'.

One of the options Matossian proposed was to set up an account in Abbas's name, and to use that to route the humanitarian and other aid, moving it outside the direct control of Hamas. It was a pragmatic workaround. Even that could cause complications, however, in creating a perception that the United States was meddling and undermining the elected government that had won power in a democratic vote that the West had supported.

The clock was ticking. The Palestinian government was desperately in need of its next funding round from Saudi Arabia,

Kuwait, Algeria, Japan and Russia to clear up two multi-million-dollar overdraft facilities. Naturally, Arab Bank was keen to see the PLC remain solvent. But if it processed the payments in breach of US sanctions, the digital trail of those payments could never be erased. This was the first lesson that anyone in the great game of financial intelligence would have learned.

'Matossian relayed the bank's desire to avert a humanitarian crisis in the territories should it stop granting credit to the Palestinian Authority,' the ambassador wrote in a confidential cable.

I reached out to Matossian, as he was the leading figure in the Middle Eastern and North African anti-money-laundering community. The Arab Bank financial crime expert was also setting up a regional Financial Crime Compliance Group to bring together key players across the private and public sectors to support collaborative anti-money-laundering efforts.

Matossian, a gracious host, agreed to meet me at his offices in central Amman. Later that night we gathered at his favourite Jordanian restaurant for an exquisite banquet. Waiters brought out platters of woodfired flatbreads, warm olives, hummus and chilled, peeled almonds as we broke bread and talked story. Matossian's love of the Jordanian people was palpable.

'Are you ever going back to New York?' I asked.

'No, I'm Jordanian now,' he replied without hesitation.

*

Ever since the United States began its regime change operation in Iraq back in 2003, Jordan has suffered from the fallout. Even in the middle of the desert, the explosions seemed to have a ripple effect that spread outwards in concentric circles to neighbouring countries.

First, the 'Coalition of the Willing' showered the country with bombs, quickly destabilising the reign of Saddam Hussein, who was brutally deposed. After that, as the reconstruction began, the Americans showered the country in bucks. Billions of greenbacks flowed through the new Iraqi government into neighbouring countries. Jordan was a popular transit point for the proceeds of corruption. People who were there at that time speak of vehicles coming across the border with boot loads of US dollars. The country experienced a massive equities boom, as foreign criminals and kleptocrats placed their ill-gotten dollars in Jordan's fledgling stock market. Citizens piled in to join the wealth-making frenzy. People punted their life savings on penny stocks, just as they had done a decade earlier through the cunning schemes of Stephen Saccoccia and the Wolves of Wall Street.

What few people in Jordan realised was that these stock-market frauds were often the 'blow-off' stage in huge transnational money-laundering schemes. Billions of dollars moved from the coffers of the fledgling Iraqi government, through the Amman stock exchange, and then on to their ultimate destination.

Sometimes that money would buy real estate in respectable markets overseas, like Australia. To a less-than-attentive gatekeeper, it would look like the not-so-squeaky-clean proceeds of a lucky punt on the Jordanian stock bubble. In other cases, the pilfered Iraqi funds were washed and then reinvested in terrorism, to destabilise the US's own development and reconstruction efforts. The Americans were, in effect, financing their own resistance.

Of course, someone would be left holding the losses when the investment merry-go-round stopped. Once again, it was the unfortunate retail investors who carried the bag as the market crashed.

The impact on the Jordanian stock market was catastrophic. Boom turned into bust and a generation of Jordanians swore off stock-market 'gambling' for life. The Amman Stock Exchange crash was a terrible yet salient reminder to the world that illicit money was the least loyal lucre on Earth. To invite it in, uncritically, was to make a Faustian bargain.

Major financial centres such as London, New York and Hong Kong prided themselves on attracting, holding and prudently managing the world's savings. In money-laundering terms, this is the 'integration' stage – where the most grubby and disloyal funds become sparkling clean and what bankers call 'sticky'. As a nation-state, if you were going to facilitate money laundering, it would be prudent to do so at the final integration stage. This means the criminal money will at least stick around to power some domestic economic growth – and the politicians can feign horror when the occasional illicit finance scandal blows up in the media.

Unfortunately for developing economies such as Jordan, the owners of all this illicit finance had no plans to stick around. Their goal was to place their money in the system, layer it to disguise the trail, and then move it on as quickly as possible to disassociate the profit from the predicate crime. Every time a transaction crosses a border, law enforcement teams need to begin a new request for cooperation from their overseas counterparts.

As Bill Majcher puts it, 'With the click of a mouse, a launderer can add three to six months to one of your investigations.

Criminals have all the money and no rules. Police? They have all the rules and no money.'

One of the tragedies of the Amman stock market crash was that the laundering of Iraq's development funds was used to finance further violent extremism across the region. Without realising it, Jordanian stock markets had acted as a recycling scheme to put US taxpayers' dollars into the hands of groups like ISIS. These fintel failures meant it was America's own money that contributed to the declaration of a caliphate in Iraq and Syria in mid-2014. American dollars were, in effect, being used to take the lives of civilians and American soldiers.

*

The world of money laundering and terrorism financing respects no borders. The entire global economy is interconnected and criminals are adept at exploiting the opportunities this creates. As such, Australia's vulnerabilities make it not only an attractive destination for the inflow of foreign dirty loot. It is also an attractive destination for raising funds to support political extremism, which flows outward to the world's geopolitical hotspots. The law enforcement community needs to track illicit money flows in both directions.

As with Australia, the fintel communities in countries like Jordan are full of brave, compassionate, dedicated and determined people like Matossian and his team at Arab Bank. Many have a background in law enforcement and may have moved in and out of the private sector; others started in banking and became passionate about combating the horrors of organised crime and terrorism. Each day they work to unravel the secret patterns and stories that money flows can reveal. Over time, these analysts develop a 'sixth sense' for their work. They can instinctively see anomalies in patterns of data that might look like a bowl of tagliatelle to anyone else outside – or indeed inside – their profession.

And in places like Jordan, this profession can be a dangerous one. Everyone I met in the sector had a story about being followed home from work after filing a suspicious activity report. In some cases they ended up sitting in court alongside the targets of their filings, which is an unsettling experience in a part of the world where the fragility of life is felt on a daily basis.

And yet these courageous men and women continue with their work, in spite of personal threats, in the hope it will make their country a better place, with less crime, less violence and less political corruption.

THIRTY-THREE

The Caymans of the South Pacific

Although Captain Cook may beg to differ, islands are usually known for their warm hospitality and welcoming cultures. With its stunning beaches, exceptional weather, friendly inhabitants and robust tourism sector, the world's only island continent is no exception. Prior to the global pandemic, Australia was known internationally for its warm-hearted, open-armed embrace of the world's travellers. But there is another type of tourist who finds Australia even more attractive, accommodating, obliging: the international money launderer.

For the launderer, of course, money is no barrier to the experience of pleasure. No luxury is unobtainable, no expense is unwarranted, no champagne is too exclusive. From the penthouse suites at luxury harbourside hotels to the comped suites in casinos, it's often very hard to differentiate between a legitimate businessman in a sharp suit and a bagman for the world's most ruthless crooks. In fact, the distinction is so subtle that, all too often, Australia's finest lawyers, accountants, or trust and company agents haven't managed to spot the difference. As a result, more than $1 billion sails into the country's waters each year from the proceeds of foreign corruption alone.

Professor Jason Sharman is the Sir Patrick Sheehy Professor of International Relations at King's College, Cambridge – and a proud Aussie living abroad. He's also a leading international money-laundering expert. Professor Sharman has looked deeply beneath the veneers of the world's dark-money markets. He has watched the southward flow of illicit funds from countries such as Papua New Guinea, which are desperate for development funds to pay for new schools, hospitals and clean water sources.

During a keynote lecture at Griffith University in 2016, Professor Sharman read Australia the riot act. He said that while billions in corrupt funds were flowing into Australia each year, only $4 million had been recovered by Australian authorities and returned to the countries of origin. 'If we're giving hundreds of millions of dollars a year in aid to Papua New Guinea in order to help that country's development, it's rather ironic if corrupt politicians from that country are taking money out of the PNG budget and putting it in Cairns or Brisbane or Sydney,' Sharman said.

China, South-East Asia and the South Pacific are the main sources of corrupt funds entering Australia. 'It tends to make for some tense relations when the Chinese government says, "We'd like that money back" and the Australian government sits on its hands and does nothing,' he said.

The clean and principled PNG politicians walk a fine line with their wealthier and generous friends to the south. They must avoid causing embarrassment or risk hundreds of millions in much-needed aid. But many have finally had enough. They want Australia to do more to tackle the proceeds of corruption, and they're speaking out about it. They want this filthy lucre found and sent home, where it belongs, to build PNG's national infrastructure.

In one case, $3.6 million in funds linked to corruption was identified in banks in Singapore. The perpetrators of the scheme were supposed to use the funds to set up community colleges in Papua New Guinea. The case also involved allegations of corruption against former PNG prime minister Sir Michael Somare, and a conspiracy to defraud by the director of a Chinese corporation.

Sam Koim, the chairman of PNG's anti-corruption agency, is one of those people who has lost patience. Koim says his country is heavily reliant on support from countries such as Australia, which are targets for these funds. He had managed to convince Singapore to return stolen funds but Australia was proving less cooperative.

'It's up to Australia to have the political will to actually take a step like what Singapore did,' he says. 'But as for the political will, I'm yet to see one that will push them to actually do something about it.'

International agencies have accused Australia of lagging in its efforts to 'get its house in order' regarding corruption.

Jason Sharman's lecture slayed rich countries – including his beloved home – for their convenient failure to detect and return these proceeds of crime. 'Rich countries provide despots from poor countries opportunities for conspicuous consumption,' he said. 'Buying the mansion, buying the Ferraris, going on incredible spending binges. It provides an insurance policy. If you're a despot, your rule is often insecure. To the extent that you have a nice place set up in Paris or London, or indeed even in Australia, if your political fortunes turn at home you have a comfortable refuge or safe haven to go to.'

Sharman believes the days of hosting boltholes for crooked despots have come to an end. Australia cannot feign horror at the likes of Muammar Gaddafi or Ferdinand Marcos while providing a bolthole for their ilk. 'It is no longer okay for one country to host money stolen by the leader of another country,' he said, referring to the introduction of a global pact in 2005 forbidding this kind of behaviour. 'The Australian government prefers to ignore the situation and adopt a resolute head-in-the-sand attitude and a deliberate policy of inaction.'

Professor Sharman said a neighbouring country had gone as far as to give Australia a new nickname: 'the Cayman Islands of the South Pacific'. PNG officials no longer believed in the mythology that Australia was the Lucky Country. They had come to believe it was just a looty country. He warned that a change of attitude might only come about in the event of a major scandal, such as the Australian Wheat Board's 'oil for food' scandal in 2005, or the RBA's polymer banknote bribery scandal.

'It's politically easier to ignore the situation than to try and fix it. But it's not good for Australia to end up a haven for the proceeds of foreign crime,' Professor Sharman said. 'Corrupt leaders have a strange relationship with the rule of law in that they don't like the rule of law when they're stealing the money but they do like the rule of law when it comes to protecting the money they've stolen. They want to go to a country that is subject to the rule of law and with a stable economy.'

*

Of course, the proceeds of corruption are not the only threat to Australia's political and economic integrity. When a country turns a blind eye to one type of crime (with victims abroad), it invariably misses other crimes with victims closer to home.

The booming Australian illicit drug market is just one example. The corrupt politicians whom Australian real estate agents woo in PNG are, of course, not great advocates for the rule of law when it comes to drug trafficking either.

This has opened a new trade route for Latin American drug cartels to infiltrate one of the world's most expensive markets for illicit drugs.

In 2020, a Cessna light aircraft departed from a remote airstrip in PNG bound for northern Australia. The plane took off but struggled to stabilise, partly because it was carrying an unusually heavy cargo. It went into a dive and crashed, leaving wreckage strewn throughout the humid jungle near Papa Lea Lea, north of Port Moresby. When the authorities arrived, they didn't find any bodies – thankfully – but they did find a suspiciously large amount of powdery residue.

In a case reminiscent of South American 'cocaine cowboy' drug flights, law-enforcement officials could not rule out the possibility that the plane had crashed due to being overloaded with cocaine. This desperate type of amateur narco flight was a relatively rare phenomenon for the Australian drug market.

Gavin Coles is a former employee of the United Kingdom's financial crimes unit who now lives in Victoria. He's passionate about financial crime, having worked on the front line of the 1990s drug wars, tracking cartel cash as it sluiced around the planet. He has worked in financial crime teams in banks in Australia, Hong Kong and the United States. These days, he's happy back at home in Australia with his wife and kids. Being a father has turbo-charged his belief in the need to prevent a klepto-economy from taking hold in his adopted country.

Coles said the COVID-19 pandemic had been a catastrophe for many criminal syndicates. Their supply chains were disrupted, as well as their cash-intensive businesses. This was forcing criminals to adapt, to take risks, and this was leading to some fatal errors.

Coles said honest people can get caught up in this twisted web. Having lost some of their laundering supply lines, organised-crime groups may approach an existing business that is struggling, and pay to move funds through their accounts. A bank's transaction monitoring systems typically cannot pick up the change in the source of funds until the outward transactions occur.

'Most financial institutions only review such transactions after the fact, especially for previously low-risk businesses, by which time the organised-crime group has the money offshore,' Coles says. 'That sort of offer will become much more attractive when people are desperate.'

In the case of the Cessna, this is exactly what happened. Police in Australia and Papua New Guinea eventually recovered 28 bags of cocaine worth $80 million at a different PNG location from the crash. They arrested five suspected drug traffickers connected to the plane, all members of a Melbourne-based criminal syndicate with alleged links to Italian organised crime. The rattled Australian pilot eventually turned up at the Australian consulate in Port Moresby. He was also arrested.

'The AFP alleges greed played a significant part in the syndicate's activities and cannot rule out that the weight of the cocaine had an impact on the plane's ability to take off,' the Australian police said in a statement. In Papua New Guinea, meanwhile, the plane crash was the talk of the town. Italian organised crime – the so-called 'Ndrangheta – had arrived with a bang. The local newspapers reported that this was the largest drug haul in the country's history.

As AFP Deputy Commissioner of Investigations Ian McCartney pointed out, 'With current interstate travel restrictions in place due to COVID-19, the attempt to import illicit drugs into Australia shows how opportunistic and greedy organised crime can be.'

The hydra of the criminal netherworld had adapted to a changing operating landscape, as the authorities desperately tried to bring them crashing back to earth.

The affair also suggested that global crime syndicates were competing for dominance in one of the world's most profitable drug markets. And to do so, they would need access to the finest professional skills money could acquire. Very soon, as it turned out, an information bombshell would detonate around the world, proving that those skills were only too readily available down in the Lucky Country.

THIRTY-FOUR

A Matter of Trusts

For more than 400 wealthy Australians, it started as the Monday from hell – and only got worse from there. On 4 October 2021, the world woke to explosive news. The offshore banking sector had suffered the equivalent of a coordinated neutron bomb attack. In newspapers strewn across some of Australia's most prestigious breakfast tables, details of the elites' financial secrets were laid bare. Cops and tax collectors woke up salivating; the world's oligarchs were rattled.

Two years earlier, the International Consortium of Investigative Journalists (ICIJ) had been drip-fed the secretive databases belonging to 14 of the world's leading financial secrecy facilitators. The ICIJ's 600 members across 150 news outlets had pored over 11.9 million confidential files detailing the wonders of a parallel financial universe. For thousands of politicians, plutocrats, royals and celebrities, it was a day of reckoning.

For Australians, the Pandora Papers were especially salacious. Unlike earlier leaks of private financial documents, which focused primarily on people in the Northern Hemisphere, these were right on our doorstep. A notorious offshore facilitator named Asiaciti Trust was one of the firms that had been hacked; two million of its files were now in the hands of journalists. If the earlier Panama Papers, leaked in 2016, were anything to go by, the tax authorities would soon be making some awkward phone calls to Australia's financial elites.

The Asiaciti files detailed the shell games played by some of Australia's wealthiest individuals. Titans of industry and pillars of society had been exposed for their financial skulduggery. The files also exposed the cunning conduits and audacious aqueducts that Asiaciti used to slosh lucre through waypoints such as the Cook Islands, Samoa, Nevis, Panama, Singapore and Hong Kong.

Asiaciti's Australian founder, Graeme Briggs, was also having a bad day. Briggs was a humble accountant who had amassed a $62 million fortune while living in Singapore. He had played a key role in establishing Samoa as an offshore tax haven, and knew exactly how to make best use of its legal and accounting intricacies.

Briggs had a pretty good idea of what was coming a few weeks earlier, when investigative journos from around the world started approaching him for comment on his clients' most secret activities. The shrewd accountant, with plush offices in Robinson Road, Singapore, was devastated. He said the data had been 'illegally accessed from Asiaciti Trust'. Briggs had inadvertently opened a Pandora's box containing all of his clients' darkest financial secrets.

In failing to secure his customers' data, Briggs had opened a porthole into the ways that the wealthy elites can exist outside of the Australian tax law.

*

At the heart of Briggs's schemes lay some miraculous structures. None was more so than the common law trust, which is known in the money-laundering world as a 'legal arrangement'. These wondrous structures are used along with offshore bank accounts, corporate vehicles, bearer shares, bearer share warrants, nominee shareholders and nominee directors to thoroughly conceal money trails.

Trusts have many legitimate uses but, like any technology, they can be used for good or for ill. Financial crime experts and tax law reform campaigners have long been concerned about their misuse. The simple legal mechanism of a trust – assets held by one entity (the trust), controlled by a second entity (the trustee), for the benefit of a third (the beneficiary) – makes it very hard to determine the 'ultimate beneficial owner' (UBO) of an asset. It is therefore much harder for tax authorities, jilted spouses, creditors and investigators to distinguish between who controls the trust and who owns it. Smart people, as the saying goes, own nothing but control everything.

'Asiaciti Trust provides legitimate fiduciary services to clients around the world,' Briggs said in a statement following the leaks. 'Our work is highly regulated and we are committed to the highest business standards, including ensuring that our operations fully comply with all laws and regulations in the jurisdictions in which we operate.'

The complex legal arrangements – the intergovernmental Financial Action Task Force's (FATF) umbrella term for trusts – are central to the international 'black money' laundromat. This has been apparent with the surge of leaks in recent years from offshore financial centres such as Panama, Bermuda, Mauritius, Liechtenstein and Luxembourg. 'A trust may be created in one jurisdiction and used in another to hold assets across jurisdictions to disguise the origins of criminal proceeds,' the FATF warned in 2014. 'It may be used to enhance anonymity by completely disconnecting the beneficial owner from the names of the other parties including the trustee, settlor, protector or beneficiary.'

Canada has similar problems to Australia when it comes to foreign property ownership and the concealment of criminal funds. The province of British Columbia has passed a landmark law that requires the 'legal owner' of real property to disclose the identities of the beneficial owners to the Land Registry. Other provinces in Canada are looking to emulate these reforms to deal with a surge of foreign money – both legitimate and illicit – that has been used to purchase property in the country.

New Zealand also overhauled its trust regime in the wake of the Panama Papers. The country improved the transparency of foreign trusts in 2017, following the Shewan Inquiry. More recently the parliament introduced the largest overhaul of trust law in New Zealand in 70 years.

Dr Gordon Hook, executive secretary of the Asia/Pacific Group on Money Laundering (APG), knows trusts all too well. He is a Canadian living in Australia, a former navy lawyer who has a PhD specialising in trusts. For many years he has led the FATF's equivalent body across the Asia-Pacific region, assessing the financial crime risks and vulnerabilities in different countries.

Hook said the intricacies of trusts can vary across jurisdictions. Launderers use this to their advantage. They love nothing more than complexity and the loopholes that come with it. Many of these complex arrangements are not directly compatible with the understanding of trusts in common law jurisdictions such as the United Kingdom, New Zealand, Australia and Canada, where the trustee holds the assets for the benefit of another – the beneficiary.

Under French law, for instance, trust assets are typically owned by the trustee for the benefit of the beneficiaries – an arrangement that is similar to that of common law trusts. In South Africa and the Netherlands, however, trust assets in a 'bewind trust' are owned by the beneficiaries, and the trustee takes on a management role. However, in the Canadian province of Quebec, trust assets are not owned by anyone. They sit in an 'ownerless limbo' referred to as a 'patrimony by acquisition' – effectively creating a separate legal entity.

'So in civil law jurisdictions you've got a variety of different scenarios: trustees legally owning assets, or the beneficiaries legally owning the assets, or the assets not being owned by anyone,' Hook explains.

*

Trusts have a number of qualities that make them attractive to criminals, money launderers, tax evaders and financiers of terrorism. Foremost among these is the opacity that a trust structure offers. In many jurisdictions, there is no requirement to register the trust deed for the trust to be effective. The trust can simply exist in a lever-arch folder on someone's shelf.

Even in jurisdictions where there is a registration requirement, this information is rarely verified. In Pakistan, for instance, trusts can be registered, but this is optional and there is no inquiry into the validity of the information that has been registered. There is also a risk that criminals may use the act of registration to create a veneer of credibility.

Offshore asset-protection trusts are commonly found in small Caribbean or Pacific island nations such as the Cook Islands, the Cayman Islands and Bermuda. They are essentially discretionary trusts with additional legislative protections, such as a tighter statute of limitations.

Purpose trusts – in particular, non-charitable purpose trusts – do not have any beneficial owners. They usually have business purposes for holding shares or structuring securities.

In Canada, the extent of criminal money laundering through real estate has triggered a number of inquiries and law reforms. Yet in Australia, there have been no such efforts to limit the abuse of trusts to hide the true owners of real estate. To do so might prove unlucky for the armies of Australians who have hitched their fortunes to the 'equity mate' economy. For professional advisers, muddying the property ownership paper trail is all too easy. 'The beneficiary's name is not on the land title,' says Hook. 'The trustee's name is on the land title, whether it's a person or a legal entity, but there is no indication on the title that the person or entity is acting as trustee for either one beneficiary or to a class of beneficiaries.'

The fact that beneficiaries' names are not usually disclosed to any public authority helps explain why trusts continue to feature so prominently in major international financial crime cases.

By default, trusts offer an exceedingly high level of personal anonymity. If third parties – including tax authorities – attempt to identify the beneficiary of a trust, they will generally only be able to find the name of the trustee. That opacity creates a veil of secrecy around asset ownership that is highly attractive to launderers, as demonstrated in the Panama and Pandora Papers, along with other major data leaks.

Trusts in some countries, such as the Cook Islands, offer even greater benefits to financial criminals, such as 'flee or flight' clauses. This means that if a specified event occurs (for instance, an enquiry by law-enforcement agencies), then the trust will flee the jurisdiction in which it is registered. As an example, a trust in the Cook Islands could automatically 'flee' to Panama or Samoa if a law enforcement agency were to ask any questions about the trust, its beneficiaries or its assets. 'It's very complex to implement,' Hook says, 'but, nevertheless, there are a lot of clauses like that in offshore jurisdictions.'

In addition, some jurisdictions have strict time limits that make it difficult, if not impossible, to pursue legal actions against trusts. The Cook Islands was popular with Asiaciti clients, for example, because there is a two-year statute of limitations from the time a trust is formed. Bad actors can leave trusts dormant for two years before using them for nefarious purposes to obtain another layer of ironclad security.

Many times the authorities have attempted to unravel the tangled web of secrecy offered by offshore trusts. In the United States, there have been landmark cases that dealt with trusts in the Cook Islands, where claimants attempted to repatriate assets to the United States. Despite the political clout of the US government, none of these repatriation attempts has ever succeeded. 'The Cook Islands regime is advertised as ironclad, and it is,' Hook says.

Trust deeds can even be drafted that are 'indefinite'. As such, the law-enforcement authorities would have to wait for the trust to vest (terminate) before securing any assets.

Even despite the risk of data leaks, Australian money launderers and other financial criminals seem as fond of trusts as they ever were. With the help of accountancy and law firms, they're in a position to go jurisdiction-shopping for the most favourable secrecy and asset-protection regimes on offer. They can layer trusts and shell companies across multiple jurisdictions to take advantage of a smorgasbord of legal chicanery.

Hook says the experience in British Columbia should stand as a warning to Australia. 'There's been a lot of news out of the province in recent years about the extent of money laundering through the real estate sector. British Columbia has passed a law that requires the disclosure of beneficial owners to the land registry. Now other parts of Canada are looking at similar laws because there are the same issues in other provinces,' he says. 'It would be safe to say there are the same issues in Australia.'

*

As news of the Pandora Papers leaks played out across newspapers, mobile phones and television screens, Australians expressed their disgust. Senator Deborah O'Neill said the revelations were a reminder of how badly the country had dropped the ball on tackling financial crime and money laundering in the real estate market. The evidence was undeniable. 'A nondescript accountant can be at the heart of a massive international abuse of power, siphoning off money and illegal activity that costs the community,' O'Neill said.

The assets in the leaks included four spectacular Tasmanian dairy farms, apartment blocks in Sydney and Melbourne, and even a Hilton Hotel in Sydney. Six layers of the 'shell game' were peeled back, with nested companies and trusts, to reveal the Hilton's ultimate owner was a Chinese steel magnate. This entrepreneur had once admitted to paying $12 million in bribes to Rio Tinto executives. The money to fund his $442 million purchase of premium Australian property had passed through a 'Russian dolls' structure of companies in the British Virgin Islands and the Caymans.

For the first time, many Australians came face to face with the extent to which their country had sold itself to the highest bidder. Waterfront tourism icons, premium farmland and apartment blocks had been flogged off like the silverware from a failing English estate. Even worse, the Australian lawyers, accountants and real estate agents in those transactions had not been required to ask the most basic questions about whether the buyer was using legitimate or criminal funds.

THIRTY-FIVE

Poking the Monster

Essex, England, 1968

At three years old, Neil is an inquisitive little boy, forever exploring the backyard of his family's post-war bungalow in Essex, England. When Dad's at work, he's usually asking Mum questions, visiting grandparents, or just playing outside while Mum keeps the house ticking over smoothly. On this sunny day, Neil's mother is inside working in the kitchen, while her boy amuses himself in the safety of their English backyard. Neil's parents moved from the crowded East End of London — what would later be known as Docklands — so they could enjoy the space and countryside of Essex. A standalone home with a garden was a dream that a young family could never achieve in bustling London.

Neil's father was working as a stockbroker, a market maker, which had bought their working-class family new opportunities. His father's father had been a ship's carpenter and shop owner, while the grandfather on his mother's side owned a haulage business and was a lorry driver. Both sides of the family were part of a tight-knit World War II community that had been galvanised by the destruction wrought by frequent Luftwaffe bombing raids. The whole family had inherited a mantra of hard work and self-sacrifice for the common good. They also believed in pulling oneself up by the bootstraps and making an even better life for their own children.

As a boisterous child playing in his own back garden, Neil has no idea of his family's history. All he is interested in at that moment is the hypnotic spin of the yellow metal spokes on his tricycle. So fast! How do they work?

Neil's pride and joy is this blue and yellow trike, which he's quickly learned to master as he pedals around the back garden, with only minor scrapes and abrasions.

The boy hops off and turns his bike over, trying to understand how it works. He starts spinning the rubber tyres as fast as his little hands can propel them. The teardrop-shaped holes in the metal wheel turn into a blur. He puts his hand on the tyre and watches the wheel slow to a halt. Again, Neil brings it to top speed with his furious spins. He pokes out a finger and, with determination, drives it inside a hole in the spinning disc.

There's a jolt. The tyre stops. Red stuff spurts all over the concrete. A shock and pain he has never felt before. Neil lifts his finger to look and the top bit is missing right down to the first knuckle. A fingertip lies detached on the ground. He howls.

It's a guttural howl, the type that chills a mother's spine. Seconds later his mother is running out of the back door. She finds her boy clutching his hand, covered in blood and crying out over his tears.

'Mummy, I wanted to know why it stops.'

'Pop', an elderly neighbour, hears the commotion from over the fence. He rushes into the back garden, finds the severed fingertip and delicately but purposefully reacquaints it with the finger, as Neil's mum gets ready to take him in the pushchair to the doctor.

*

Deira, Dubai, United Arab Emirates, 2017

The Gold Souk was buzzing. The financial crisis of 2008 was a distant decade-old memory. Neil Jeans and I were walking through the marketplace as spruikers lured us – a pair of typical Aussie tourists – expertly inside their lairs. Like the goldsmiths themselves, they possessed the lines, techniques and charisma that had been fine-tuned and handed down over hundreds of years. Window displays were draped in exquisite gold jewellery. Not just necklaces but entire intricate breastplates; pieces fit for any Middle Eastern princess. The detailing in the gold work was flawless. It was easy to see why historic Dubai is still one of the world's great gold-trading centres.

Earlier in the day we had visited the Old Fort, pockmarked with bullet holes, where the Dubai princes had defended their city from invaders. The territory has a tiny population, just a few million Emiratis, yet it has been a hub for global trade and commerce for hundreds of years. Even to this day, Dubai's trade routes for financial services, gold, shipping containers and other commodities help to power the world's 'just in time' supply chains and financialised economy.

Jeans and I were in Dubai at the request of the government to help educate the business community on how to detect dirty money ahead of an international review. We'd been working with real estate agents, lawyers, accountants and gold refineries to improve their financial crime detection skills. It had been a whirlwind tour through the role played by free-trade zones, gold re-stamping, illicit tobacco, banking and finance, and trade-based money laundering.

As an ex-UK police officer with the National Crime Squad (NCS), Jeans was also well aware that Dubai provides refuge to many kingpins of the underworld. Outlaw motorcycle gangs, drug syndicates and money launderers are increasingly setting themselves up in offshore jurisdictions to sit just out of reach of domestic law enforcement agencies.

As a proud Australian national now, Jeans goes so far as to support the Aussies when they play England in The Ashes (although he maintains that, with two passports, he will always be on the winning side). But when it comes to tackling serious and organised crime, Jeans is a true believer that there are no national borders. The threat is global, intangible and constantly evolving, like a serpentine Hydra that extends its poisonous heads into all of the world's major financial and trade routes. Lopping one head does little to restrain this destructive force.

On this day though, no one would have thought the jovial-faced chap was anything other than an Aussie on a stopover from London. With his checked shirt tucked under his belt, blue cap, jeans and neatly trimmed stubble, he looked every bit a curious tourist. We walked through spice markets, with the alluring aromas that had drawn mariners to these shores for hundreds of years.

We travelled by boat as families traipsed up and down the Dubai Creek, *Khor Dubai*, just as traders have done since the city's birth. The ancient Greeks used to call it the River Zara, coincidentally my own daughter's name.

'Today, Dubai Creek is the main artery for trade in the emirate. On both sides of the creek, there are hundreds of *dhows* of different sizes, loading and unloading a variety of goods,' a plaque in the city's main museum read.

Emiratis only discovered the good fortune that would bring them extreme wealth in the early 1900s. For Dubai it was location more than oil. As a ferociously resourceful nation, Dubai has seized on this opportunity. It has poured the Emirate's relatively modest oil wealth into building one of the planet's greatest trading hubs. It has also built a financial centre from scratch.

Later in the day we tied on the traditional headscarves, joined a caravan of white Toyota Land Cruisers, and took off to the desert. Unlike much of the Arab world, the ever-pragmatic Dubaians were happy to serve us cold beer as we watched dancers twirl like dervishes under a star-speckled night sky.

As he drew from the richly scented tobacco of a traditional hookah pipe, Jeans shared with me the incredible journey that had led him through the world's hidden money markets, across continents and deep into the darkest heart of Australian financial crime.

'My mother always used to say that one of my most overused words as a child was "why",' he recalled with an exhalation of laughter and smoke. His right hand was holding the hookah pipe and revealed a scarred knuckle, where the top segment had been reattached. Even if it has cost him dearly at times, and put him in situations no sane person would choose, Jeans has never recovered from that congenital curiosity.

'The word "why" was never far from my lips. I think that basically underlines my philosophy and, to a certain degree, my psyche. I'm a pretty inquisitive person, never really accepting the status quo. That has evolved into basically somebody who is passionate about joining the dots, solving crimes, cracking puzzles, understanding the "why". It's led me on a career journey that's been far reaching and far more interesting than I could ever have hoped.'

That's an understatement. Jeans is one of a handful of people who have managed to peel back the financial sector's veneers of respectability, going deep inside the world's black money laundromat.

When he'd left school, Jeans wanted to be a copper. He was thwarted by the height restriction at the time. He was just under the mandatory cut-off at 5'6". It was a strange rule that assumed all coppers would be out on the beat, physically imposing their will on feisty ne'er-do-wells and criminals. In truth, Jeans wanted to satisfy his curiosity for crime and adventure as a detective.

Having missed out on the police, Jeans instead became a stockbroker when he left school. He was fortunate that his dad could make some introductions. Jeans soon went off to the City of London to learn the fine art of making money.

In 1991, when Neil turned 26, the UK police modernised and started to recruit from a more diverse range of applicants. Unlike the old days, they now saw diversity as a strength. Jeans left his career in the City, jettisoned eight years of financial markets experience, and took a risk. He would try to make his mark on the City of London afresh – not as a moneyman but as a detective.

Around the same time, the UK was part of a globally coordinated push to criminalise washing and concealing the proceeds of criminal activity. Jeans had no idea then, but his career paths were about to converge. His eight-year City apprenticeship would be the perfect foundation for the emerging tradecraft of financial crime investigations.

Jeans already knew how money moved. He understood the financial markets deeply. Another thing the stockbroking world had taught him was that 'the most valuable commodity in the world is information'. He would soon exploit all of this knowledge in his new role with the UK Police.

*

It's 1994, just three years into his new career as a police officer.

Jeans sits in his musty lair, deep within the bowels of the Southeast Regional Crime Squad's secure facility in Citadel Place, near Vauxhall. His new home is not far from the MI6 building, opposite the UK Houses of Parliament and Big Ben. But he can't see any of that. There's one window, up high, with fluorescent lights illuminating a constant swirl of dust. He's surrounded by wall-to-wall boxes. Two wooden desks are in the centre of the room. One houses a greenscreen computer. The other holds orderly piles of small pink slips — trading receipts for US share purchases that have been seized from businesses based in the Channel Islands specialising in company formation.

The days have blended. It was November when Jeans arrived, one of three new recruits into the UK's top-secret National Financial Crimes Unit. The unit had been set up to target the most sophisticated organised-crime groups operating in the UK and internationally. As a rookie cop with

303

less than three years' experience, Jeans couldn't believe his luck. He had an investigator's natural instinct but even his mentors were surprised when he received a phone call 'inviting him to apply'.

'Well, best you apply then,' was his chief inspector's advice.

On day three, Neil realised why he'd been hand-picked. Stephen Saccoccia had recently been jailed in New York for 660 years. The charges were relatively new: laundering money for the competing Cali and Medellin Colombian drug cartels. One of Saccoccia's ingenious schemes appeared to use offshore shell companies and the US securities markets. As part of a cross-border investigation, the UK's crack financial investigations squad had seized masses of trading receipts from firms that had handled trades for some of the companies linked to Saccoccia's mob. They had boxes and boxes of pink slips bearing what looked like dot-matrix hieroglyphics. The problem was the cops didn't really know what to do with them. They needed someone who understood stockbroking.

Four months later, on a Thursday morning in March, Neil wonders what he's got himself into. He joined the police, in large part, because he loves the camaraderie, the excitement and the banter, and he wants to lock up bad guys. Yet here he is spending 60 hours each week locked, alone, in this bunker. He'd arrested criminals who got better terms. He's logging 12-hour days, filtering trading receipts and punching data into Watson — the brand-new-but-still-clunky police investigative tool.

Neil looks up at the mass of boxes remaining to be opened. In another four months, he'll be able to start running search strings, looking for patterns that his expansive investigative mind hasn't yet noticed.

As he punches the keyboard with his scarred middle finger, Neil has a flashback to that three-year-old boy in Essex. He's still testing ideas, asking 'why' when others have given up, poking things and seeing how they react. And this day, his finger even seems to ache.

Jeans is building pictures in his mind. He's starting to connect the dots on Saccoccia's network, his criminal structure, and narrowing in on the 'why'. It's mind-bending, brain-numbing work, long before computers could automate these mundane tasks with 'graph analytics'. Like all investigators, he's hunting that Eureka moment; the connection that will flash in his intuition like a Piezo spark, igniting a furnace.

But the big breakthrough is proving elusive.

The only way to survive this lonely toil is routine. When the wall clock ticks on to a straight-up 12.30pm, Neil leaves his bunker. He flashes his ID, shares a few jokes with security and trudges out into the dreariness of Vauxhall in March. It's grey and rainy but a sheer joy to be outside. Neil always walks the mile to his sandwich shop, regardless of weather, just to clear some of the data from his head. A boot-powered internal reboot.

He wanders past the same dilapidated council flats, which conceal so many sad stories, on to his favourite sandwich bar. The lady behind the counter greets him with a perfunctory, 'Coronation chicken bap?'

'Yes thanks, just for something completely different,' he replies. In his civilian work clothes, the counter lady has no idea this friendly, wickedly humorous man of 29 years is trying to unravel one of the global cocaine trade's largest and most complex international laundromats.

Neil leaves with his bap, taking the long route past the newsagent, despite the rain. In massive bold type, an A-frame advertises the breaking news from the *Evening Standard*.

'Lord Pilkington defrauded by stockbrokers.'

Ha! Happens to the best of them, he muses, and fumbles for the 25p rattling loose in his pocket.

Back in the lair, Neil rifles through the paper in the correct order. First the back page, the football, then onto the cover story.

The lead story is lurid. It's awash with the tabloid Schadenfreude of Lord Pilkington, a leading industrialist and former owner of Pilkington Glass, falling victim to the crooked penny stock spruikers on Wall Street. Neil reads the narrow newspaper columns with amazement. For a moment he thinks he's reading his own pink slips. The brokers, the companies, the trades. It's all the same names.

These are the moments of sweet serendipity Neil will have many times throughout his career. Right place, right time. He drops his bap on the table, grabs the newspaper and marches into his boss Gordon's office. A couple of knocks and straight in.

Neil starts to detonate a bombshell. Those boxes full of receipts are the laundering side of the world's biggest penny stock fraud, he suspects, which in turn is the last stage of Saccoccia's epic drug cartel laundering operation. The penny stock fraud is the cherry next to the pie, for criminals who just can't resist.

Gordon is gobsmacked by this lead. It's the stroke of luck every major investigation needs. He calls Clark Abrahams, a contact at the US Securities and Exchanges Commission

306

in New York. Neil can hear the friendly American's accent through the tinny transatlantic phone line. Gordon asks for a contact in the Office of the New York District Attorney, which was leading the investigation into the stockbrokers who defrauded Lord Pilkington.

The next day Neil's head is still swimming. Is this real? Will they call? What if he has it all wrong?

First thing New York time, Friday morning, Gordon's phone rings. He picks it up and he and Neil hear the voice of John Moscow for the first time. Moscow is already a legend in the financial crime investigation community as the Manhattan assistant DA who took down Bank of Credit and Commerce International, the Luxembourg-based bank 75 per cent owned by the ruler of Abu Dhabi, for laundering money for figures such as Saddam Hussein, Manuel Noriega, Hussain Muhammad Ershad, Samuel Doe, and for criminal organisations such as the Colombian Medellin Cartel.

By 4 pm that afternoon they have launched a joint investigation with the New York DA's Office. Neil and Gordon's airline tickets for Monday morning have been issued.

The boy from Essex has stuck his finger into a big one this time. A real big one. He's going to New York.

*

As we watched dancers swirl in the Dubai desert, I was captivated by this tale of serendipity, adventure. The desert air was warm, invigorating, and scented with apple tobacco. As I ordered another beer, Neil Jeans unravelled the next three years of his career with the organisation that evolved into the UK's National Crime

Agency (NCA). His hunch about Saccoccia's links to the Wall Street penny stock frauds had turned out to be spot on. Gordon, the head of the unit, became his investigative partner working between London and New York. Jeans had been on cloud nine.

As US prosecutors had already established, Saccoccia's ingenious laundering scheme had included ramping worthless 'pink slip' stocks through off-market trading in the 45 days before the companies went public. These off-market trades created a smokescreen that allowed drug cartels to settle their debts, buying and selling each other worthless scrip hundreds of times via offshore accounts. It was criminal money laundering in plain sight. The entire market for these initial public offerings was artificial. Even the initial seed capital for the companies was Colombian drug money.

The joint UK–US investigation found that these criminal groups couldn't resist making even more dirty money on the launder. Rather than letting the stock value slowly return to zero, they would engage the wolves of Wall Street to sell the overpriced stocks via 'boiler rooms' to naive elderly retirees.

'Because of my experience as a stockbroker I got the job of debriefing all the stockbrokers. I was handling the cooperating witnesses as informants. These were the people who were doing the pumps and dumps for the laundering operation. They were on the inside and most of them were linked to Russian or Italian mafia,' Jeans recalls.

Some of the cooperating witnesses died before they could make it to court – one of the downsides of breaking the underworld's *omerta*.

'The stockbrokers were ultimately prosecuted for their pump-and-dump schemes. We had 47 victims who were brought in as witnesses. These were retirees who had lost their homes, their life savings,' Jeans remembers.

Moscow was tasked with questioning the devastated victims in court. Most of them were elderly, trusting, salt-of-the earth Americans. Jeans recalls that Moscow always opened his line of questioning the same way.

'Tell me, sir, what theatre of war did you fight in during World War II?'

By the end of the three-year investigation, and the prosecutions, Jeans was exhausted but exhilarated. He had been given a crash course in the global black money laundromat, he had seen first-hand the inner workings of organised crime, he'd won over informants and lost others to murder, he had tracked incalculable sums of money and witnessed the carnage it so often leaves behind.

He had seen first-hand that white-collar crime isn't clean. It destroys lives of the innocent and the vulnerable.

It was an experience that had already changed the course of Neil's life. He was in on the ground floor of the anti-money-laundering game. This journey would eventually lead him to Melbourne, Australia, where he would play a critical role in two cases that would rock the foundations of the cosy banking establishment.

Few people were aware of it, as the civil cases had never made it to court, but Jeans had been a crucial part of the AUSTRAC alliance. He'd played a critical role in prosecuting two of the largest banks in Australia, leading to the largest fines in Australian corporate history and a new corporate culture. He had been the expert witness in both the CBA and Westpac cases, working closely with Sonja Marsic and her small team of lawyers.

While Marsic was an expert in law, she had needed a Neil Jeans to help her decode the banking and criminal underworld's darkest secrets and to apply his formidable skills to building their case.

After a career slaying some of the criminal underworld's giants, however, Jeans wasn't ready to give up. He'd helped to bring Australia's two largest financial institutions to heel. Next he would set his eyes upon on a new target: the gatekeepers behind the great Australian property Ponzi scheme. These were the same types of gatekeepers that had been involved in the crooked share trading and money laundering undertaken by Saccoccia and his associates three decades earlier in New York.

Neil Jeans's journey to the dark heart of financial crime had come full circle.

THIRTY-SIX

Inquiring Minds

By late 2019, no one in Australia could pretend the country didn't have a dirty money problem. A slew of media reports on international laundering made it clear that Australia's addiction to dirty money was more than an economic, political and social problem. It was also infiltrating and undermining national security. Behind the scenes, the potential for illicit fund flows to be used to manipulate or undermine the Aussie economy had become a top-tier concern in Canberra. Senior intelligence figures were warning that Australia's strong economic relationship with China, for example, could influence the handling of issues such as freedom of navigation in the South China Sea or Taiwanese independence.

In 2020, a 'compromise' of senators (as in, the collective noun) ordered an Inquiry into Foreign Investment Proposals. This was an opportunity to finally blow the edifice of economic respectability to smithereens. The report highlighted the vulnerabilities that Australia had opened up through its financial crime failures. One of the topics for the review was the extent to which foreign investment could be used to facilitate money laundering. The review was also exploring the gaps that had arisen between agencies such as the AFP, AUSTRAC and the Foreign Investment Review Board (FIRB).

The AFP told a hearing in Canberra that it had been working with counterparts in other countries, including China, to target illicit funds. It was also working closely with AUSTRAC to detect illicit money flows. This work had been hampered, continually, by the lack of intelligence from non-financial businesses and professions.

Peter Whish-Wilson, Greens senator for Tasmania, said that Australia's policy stalemate on the long-promised 'Tranche 2' laws meant that laundered funds could be used as a tool of foreign political influence in Australia.

Whish-Wilson said that while Australia dithered, New Zealand had pushed ahead with both phases of its AML regime. It had leapfrogged Australia and was regulating lawyers, accountants and real estate agents in addition to 'phase 1' businesses such as banks, casinos and insurers.

Organisations ranging from the AFP to the Uniting Church told the senators that Australia had become an attractive transit point and destination for dirty loot. This, in turn, was challenging the country's democratic institutions.

Chris Collett, AUSTRAC's deputy chief executive, told the inquiry that the agency was working closely with partners through the Fintel Alliance and other channels to tackle offshore money-laundering threats. Agencies such as AUSTRAC are barred from commenting on government policy decisions, so Collett chose his words carefully on Tranche 2.

'From an intelligence point of view, any intelligence officer will always value more data. But that has to be weighed up against, for want of a better term, a cost-benefit issue. These matters involve regulatory burdens for the sectors involved. It's certainly important that any decision the government may make is done in collaboration and consultation with industry and it weighs up those competing issues,' Collett said.

Whish-Wilson told the inquiry that the FATF had placed Australia on an enhanced follow-up program over its failure to pass laws to cover gatekeeper professions.

'I remember Senator Brandis saying in 2016 that it was a priority for the government and we're still waiting. I'm particularly interested in why they're important. The Australian Criminal Intelligence Commission (ACIC) reported in 2017 that the most common professions exploited by organised crime included lawyers, accountants and real estate agents and brokers,' Whish-Wilson said.

Collett said he agreed with the ACIC's perspective that those professions could be exploited by serious and organised criminals. The AUSTRAC official said the agency did not have a 'specific number' on the amount of money that is laundered through real estate in Australia every year, as it could not access that data under the current laws.

The inquiry heard the federal Treasury had also ramped up its investigations into foreign property purchases amid a heightened geopolitical risk climate. Enquiries from Treasury and the Foreign Investment Review Board (FIRB) for AUSTRAC assistance on laundering cases involving foreign property purchases had surged by 800 per cent, the inquiry heard.

In some cases the agency was replying with a 'nil response'. This meant it did not hold any intelligence on the parties to those suspicious property transactions.

The Uniting Church said these failures were a national disgrace.

'Such businesses should have a duty not to be a party to or facilitate any transactions where there is an obvious risk of money laundering or where the funds involved are likely to be the proceeds of crime. The businesses that should be captured in the amendments include real estate agents concerning the buying and selling of property, lawyers, accountants, notaries and company service providers,' the Church said in a submission to the inquiry.

'There is a significant risk of money laundering through real estate professionals that have set up Chinese-based offices to attract Chinese investment into Australian property if the real estate businesses in question do not have significant anti-money-laundering processes in place,' the Church said.

*

In a rare splash of literary flamboyance, the Senate's report was titled 'Greenfields, cash cows and the regulation of foreign investment in Australia'. The inquiry did not make any recommendations, however, to limit the flow of foreign criminal funds into Australia. This was despite the report acknowledging that laundered funds were 'difficult to identify'. In one case discussed in the report, Operation Gethen, the AFP worked on a tip-off from the Chinese police to seize $17.3 million in the proceeds of a mainland real estate and bank loan fraud. The funds were washed in Australia through property purchases. This included six properties in Melbourne and more than 3,000 acres of premium coastal farmland in Musselroe Bay on Tasmania's north-eastern coast.

'The AFP told the committee some foreign companies operate with a sophisticated veneer and it is difficult to identify wrongdoing,' the report said. 'No alarm bells would have been ringing.'

Stefan Jerga, who led the AFP's criminal asset confiscation team, put it this way: 'In the real estate context, unless somebody is bold enough to put a pile of cash on your desk and say, "I want to buy the property with cash," a lot of other indicators might not be that obvious.'

The absence of any effort to address the elephant in the room left many of the participants gobsmacked. Whish-Wilson and the Greens were livid. They took the view that Labor and the Liberals had baulked at a historic opportunity to close the Australian dirty money sluice gates.

The Greens senator insisted on including his additional comments at the back of the report, under the banner 'Still in the dark'. The inquiry was originally established under a motion from Senator Whish-Wilson and he felt it had missed its mark, spectacularly.

'We should stop pussyfooting around,' he wrote. 'Australia has become a hot-spot for illicit capital, and money laundering through real estate in particular.'

Whish-Wilson castigated the Senate for overlooking the fact that seizures of criminal property, such as the dairy farm in Musselroe Bay, had only been possible following a complaint from the Chinese MPS. To make matters worse, when the Musselroe Bay farm was seized, it had a development approval for an 18-hole golf course, a resort, 40 villas, 200 units and 100 rooms. This was a profound insight into the potential for property development to wash dirty foreign funds – not just in the purchase stage but also through subsequent development and construction work.

'So lax is Australia's AML/CTF framework that, as the inquiry heard, the action taken by the AFP to seize assets in relation to the Musselroe Bay development only occurs following a tip-off from Chinese authorities. We're literally dependent on the host country police telling us if their citizens are using Australian real estate to wash hot money,' he wrote in one scathing passage.

'For Australia's foreign investment approval process to have any integrity, Australia's AML/CTF framework must be strengthened. A failure to do so, coupled with ongoing secrecy around foreign investment approvals, will foster an environment where illegal activity is tolerated and where corruption can flourish.'

*

In June 2021, a draft of the Senate report on foreign ownership and illicit money was circulating in Canberra. Some of the senators were deeply disappointed by the failure to call out Australia's secret addiction to dirty lucre, regardless of where it originated. Yet again, it seemed as though Australia was happy to advertise itself as an equal-opportunity laundromat for the world's most wretched financial refuse. It was happy to take the tired, tempest-tossed bags of money that crossed the wide brown land looking for a sympathetic home – or at least a place to rest, before continuing its journey through the world's black money markets.

Far from closing the sluice gates, Australia was lifting a lamp beside the Lucky Laundry's golden door.

By late June, Deborah O'Neill had had enough. Senator O'Neill was known around Parliament as a lady of principle, a tough operator, and someone who was willing to stand up when integrity was on the line. Even if this meant standing up to her own party's factions. Before joining politics, she'd been a life-long educator, including posts as a high school teacher and uni lecturer. On top of these attributes, O'Neill had a voracious appetite for learning herself. Over a decade in politics she'd developed a thorough understanding of the arcane world of money and its serpentine ability to tickle the dirtiest armpits of power.

In March 2020, for example, Senator O'Neill was the only politician brave enough to call a Senate inquiry into the role of the powerful 'big four' auditing firms, following a spate of corporate collapses. The inherent conflicts when a single organisation provided accounting, consulting and auditing services – to the same clients – was something that no one had previously been willing to touch.

On June 22, 2021, Senator O'Neill convinced Labor to join forces with the Greens and independent crossbenchers in demanding a parliamentary inquiry into the country's anti-money-laundering regime. The surprise announcement came on the back of strong lobbying from Greens Senator Nick McKim, who was calling for a hard deadline for the passage of the 15-year-old Tranche 2 law reforms.

Senator O'Neill said she had drafted the terms-of-inquiry broadly enough to examine 'what Australia needs to do so we are no longer one of the world's money-laundering weak links'.

Dr Daniel Mulino, a Labor MP, said that since 2013, the Coalition government had repeatedly missed the deadlines in its own AML/CTF reform timetable.

'Strengthening Australia's AML/CTF laws and implementing Tranche 2 legislation has apparently been this government's policy since it was elected, but we've seen no action. While other countries have strengthened their AML/CTF defences, the government's inaction has left the door open for illicit capital to flood into Australia,' Mulino said

On the night before the vote, Labor and the Greens were still unsure whether they had the numbers. They needed to court at least two of the crossbenchers.

Rex Patrick, independent senator for South Australia, threw his chips on the table. 'This is an area that concerns me and needs to be examined in detail. I will be supporting the move for an inquiry,' he told me that evening.

It was touch and go. Then, on the morning of the vote, Pauline Hanson's One Nation joined the fray, giving the inquiry a genuinely rare moment of cross-spectrum political support. They had drawn votes from the hard left to the hard right; they had the numbers. With the inquiry now guaranteed, the Coalition government also threw its support behind a review. The inquiry was referred to the Senate Standing Committee on Legal and Constitutional Affairs, with Labor Senator Kim Carr as chair.

Was this the moment Australia needed to finally tackle the national addiction to dirty money?

*

On 9 November, 2021, the inquiry opened for two days of public hearings. In Canberra, the first session featured anti-money-laundering stalwarts Neil Jeans, Paddy Oliver and financial crime software entrepreneur Anthony Quinn. In the middle of a pandemic they made their way to Canberra for the hearings. They weren't there to pull any punches.

Jeans, who had worked tirelessly as the expert witness in the Commonwealth Bank and Westpac cases, laid it all on the line.

'It's my experience from my time in law enforcement that businesses within the [legal, accounting and real estate] sectors can be used – either unwittingly or wittingly – to launder the proceeds of transnational organised crime,' he told the assembled senators.

'Australia is increasingly considered a laggard in the area of AML/CTF and consequently it's perceived as an attractive haven for criminal proceeds.'

Senator O'Neill pounced: 'You indicated that 195 countries have been able to get Tranche 2 done. Australia is one of five that have been increasingly considered a laggard, Mr Jeans, and, by failure to implement Tranche 2 are attractive to organised crime?'

'That's correct,' Jeans responded. 'We are really one of three countries that have failed to take action out of the 177 [countries] that have been assessed ... those are Australia, Haiti and Madagascar. One thing they have in common is they're all islands, but I think we're the biggest island.'

Even in the gravity of a Senate hearing, Jeans couldn't contain his penchant for the mischievous one-liner.

Senator O'Neill smiled. She had clearly been doing her homework and appreciated the jibe. 'The reality is there's work to be done and it isn't being done. That not only puts us at risk in terms of the movement of money, being a honeypot for organised crime and financial crime more broadly, but it puts us at risk of going onto the greylist.'

Jeans explained to the Senate the implications of being greylisted by the influential FATF. This was the ignoble listing that had cost Pakistan's struggling economy US$38 billion over a 13-year period. He warned that Australia was naive to think it couldn't happen here.

'The greylist is basically a list of increased monitoring. As a data point for the committee, Turkey was put on the greylist a couple of weeks ago. Turkey is also a full member of the FATF. It's one of only two members of the full members of the FATF that have been put on the greylist — the other one being Iceland,' he said.

Iceland was removed quickly after the government took immediate action as they 'understood the economic impacts of being put on the greylist'.

'What the greylist says is that other countries should have regard to the weaknesses in a particular country's regime and make sure those risks are appropriately mitigated. They don't necessarily recommend enhanced due diligence on everything, but what we see by definition is that this could have impacts on the financial institutions being able to operate internationally, because they would be required to be subject to more scrutiny on a transaction-by-transaction basis. There could also be an impact in relation to access to capital markets. So this has a real-world economic potential impact,' Jeans said.

Senator O'Neill's forensic line of questioning was forcing Australian politicians of all persuasions to see the pachyderm in the parliament. The country could not act as a global black money wash-house with impunity. There were real-world economic costs, in addition to the social, political and cultural price.

The penny was dropping. 'In terms of financial access and Australia's role as a significant financial hub for the Asia-Pacific, could you reflect on what would happen to our status if we end up on the greylist, in terms of our regional capacity to play?' Senator O'Neill coaxed.

'Again, it would be the same. Singapore, Hong Kong and Indonesia are also members of the FATF, so they would have to take notice of any greylisting. That would ultimately impact the ability of Australia to do business in those countries, including China, Japan and other countries, and New Zealand as well. The FATF greylist is not the only greylist. The EU have their own separate greylist,' Jeans explained.

When Senator Nick McKim took the microphone, he seemed angry at Australia's failure to live up to the values it espouses on the world stage: transparency, credibility, integrity.

'Is it your argument that Australia's actually more attractive to people who want to clean dirty money because we're such a laggard in international terms and because we are – along with Haiti and Madagascar – one of only three countries that's not moving significantly, or have already moved, in that area? Is that your evidence?' Senator McKim asked.

'That is my evidence, yes,' Jeans said.

*

Later in the day, the Senate heard from Serena Lilywhite, chief executive of Transparency International (TI) in Australia. Lilywhite had been campaigning for years to plug the loopholes that allow kleptocrats to wash their ill-gotten gains in Australia with impunity, while lawyers, accountants and real estate agents take their cut and feign ignorance.

'Money laundering is not a faceless crime. I request the committee give this consideration. It has devastating impacts both in Australia and overseas, and it can reasonably be argued it is driving up property prices in Australia and locking many Australians out of owning their own home,' Lilywhite said.

'Money laundering into Australia's property market is coming from countries far and wide – from Sudan, China, Malaysia, PNG and Russia, among others. It also shows that money laundering is linked to a variety of people – Sudanese generals, Malaysian bankers, PNG's political elite and Chinese high rollers through casinos and property.'

Lilywhite floored the Senate with examples of how easy it is to procure companies, trusts and even nominee directors with 'an Australian-sounding name' to help foreign criminals and kleptocrats to conceal and secure their wealth. This is not money that's flaunted and hung out for show; it's money that requires the highest level of discretion.

'There are current loopholes in our system that allow for non-licensed third-party providers to actually sell nominee director or shareholder services. That effectively hides the real identities and the ultimate beneficiaries. It allows for these sorts of opaque business structures to flourish,' Lilywhite said.

The Senate was left with no illusions that money laundering had become as Australian as meat pies, white zinc, and power chords screaming from a dirty Marshall amplifier.

'It sounds like AC/DC might have had it right,' Senator O'Neill quipped, referring to the band's 1976 album title. 'It sounds like you can do dirty deeds very cheaply in Australia at the moment. A $2 company and off you go; no one will know what's going on.'

As if to ram home the Senate inquiry's importance, Lilywhite was in the middle of selling her own family's home. The property was going to auction that weekend, a mere four days' time. Even the head of TI in Australia had a personal story to tell about skulduggery in the booming Aussie property market.

'I was surprised to learn that there was an expression of interest in our family home from a professional services firm based in Sydney,' she explained. 'It has advised our real estate agent that it's acting on behalf of a high-net-worth individual based overseas. You can imagine what I thought when I heard that.'

If the Senate inquiry into money laundering needed a ray of sunshine – of hope – there it was. Across two days of hearings, ordinary Aussies were telling their politicians – directly – that they demanded change. They made it clear that Australia could do much, much better in the globally coordinated fight against financial crime. That might come with some economic costs, but continued inaction would be far more expensive.

Although she had no idea where the funds came from for her potential overseas purchaser, Serena Lilywhite did not want to sell her cherished family home to potential criminals or corrupt foreign politicians, regardless of the golden egg that goose might lay.

You can rest assured that, on this occasion at least, the foreign property bidder represented by a slick professional services firm did not get lucky at auction. For once, Australia's jewels were not available to the highest bidder, with a wink and a nod, and no questions asked.

THIRTY-SEVEN

The Heart of the Matter

North Melbourne, 1968

'Paul, can you grab me that rag over there,' says Branko Jevtovic. Paul looks up at his father, wiry and lean, dusting his hands, with veins bulging like a footballer's forearms. The rich sting of paint thinner hangs in the air. Branko's white overalls are covered in dust and paint. Behind him, a car shines proudly, with a new lease of life — as flawless as the day it rolled off the Melbourne production line.

'Good as new, Tata!' Paul says. Paul is only nine years old but has already inherited his tat's first-generation Aussie work ethic. PJ knows more about panel-beating than most of the shop's apprentices, or so his tata likes to tell his friends.

After cleaning his hands, Branko ruffles Paul's mop of dark hair — the blessing of a Serbian and Greek bloodline. Branko is only 32 but he's now been away from his country of birth for more than half of his young life. The horrors of war, the marching menace of communism, the desperation and daily

324

worry of poverty. It all seems like an ocean, a hemisphere and another lifetime away.

Whenever he gets the chance, Branko reminds his son how fortunate they are that, as a kid just seven years older than Paul is today, he happened to stand in the immigration queue — all alone — that led to the Lucky Country.

As they wash down, Paul is bursting with energy. For a sports-mad kid, washdown triggers a Pavlovian response. He can already smell the beaten grass, hear the whistle, feel the thump of leather boot hitting leather ball.

'Can we go over the road, Tata?' he asks, eyes pleading.

'Sure, son, why not? Let's do that. We can't be long. Your mother will have dinner ready,' Branko says.

The late-afternoon traffic is rolling down Ardern Street. Paul loves it when someone walks him across the busy road to North Melbourne Football Club — the home of the 'Shinboners'. Training days are the best. There's no fence or barricade to separate him from his heroes, just the energy and drama of the game up close.

As they weave through the traffic, Paul peers through the wooden stands. A football flies through the air and is plucked from its trajectory by a magic-handed goalie. The muffled voice of a coach, shouting encouragement from the sidelines, draws him in like a magnet.

'What's he saying?' Paul wonders, listening intently over the Melbourne afternoon rush hour, as he bolts through a gap in the cars.

'Slow down!' Branko cries.

But it's too late. Paul has already clambered up the wooden stands and is watching dark-haired men of European ancestry fight wars of immense consequence on the turf at this hallowed ground.

*

Paul Jevtovic's late mother, Elizabeth, had arrived in Australia from wartorn Europe when she was just two years old. The good life, here in Australia, was all she knew. At 16 she fell in love and married the proud, handsome, hard-working Serbian-speaking Branko Jevtovic. He was determined, stoic, brave and adventurous. He told amazing stories.

When the tyranny of communism swept through Eastern Europe, Branko was still a boy. But he already knew he couldn't stay in Yugoslavia. At 16 he joined a group of men and left behind his entire family, and his home in Kragujevac. Branko had no idea where he was headed, or that he wouldn't be able to return to his birthland in Serbia for three decades. His group travelled to Austria where they had heard of an emigration camp. Once safe there, these hopeful boys found themselves standing in a queue as their destiny was determined with the whimsy of a chook raffle.

'Australia.'

The word was strange. Like Austria but more exciting, he thought. Full of hope. Young Branko now had a whole new language to learn: Engleski.

As soon as he arrived in Australia, Branko needed money, a job. He would find work through a compassionate Aussie who owned a panel-beating shop. The Yugoslavian teenager's career, like his new nationality, would be delivered by the hand of fate.

Life was fragile and Branko didn't have time to waste. He was destined to fall in love and become a father at 21.

Before the whirlwind romance had passed, the young couple had been delivered a miracle: a beautiful baby boy. He was the first of the Jevtovic bloodline to be born as an Aussie. They gave him the Biblical name of Paul, which would soon prove fitting. Paul's magnetic personality, sense of adventure and irrepressible sense of justice didn't take long to surface.

As a kid who was different, in 1960s Australia, Paul's parents thought he would need this natural charisma. They needn't have worried. Six years later, it was his first day of school. Nerves mixed with wonder. His young parents could afford a public school uniform but not the shoes just yet.

Never mind. His great-grandmother, Nana, had also immigrated to Australia – and she too had small feet. Paul's chest swelled with pride as his beautiful young mother Elizabeth, just 22 years old now, tied the laces on his new leather shoes. He was old enough to be walking in his great-grandmother's boots. Amazing! And off he skipped to his first day at school.

Before he knew it, Paul would have a whole new group of mates. Kids who, like him, loved every sport you could list. Swimming, Aussie rules, athletics, football, cricket. In Australia, there was a game for every season.

As if he needed it, young Paul now had two more reasons to love his home in Australia. He had his first real mates. He had sport. And to top things off, he had the coolest pair of leather shoes in the whole class.

*

There would be many times in his career when Paul would need the skills he learned on that grass paddock, in a team, ferociously hunting a leather ball as though it were a criminal gang. He would also need the tenacity, work ethic and attention to detail he learned in his dad's panel-beating shop. And there would be something else that would never leave him: the memory of how it felt to be dressed in those third-hand leather shoes. No matter how tough things got, no matter how great the challenge, that memory would ground him and give him courage. After all, he was walking in the footsteps of a long line of survivors.

Without doubt the most publicly visible of these times would be the day he decided that enough was enough. The day he determined that a rogue Australian banking giant had been flagrantly ignoring the criminality in its midst. It had shredded its social licence. It had betrayed Australia's trust. And it needed to be brought to heel.

That act of courage, and principle, would change the course of Australian corporate history.

'Our way of life is very, very special,' Paul Jevtovic told me as he left AUSTRAC in 2017. 'We live in the greatest country in the world. I come from a migrant family that came to this country, and this country has given my family a life and so many families a wonderful life. My public service has been driven by that. We can't just keep taking from this country – we have to give back.'

Jevtovic believes Australia is fighting a war against forces that want to undermine the key pillars of our way of life: freedom, democracy, the rule of law, political integrity, safety, diversity and mutual respect. For this son of Serbian immigrants, this work is not a job but a calling.

When he took on the role of chief executive at AUSTRAC in November 2014, the life-long organised-crime fighter had a clear vision and a clear mission. He was also fortunate to have a clear mandate from the government: to transform the country's financial intelligence infrastructure.

It was an ambitious quest. And to achieve this goal, he knew, he would need to go well beyond his agency's headcount. 'We're at our best when we're in partnerships, when we're bringing to the table that diversity of skills and thinking and experience. That's when we are at our strongest,' he told me, with a precision that suggested he'd delivered this message once or twice before. And he had. During a 2015 roundtable with the country's biggest reporting entities, he had noted, 'We don't want to have 300 people at AUSTRAC working to keep Australians safe. We need to have 14,000 reporting entities working with us. We need 26 million Australians to be supporting this work. We want to partner with you. And we will trust you, until you give us reason not to.'

This was classic Paul Jevtovic, according to those who have worked closely with him over his four decades in the public sphere. As a leader, he has an incredible ability to inspire and motivate his teams. But he also has clear boundaries, and betrayal of the trust he places in his partners is not looked kindly upon by a man whose life's work – and at times even his life – has depended on teamwork. More than one Australian-listed company's board has discovered this the hard way, along with the financial consequences of breaching AUSTRAC's trust.

Another of Paul's defining beliefs at the Australian Crime Commission (ACC) and AUSTRAC was that these agencies needed the support of their stakeholders – in government, business and the public in general. This required those agencies to strive for excellence and, in AUSTRAC's case, to become much more transparent.

'For most government departments, their future is assured. If something goes wrong they'll still be here tomorrow. At the ACC that was never the case. It had to fight for its existence,' says Dr Maria Milosavljevic, an expert in technology, big data and AI, and one of the people who worked for Jevtovic. 'Paul's rationale was that the only way the ACC could ensure its existence was to provide intelligence that nobody else could deliver. He took that view to AUSTRAC.'

Jevtovic's willingness to try different things – often daring things – was forged in the furnace of his difficult work in law enforcement. His view was that government agencies needed to take calculated risks in response to unprecedented threats, particularly in the area of fighting organised crime and violent extremism.

'One of his real passions was for investigating money laundering,' says John Lawler, former head of the ACC. 'He led some of the cash money-laundering projects that the Crime Commission got involved in. That work had stunning results in relation to the cash seizures.'

Paul Jevtovic's incredible story exemplifies what makes Australia great. It is the story of how one person from humble origins can change the course of history, simply by standing up for what they believe.

But as Paul is the first to say, this was not his story. He was simply fortunate to land – through the blessings of circumstance – in the right place at the right time. Sure, he made a decision of conscience, and that decision somehow sparked a wildfire. But it was his humility and integrity that drew others to his cause. He was supported in his career by other great women and men. People the likes of John Lawler and Maria Milosavljevic. He was part of a team within government that utterly abhorred corruption, an agency that cared deeply about its work and a small clique across the business community who wanted to join the fight against organised crime. He was an ambassador for trying to do what's right.

Jevtovic's experience isn't the archetypal story of 'one good cop' against a crooked system. It is the story of every single good cop who worked, day in, day out, to uphold one of the greatest free and liberal democracies the world has ever seen. His is not a story of law. It is a story of justice.

Like his father, Branko, and mother, Elizabeth, Paul embraced the life and opportunities Australia offered. And this great southern land, in turn, embraced Paul. His experience is not about the power of one but the power of many.

We Gotta Carry Each Other

Ho Chi Minh City, Vietnam, August 2019

For the pair of us, both seasoned travellers, this is going to be our first ever night in Vietnam's electric business capital. It's 7 pm on Saturday and we're just two wide-eyed Aussie tourists clinging to the back of mopeds, burning through the neon blur of what was once Saigon. The city, its energy and its people already have us hooked.

On Monday morning, Warren Lysaght and I will arrive at the Sheraton, in immaculately pressed suits, to help deliver a three-day training session on counter-narcotics investigations. The program is being delivered by the US Department of Justice's Office of Overseas Prosecutorial Development, Assistance and Training team as part of their international outreach and capacity-building program. We're told this is the first time a DOJ program has been delivered in Vietnam, which makes the experience extra special.

Warren is here to talk about laundering from a police perspective, how he's followed the money across international

332

borders to dismantle drug-trafficking syndicates. Although he helped lead the Strike Force Bugam job from Australia, busting open a Vietnamese–Australian crime syndicate, this is the first time he's had an opportunity to make the trip across to Vietnam itself. I'm here to talk about public–private financial crimefighting partnerships, bringing together the might of industry and government for a common cause, and the use of cutting-edge technology in narcotics investigations.

We're both ecstatic to finally be in 'HCMC' and are gearing up for an intense week. On Monday, the Vietnamese police will arrive in pristine army-green uniforms with red-and-gold-barred epaulettes. Their English will be only slightly better than our grasp of Vietnamese. That is, slightly more than non-existent. But with the help of a multilingual translation team, an incredible week of friendship and skill sharing is destined to follow.

Right now, though? Well, it's still Saturday night in a sizzling new city. We have some exploring to do. Back at the hotel, our American hosts laughed at our curiosity. Aussies are known around the world as intrepid travellers; we have a reputation to uphold. There's no way we're going to let our countryfolk down and sit in the Sheraton lobby, missing an opportunity to experience this city at night. We would, we promised our hosts, endeavour not to have a run-in with one of the delegates at next week's event. That could prove awkward.

Now, sitting on the back of mopeds, with our lives in the hands of someone we've just met on Grab, Vietnam's ride hailing service, the traffic seems chaotic. After a few near misses that are in fact just hard-right turns, we settle in. The mass of motorbikes starts to feel almost organic. The riders merge together like blood cells down an artery, pulsing red, slowing and then surging, with scant regard for the dumb inefficiency of traffic lights. Sirens, horns, movement, exotic smells coming from street carts. This neon-lit city feels like an unfathomably complex movie set — a theatre with so many stories to unfurl, all competing for our attention.

The drivers drop us in District 1, in an area we're assured is the epicentre of epicureanism. A city of nine million is going to be difficult for two blow-ins to navigate. But we have one small thing working in our favour. One of Warren's Vietnamese-born colleagues from Strike Force Bugam has given him the 'List'. These are off-the-main-road places, down alleys, that offer the best taste of Vietnamese street food. Our mission is pretty straightforward: on this first night, we won't get too ambitious. All we aim to find is the best bowl of pho this city has to offer.

Walking down alley after alley, I'm starting to doubt either Warren's mate's street cred, or his own navigation skills. Besides, who can trust a Cupertino-made mobile phone map in the noodle-like chaos of central Ho Chi Minh City's alleyways? We pass small groups set up on the side of the road, laughing, drinking, eating street fare.

Bugger the List, I think. We're 6800 kilometres from Sydney. That's close enough. The locals can lead us from here.

In front of us, a dozen Saigonese are perched around a knee-high wooden table, seated on blue plastic footstools, centimetres from the sporadic traffic. Three things catch my eye: their array of Vietnamese culinary delights, their laughter and a large PA speaker with a microphone resting just behind them. These people will know what's up. In the middle —

commanding the audience with heroic gesticulations — is an ageless man in a white shirt and black beret. He's more portly than the average Vietnamese, strongly built, and carries an air of effortless authority.

'This guy must be either a muso or a retired Viet Cong colonel,' I whisper to Warren. 'Either way, he'll know where to get good tucker.'

I stop, smile and try to communicate with the group, ashamed to be so bereft of local language skills. Gesturing pathetically, we mime a charade of chowing down on a bowl of steaming noodles, topped with crushed nuts and a sprig of mint.

The group look at these two hopeless Aussies, lost in the backstreets of HCMC and fall apart laughing. Pity over this woeful mime performance, it must be said, has probably helped us. A few of the group know some English and stand up to help these aimless fools in a foreign city. The next thing we know, two more blue stools have emerged from the dark, two beer tops go spinning through the air, and we're settling down in the midst of a Saturday-night family gathering.

How magical is travel? How kind is the human family? How unbelievable is Lady Luck? As brazen as our dreams are, she is about to deliver us what we've come for: HCMC's finest pho, in the company of our 12 oldest Vietnamese friends.

Generic Android phones, with Google Translate, appear from pockets to provide sense to our discussion. We show them on digital maps where we hail from and they embrace us like family. Questions in broken English fly as fast as ping pong balls across the table. A warm wind caresses my neck as each scooter zips past.

More food arrives. As a visitor, this generosity is embarrassing. They refuse a handful of dong, feigning deep insult at the gesture. The only thing I can do is race into the small shop next door and ask for more Bia Saigon and cigarettes than I can carry in a single trip. The table roars as more sustenance arrives. Ice appears in a plastic bucket. There's clearly a shared language between Vietnam and Australia. And I suspect it involves Eskies. I can't help but fog up at the thought of all those young Aussies, less than half my age, arriving here 50 years earlier for the business of war. If only they'd been able to break bao buns, laugh and drink ice-cold beer with their Vietnamese comrades.

A street-cart vendor walks past with racks of dried squid. He's accosted by the group and runs his product through a hand-driven roller. The table cracks up as we choke on the chewy, pungent substrate. Bubble gum dipped in fish sauce? It's both an acquired taste and an acquired skill to masticate, but we get there.

I point to the PA speaker and strum an air guitar, asking if they're musicians — another of the great international languages. Within seconds, thin wire cables with alligator clips emerge from a scooter battery and are hooked up to an inverter. Green lights fire up on the amp and then 200 watts of Vietnamese pop music begins blaring down the alleyway. The colonel's wife picks up a wireless microphone, clicks the switch with a ruby red fingernail, brings up a backing track on YouTube, and commences to belt out a stunning rendition of an unnamed Vietnamese hit. As a life-long musician myself, this is simply too much. I howl with delight, thanking the spirits of travel and adventure and serendipity for leading us ... here. Now.

Warren and I stand up and perform what must look like our best two-man Mexican wave as the colonel's wife hits a high trill. The melodies are exotic, in scales that are foreign to the Western ear. Bowls of pho arrive. Neither Warren nor I are smokers, but we will be tonight. Fragrant nicotine smoke mixed with cloves fills the air. I'm handed a dart, draw in heartily and try to stifle a cough, so as not to offend our hosts. Or, worse still, look soft.

When the song ends, the group erupts. Next thing, the microphone is thrust into my hand. The colonel's wife brings up YouTube on her phone and hands it to me. Out of the corner of an eye, I can see Warren buckling in half with laughter. There's no crawling out of this. I might love music but I don't have a catalogue of Vietnamese folk songs on standby. What to sing? What can be universal? There's only one option ...

A 12-string acoustic guitar plucks out a chord in the key of B minor, via the medium of YouTube, and our new friends erupt. No matter where you are in the world, people of all creeds and colours know the intro to 'Hotel California'. Our guests blow up. I gird my loins. Tonight there is no option of missing those raspy Don Henley high notes in the chorus. Thankfully, either the atmosphere or the clove ciggies are helping to loosen the pipes. I needn't have worried, as even people who know no English know the chorus to Eagles' songs. All 14 of us break out in a unified choir of call-and-response melodies.

After that, no matter how woefully we deliver our songs, we're part of this gang. Warren is handed the mic and — to my amazement — it turns out this burly copper with the shaved head has the tonsils of an angel. The Who's 'Behind Blue Eyes' leaves not a dry one in the street. If only Pham and Do, serving out multi-year sentences in Sydney, could be here to witness this surreal moment.

As these strange tourists embarrass themselves in song, a crowd has gathered. The locals are perplexed by this ... strange and exotic scene. We're getting the ultimate insight into Vietnamese street culture, gifted to us by the simple spirit of human generosity. Perhaps the old ghosts of HCMC know that we come in peace, as volunteers in the spirit of cross-country collaboration, and have delivered us this experience in return?

After the gang has sung their overflowing hearts out, the colonel is handed the mic. The table quietens. Raucous laughter is replaced with respectful whispers. Our corner of the street hushes. The colonel stands up as sounds from a Vietnamese folk instrument weave delicate tapestries around us. There's a hint of the minor third — what is this ... Saigon-blues-folk? A sonic legacy of the American war presence? He looks wistfully into the distance, his eyes piercing through the concrete buildings opposite and falling upon some place in the distant past. His voice is deep, rich, with a resonant vibrato. We have absolutely no idea what the words mean. But I can promise you, he sings of longing, of love that has been lost, of valour, bravery, suffering, and he also sings of acceptance. He sings a song that reaches into our very souls and plucks those heartstrings, as expertly as Joe Walsh or Don Felder bending the high notes on a Fender Telecaster.

I wonder, is he perhaps singing about Aussie friends he lost in the field of battle, defending Saigon 50 years ago? Or is he singing of the day the VC kicked our allied arses all the way back to Australia? We'll never know. What we will know, for sure, is that it's a song of peace, forgiveness, and human connection.

As the colonel's last note trails off into the annals of time, silence falls upon the street. A few seconds pass. And then, mania. Bedlam. Hugs are shared, backs are slapped and Detective Sergeant Lysaght and his Companion Lynch both bow in respect.

What a moment. So often, when travelling, people of humble means turn out to be the most generous — in food, in time, in spirit. This beautiful extended family, living in central HCMC, in houses so small they host dinner parties on the street ... they are not poor. They have the greatest living room — and indeed the greatest pho — in all of Old Saigon. They bathe in a sense of connection, of sharing, of serendipity, of chance encounters. This is something that no political kleptocrat can ever experience while living in exile, trapped in a harbourside gin palace in the heart of the Lucky Laundry. This, right here, is living.

As we share more songs, more laughs, more pungent cigarettes, I feel a sadness for Australia. I feel sorry that, in the rush to acquire affluence and matching stainless-steel appliances, we've perhaps left something behind in our modest post-war cottages. I feel sorry for the demise of front-yard cricket matches, cubby houses in trees, people strumming guitars on porches, and neighbours hand-watering lawns while listening to the cricket.

When the microphone arrives back, I'm caught fumbling, not expecting the privilege — and immense pressure — of an encore performance. My mind, perhaps rendered dull by Tigers and Bia Saigons, unspools like a buckled cassette tape.

Every decent song ever written deserts me. What to sing? It has to be universal. But not too corny. And we've already used up our shot at The Eagles.

I tap clumsily at the colonel's wife's phone. 'One U2 karaoke'. In seconds, the bassy, muted, minor key strumming of Edge's guitar kicks in. With eyes shut, the words roll off my tongue. Bono may have delusions of grandeur, but in this moment he actually is my saviour. It's a song I've secretly rehearsed — in a karaoke session in one of Tokyo's Ginza bars, back in 2007. With the language barrier, this rendition will have to pack every ounce of Bono's bathos I can muster.

As the chorus kicks in our friends join, in broken English. My eyes open to see them swaying together, holding lighters aloft. Ha! Absolutely hilarious. I'm not sure whether to laugh or cry, so just bellow more loudly instead.

*

When we leave that night, we embrace like old friends. The colonel locks eyes and gives us both a firm two-handed shake. Is he also saying goodbye, in some way, to a young Aussie soldier from the 1970s? Warren and I will never know for certain. What we do know, for certain, is that our trip has already peaked on day one.

The locals watch two Aussies walk off singing, laughing into the buzzing night air, feeling good about humanity. Feeling good about the fight against darkness and greed. Feeling good about the future we're all helping to leave, as members of the human family, to the next generation of our sisters and brothers.

How incredible are people, the vast, vast majority of whom will give a meal to a stranger in a dark alleyway, share the shirt off their back and offer profound acts of friendship to a person they'll never meet again?

Despite what we will discuss on Monday morning, with government officials who are gathered to plot war against the most odious human crimes imaginable, we aren't perturbed.

We both believe, in that moment, that the world is beautiful and the human story has many incredible, exciting chapters yet to unfold.